ORDINARY PEOPLE, EXTRAORDINARY TEACHERS

S. Giridhar is one of the earliest members of Azim Premji Foundation. He joined the Foundation more than twenty years ago after spending a similar amount of time in business management roles. When the Foundation established Azim Premji University, he became its first Registrar and Chief Operating Officer. For many years now, Giridhar has been writing regularly, drawing from his rich experiences and observations on the ground. His other passion is cricket and he has co-authored two acclaimed books on the sport: *Midwicket Tales: From Trumper to Tendulkar* and *From Mumbai to Durban: India's Greatest Tests*.

S. GIRIDHAR

ORDINARY PEOPLE, EXTRAORDINARY TEACHERS

THE HEROES OF REAL INDIA

First published by Westland Publications Private Limited in 2019

Published by Westland Books, a division of Nasadiya Technologies Private Limited, in 2022

No. 269/2B, First Floor, 'Irai Arul', Vimalraj Street, Nethaji Nagar, Allappakkam Main Road, Maduravoyal, Chennai 600095

Westland and the Westland logo are the trademarks of Nasadiya Technologies Private Limited, or its affiliates.

Copyright © S. Giridhar, 2019

ISBN: 9789395073240

10 9 8 7 6 5 4 3 2 1

The views and opinions expressed in this work are the author's own and the facts are as reported by him, and the publisher is in no way liable for the same.

All rights reserved

Typeset by SÜRYA, New Delhi

Printed at Saurabh Printers Pvt. Ltd.

No part of this book may be reproduced, or stored in a retrieval system, or transmitted in any form or by any means, electronic, mechanical, photocopying, recording, or otherwise, without express written permission of the publisher.

CONTENTS

FOREWORD — VII

WHY WE MUST SUPPORT GOVERNMENT SCHOOLS — 1

1. THE HEAD TEACHER AS CEO — 19
2. REFLECTIVE PRACTITIONERS: — 73
   A COMMITMENT TO LIFELONG LEARNING
3. EQUITY AND QUALITY: — 121
   THEY BEGIN IN THE CLASSROOM
4. TEAMWORK: THE PULL OF A SUPERORDINATE GOAL — 175
5. HEROES: THEY RECOGNISE NO BARRIERS — 213

THE LAST WORD: — 245
WHY THESE STORIES MUST BE TOLD
BY ANURAG BEHAR

ABBREVIATIONS — 254
GLOSSARY — 256
ACKNOWLEDGEMENTS — 265
REFERENCES — 271
NOTES — 274

FOREWORD

I joined the Azim Premji Foundation in 2002 when it had just been set up. We were such a small outfit then that on one of my early field visits to Hemmanahalli (Maddur block, Mandya district, Karnataka) when I returned with a medium-sized watermelon, everyone at the office could partake of it. Until 2010, before the Foundation established the Azim Premji University, I was in the thick of field work being carried out in a dozen districts of Karnataka, Rajasthan, Gujarat, Uttarakhand and Madhya Pradesh where we had partnered with respective state education departments to contribute to improving the quality of government schools. I moved to the University when it was established, from my role in the field.

The Foundation's work with government schools expanded dramatically after 2011. By 2017, the Foundation had established 'field institutes' in forty-six districts, with a team of around one thousand five hundred people engaged closely with public (government) school teachers and other functionaries of the system, supporting and contributing to developing their capabilities. The resource persons at these field institutes, in partnership with the education department, conduct capacity-building workshops (and use multiple other modes) that cover subject-matter, pedagogy and the broader aims of education. Over time, the field institutes have been able to build a community of teachers, have helped them form groups called Voluntary Teacher Forums (VTFs, see glossary) and several subject-specific WhatsApp groups. To further facilitate learning among the teachers, the field institutes have set up Teaching Learning Centres (TLCs) where teachers share learning resources among themselves. While many of these district institutes have been established in the last few years, around seven to eight of these in Karnataka, Uttarakhand and Rajasthan have been in operation for over fourteen years now.

The Foundation has a systematic mechanism to assess the effect of its work but being a largely quantitative approach, it doesn't capture the human aspect, fascinating nuances, and rhythms of school. To capture all this, a qualitative study of identified 'good' schools in the five districts where the Foundation had worked for some time was initiated. For this, immersive visits to schools to gain insights into the kind of processes and practices contributing to change in school culture, quality of pedagogy, teacher-student interactions, beliefs and practices of teachers, and the role of leadership in transforming a school were imperative. I volunteered to undertake this. Though I had been engaged with the Foundation's work in the field earlier, I had not been involved with field operations since my move to the University. I had an understanding of ground realities that I had gained in my early years but at the same time could also maintain a certain distance. I would have the benefit of 'then and now'.

Qualitative studies are conventionally done in small samples but I was keen to have a sizable number of schools—around twenty-five—in each district. I decided that I would cover schools spread evenly across all blocks in a district with the exception of Yadgir district where the Foundation's work in the district had been focused around the Surpur block. I asked colleagues in our field institutes to send me a list of around thirty schools from each block that in their judgment were 'good' and where a teacher or head teacher was doing exemplary work. From this pool of around six hundred schools, I selected one hundred and ten. Starting March 2017 until November 2018, I visited these schools in Uttarkashi and Udham Singh Nagar in Uttarakhand, Sirohi and Tonk in Rajasthan, and Yadgir in Karnataka.

The significant thing to note here is that without much difficulty, my colleagues identified the required number of schools in each block. Given that on an average, there are two hundred primary and upper primary schools in a block, this implies that the people engaged with schools and teachers are able to identify at least 15 per cent of them as 'good' or 'exceptional'. One must remember that however deep the engagement on ground, it is impossible for them to know every school and teacher, therefore, they can call out good schools only from those that they interact with regularly. If one were to ask local representatives of other such organisations working in the same area, I am sure they would identify many more that may have not figured in this list provided to me. What I am therefore saying, is, that if one were to reach out to all the people and organisations working with schools, one would have a longer list of good schools, perhaps 20-25 per cent of the total number of schools and not the 15 per cent that constitute my list. That people on the ground can identify one out of every four to five government schools as a good school is an eye-opening statistic at a time when the news in popular media is usually about a dysfunctional public school system. The odd mishap in midday meals, the truant school teacher who runs a grocery shop or who misspells the days of the week are more newsworthy than the stories of teachers who are doing stellar work in anonymity.

When I began my visits to schools, starting with the Surpur block in March 2017, my anticipation was tempered by the anxiety and uncertainty of what I would discover. What if many of these schools and teachers did not really turn out to be good, leave alone exceptional? But my apprehensions were misplaced. As I visited the schools, I found that in over 75 per cent of the cases, the teachers were indeed special. At the end of each day, as I transcribed from my handwritten notes, I relived the time I spent in the school, the conversations with teachers and children. I marvelled at the indomitable spirit of the teachers and my notes seemed to take a life of their own. That one in four to five government schools is trying very hard to provide good education to its students, may not, after all, be a rose-tinted view of public education in rural India.

My conversations with teachers provided scintillating insights into their lives, hopes, difficulties and frustrations. They were open and forthcoming and giving of their time and themselves. I observed the work of these teachers and tried to understand their perspectives on education and whether these translated into equity and quality in the classroom. We spoke about pedagogy, children and learning, and their own growth as professionals, over time. I was also accorded the privilege of getting a glimpse of their everyday lives and routines. It is because of their generosity that I have been able to collate these stories. If I have not succeeded in drawing insights from every school that I visited, the failing is mine.

In putting together these stories of heroic teachers, I have consciously stayed away from drawing comparisons or correlations with the various 'theories of change', nor have I tried to straitjacket the efforts of teachers into popular management terms such as 'circle of influence' and 'circle of control'. I have also resisted the temptation to map and measure the schools on well-known 'frameworks of school quality'. I have, instead, stitched this chronicle together as a series of stories that the readers can choose to read in any order they wish. What connects the stories from Hemmadagi in Karnataka to Gangani in Uttarakhand is the proud refrain of the teachers, '*Idhu bari sarkari kelsa alla*' or '*Yeh sarkari naukri nahi hai,*' (this is not just a government job) thereby conveying the true meaning of government service in the trenches.

WHY WE MUST SUPPORT GOVERNMENT SCHOOLS

The one hundred and ten schools that I visited may not be representative of the one million government schools in India but they certainly are of the many 'good' schools in rural India. Often in these remote and lonely outposts, it is the teachers who are determinedly working beyond their call of duty with just one firm belief that *every child can learn*. Devising their own strategies, committed to consistently improving their own capabilities, these unsung heroes have, without exception, demonstrated this spirit in every school that I have been in for the purpose of putting together this collection.

There is a good reason I use the cliché 'unsung heroes' for these teachers. We do not see them travelling long distances by bus or shared autorickshaws to reach their village schools on time. We do not see the lady teacher climb the slushy hills in the monsoon because the school, a few miles from the main road, only has a mud path leading to it. We do not recognise her agility and purposefulness as she sprints from one classroom, leaving the students with tasks that can be attempted without her supervision, to attend to another because she is the only teacher for all the classes from I to V. We forget that many of the students get to eat only cold leftovers before they come to school and go back to homes where there is no reading material nor an environment for learning. We do not realise that the report card prepared by the teacher for the parents' perusal is acknowledged with a barely legible scrawl, if not a thumb-impression. We do not appreciate the fact that visiting homes to exhort parents to send their children to school is not prescribed in their service rule books but is an unspoken covenant among conscientious village school teachers.

The challenges that come in the way of schooling in our country are unique to each district. In Uttarkashi, the terrain and climate are a logistical trial for children and teachers alike; in the plains of Udham Singh Nagar, the pupil-teacher ratio is inimical to a conducive learning environment; Yadgir in northeast Karnataka grapples with the problems of irregular attendance because of the migration of parents in search of livelihoods; and Sirohi in southern Rajasthan which has a significant tribal population (Garasias, Bhils and others) who speak their own dialects, needs teachers who can use a mix of Marwari, the local dialect and Hindi to initiate any interaction in the classroom.

In recent years, there has been a massive migration of children from public to private schools. Parents do this by imposing hardships upon themselves since most of them earn their livelihoods as village grocers, autorickshaw drivers and small-holdings farmers. They fork out almost 12-15 per cent of their monthly earnings (of around Rs 7,500) on their sons', yes just the sons', education in private schools. It is understandable if parents move their children to private schools because the government school is dysfunctional, but in a majority of the cases, the reasons are as superficial as, 'they have a nice uniform with tie and shoes', 'English seekhega,' or bizarre ones like, 'my biradari (community) will think we are kanjoos'.[1]

Standing at a bend on the road in Purola town in the Yamuna valley, I saw groups of boys in ties and shoes, waiting for their school bus even as groups of girls walked past them to the nearby government school. That one sight was a clear expression of parents' priorities with regard to their children's education—private schools for boys and government schools for girls. As for the English that their parents think they would learn, these boys, sadly, could not hold a minute's conversation with me in the language.

The manner of migration is such that to a great extent only children from disadvantaged backgrounds have remained in government schools. In the last ten years, the number of private schools has increased by over 75 per cent while government schools have grown only by 15 per cent. In 2006, only 25 per cent of our children were in private schools but this figure has risen to over 38 per cent by 2016. In contrast, the number of children studying in government schools has gone down by over 7 per cent. (see Graph 1). What our school education has seen is a gigantic centrifugation that leaves the most disadvantaged in government schools, thus aggravating the strain on the already thin social fabric of our country.

But the uplifting story of the outstanding teachers in this book, tells us that in their respective schools and villages, they are not only arresting this trend but bringing back children from private schools to their own. And they are doing this by demonstrating to the community that children in their schools are learning better. What is heartening is that even the large annual survey ASER 2018, states that migration to private schools has plateaued in the last two years and some states have even seen a small increase in enrolment in government schools.[2]

*

There is change in our government schools if one cares to look for it. In a survey my colleagues conducted in 2005 in

Graph 1: What government schools are up against

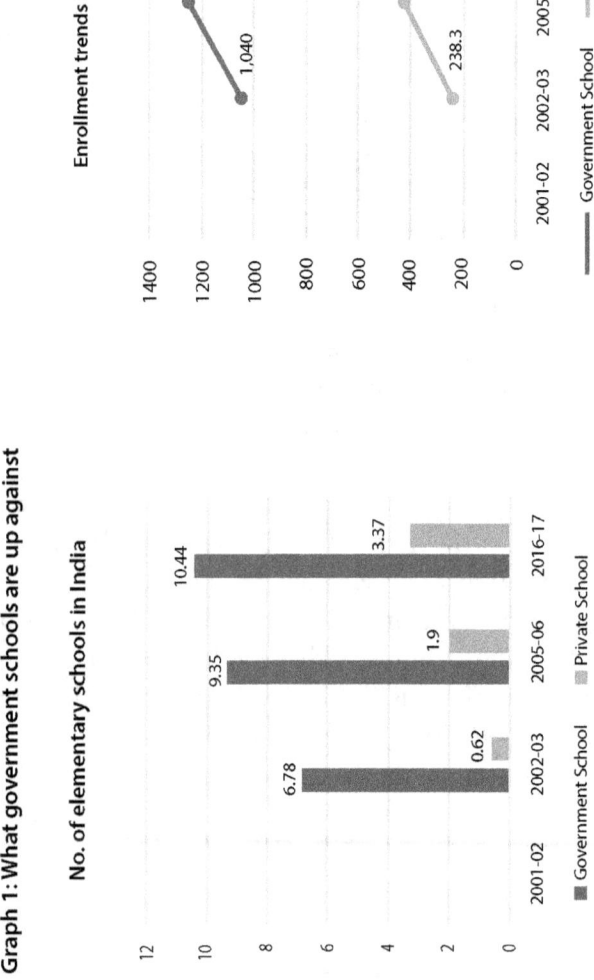

(Numbers are in lakhs)
Source: District Information System for Education (DISE)

northeast Karnataka, only four out of ten schools had obtained uniforms and books in time for the start of the academic year.[3] Today, this number has more than doubled. Nearly every school I visited had planned and procured books and uniforms well in time, even if it meant that their teachers had to sacrifice some holidays. In most schools that we visited, attendance was over 90 per cent. In the Surpur block in northeast Karnataka where attendance, for years had stubbornly stuck at around 65 per cent, it has now moved close to 80 per cent. In each of the hundred and ten schools, punctuality and presence of teachers were a given. In rural government schools, even these basic requirements of punctuality and regular attendance of children are significant signs of a vibrant culture. In the same survey of 2005, some or the other form of student fights or corporal punishment was observed in seven out of ten schools. In contrast, in the schools that we visited this time, there was no sign of the 'cane' nor physical fights among students beyond the usual pushing and shoving. In 2005, the researchers had noted that around 15 per cent of the head teachers were not in school when they visited because they were away at the Block Education Office on some errand or the other. Not so today. Nearly every head teacher was present in the schools that we visited. A major reason for this is that head teachers are able to meet incessant demands for information from their headquarters by seeking help from their younger colleagues who are more IT- and internet-savvy.

This is also perhaps a good place in this essay to put to rest the bogey of teacher absenteeism that is a favourite flogging horse in public discourse. A study by the Foundation in 2017, across six states, in a sample of six hundred and nineteen schools covering two thousand eight hundred and sixty-one teachers, showed that teacher absenteeism, that is, absence without legitimate reason or truancy is less than 2.5 per cent.[4] The study noted that in difficult circumstances that one would often associate with high teacher absenteeism, these teachers and head teachers showed remarkable commitment (manifested in no perceivable absenteeism) and high levels of engagements in classrooms.

Ten to fifteen years ago, I would come across the odd heroic teacher during my field visits. This time, what I saw among the two hundred and fifty to three hundred teachers spoke of a journey of growth, self-expression and commitment that comes from an upward curve in the area of self-development. There were multiple strands that demonstrated this transformation. One such change is that more teachers are writing a daily diary, reflecting on their school-day—the joys and struggles of teaching. The diary of a school teacher is a kaleidoscope of emotions but when it is introspective, it becomes a symbol of the learning teacher who wants to improve each day. The diaries of some teachers are so rich, they could be made mandatory reading in teacher education programmes. This is remarkable progress from twelve years ago when teachers would be hesitant to even read academic articles. In 2005, when newsletters like *Pravaah* were sent to schools in Uttarkashi, teachers would have to be called together once in a few months and coaxed to read and discuss some of the essays. But by 2017, *Pravaah* had become a sixty-four-page publication with a number of articles contributed by teachers themselves.

Many of these teachers make up for their inadequacies in subject knowledge by their commitment to continuous self-development. There can be no greater evidence of this than the fact that some science teachers, acknowledged for their excellence in teaching the subject, have no formal degree in science. The lesson plans and activities, the worksheets and experiments that they had constructed were indicative of their efforts to learn and teach the subject. Many teachers have acquired further educational qualifications through correspondence courses. When I spoke to them, their self-appraisal was honest and spontaneous: 'My school can only be classified as "B" category today but I hope it will reach "A" in the future,' or, 'There are at least twenty schools that are better; you must visit those (naming a few)'. They also expressed their frustrations openly, accepting their limitations of subject knowledge, the wicked inadequacy of not being able to teach English as well as they would like to and the enormous struggle for resources. But what was not lacking was the recurrent theme of personal ownership and pride. Confident that the community would sooner or later perceive the quality of education that their children were receiving, one teacher in a memorable turn of phrase, said to me, 'Mark my words, there will be a reverse migration from private schools to our schools.'

Are the children learning better? At each of these schools, the answer to the question is a definitive 'yes'. We saw a variety of classroom activities and children's portfolios—from neat handwriting to the ability to read and write completely new sentences; the ability to solve not merely algorithmic but word problems; the ability at mental math and higher order thinking; and, the spirit of the 'quicker' children to help their friends with their work. The teachers in these schools know the learning levels of each child in every subject. Many implement continuous and comprehensive evaluation (CCE, see glossary) in true spirit, going beyond the prescribed formats to record rich observations in individual child portfolios and then using these to plan additional support for identified children. If schools are a true microcosm of our society, then the schools that I visited, where equity and quality have reclaimed their place, give us hope of an improved school education system that provides quality schooling to every child.

*

Let us also take cognisance of the complex nature of the education system in our country. On one axis, we have socio-economic churning that is creating a sharp divide between public and private schooling and on the other is the sheer size and complexity of running over a million schools in a vast and diverse country. A typical block/taluk of a district has around two hundred and fifty elementary schools with over one thousand teachers and a typical district comprising six to seven blocks has around two thousand schools. Since Scandinavian countries are considered exemplary in the domain of public education, it might be relevant to point out that the total number of elementary schools in Norway would be the same as the number of schools in just one largish district in India. If one spends time with the block functionaries in our rural regions, one will appreciate the impossible amount of multi-tasking that is demanded of them. I spent days with a Block Education Officer (BEO) 'shadowing' him to understand his routine, rhythm and the demands of his office. He did not waste a single minute of his precious work day. Driving his jeep to the ground, he visited schools spread across several clusters in the block; convened meetings during these visits and through it all, was also constantly in touch with his staff on phone. His white shirt would get grimy by noon and he could not have worked harder. Admittedly, this BEO belongs to a small minority. The majority of his peers are overwhelmed by political pulls and pressures. The hierarchical system suffocates even the most sincere, talented and well-meaning functionaries. As a result, many are unable to provide their best attention to teachers and schools in their jurisdiction.

Good teachers try and do their best within these constraints. But in this long and lonely trudge, with limited resources, inadequate academic and administrative support, there comes a time when fatigue and a sense of resignation creep over many of them. A teacher's job is very different from most other professions—each class is different, each cohort is different, each day is different too. The energy a teacher needs to bring to the Classroom each day is a unique requirement of this profession. They deal with many stressful tasks simultaneously—winning back enrolment from private schools; earning and maintaining a rapport with the community; communicating the school's vision and goals to parents; ensuring that parents attend school events to stay updated with their children's progress and in the process stay invested in the school—all this while also fulfilling the basic promise to parents that their children will be safe and learn well. This energy and passion that devoted teachers and head teachers bring to their schools is the first casualty when they succumb to the feeling of 'no one cares' or 'I am fighting a lonely battle'.

These teachers need support from the system. For them, this 'systemic support' is represented by their supervisors at the block and district levels and by the community they serve. All that these resilient teachers need is some recognition of their efforts and simple, visible actions that demonstrate support. What could be the ways in which BEOs and District Education Officers (DEOs) demonstrate support? A few suggestions came from the teachers and the head teachers. While these may seem mundane, their strength lies in their simplicity:

- Many of these schools desperately need more teachers so that teaching and attention to children's learning

can be better. They should not be made to plead for such resources especially if they have proven to be 'performing' schools.
- In many villages, the head teachers are strained beyond their capacity in trying to get disparate community elements to come together for the common cause of their school. A supervising functionary should help the head teachers in these situations.
- Good schools are often the result of a dynamic head teacher's leadership so when that leader is transferred and a less effective person steps in, the BEO can guide and enable the new person to ensure that the school's quality does not slip.
- All teachers spoke of the importance of winning the community's trust and confidence, and of increasing enrolment by winning back students from private schools—the biggest affirmation of the community's endorsement of their quality. Only one in five good schools are adept at communicating their attributes effectively to the community, the others need help with this. For these schools, the BEO and their team can create communication campaigns. Most schools already use large platforms such as Annual Day and Independence Day programmes to showcase children's learning and talent to the community. If the supervising officers can be seen by the community at these gatherings, it would motivate parents to enrol their children in these schools. Instead of leaving good schools to their own devices, government functionaries and NGOs working on the ground must support them with information, collaterals and ideas that they could use to create campaigns for enrolments. Illustratively,

Graph 2: Significant improvement in enrolment and retention

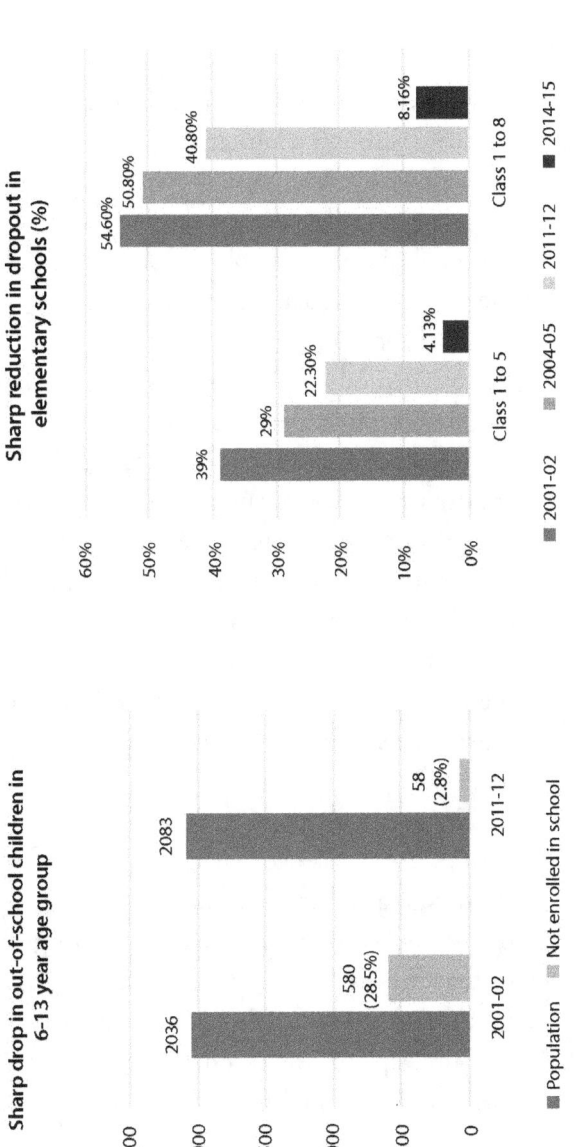

(Numbers are in lakhs)

Source: District Information System for Education (DISE)

such a communication campaign can have the following elements:

- A visible commitment to learning outcomes of children through a poster in simple language that can be displayed prominently in schools and public places in the village. It is a classic example of a clear and easily implementable action at scale. Recently, the education department of Karnataka has created one such poster.
- Announce and display the results of independent national or state level school quality assessments as evidence of children's learning; and, the list of children who have secured admission to Navodaya and Morarji schools (see glossary for more information about these schools) since this is a huge achievement for the community.
- Showcase the school's all-around achievements at the block and district level competitions in sports, music, arts, debates, essay-writing, science and maths.
- Use large events like school fairs/melas on specific themes from science, civics, history to showcase children's talent and learning.
- Invite the community to the morning assembly so that they can witness the attention given to all-round development of children and to also observe the upkeep of the school—classrooms, library, garden, kitchen and toilets.

A combination of these activities would create a picture of sustained quality and inform the community that their children are provided ample opportunities to learn and grow in a safe and caring environment.

*

The World Bank report of 2017 estimates that by 2021, India will have three hundred and seventy-two million children in the age group of 0-14 years and three hundred and sixty-seven million in the youth group of fifteen to twenty-nine years.[5] Only the quality of education will determine what these children and youth will make of their lives and how they will contribute to society. Children from disadvantaged socio-economic backgrounds in rural India are the worst sufferers in a system that does not offer equitable quality of education. This is a moral burden each one of us has to bear.

The late J.P. Naik, the doyen of Indian education during the twentieth century, titled his seminal work on Indian education as, *Equality, Quality and Quantity: The Elusive Triangle in Indian Education.* [6] Through some of its landmark initiatives, such as the Sarva Shiksha Abhiyan (SSA), India has been able to address issues of access and retention by providing a primary school in every habitation of the country with midday meals (the largest such programme in the world). As a result, enrolment has risen from 72 per cent in 2002 (when fifty-nine million children, of two hundred and twenty million in the age group of 6-14 years were out of school) to over 99 per cent in recent years. The attendance in schools has gone up and retention till Class VIII has risen from 42 per cent in 2002 to around 80 per cent in recent times. (see Graph 2)

But the elusiveness that J.P. Naik pointed to is borne out by the fact that the third vertex of this triangle, namely, quality of education has remained unattainable. Often, suggestions for improvement of the quality of government school education have harped on teacher accountability and incentives; the use of technology in schools; and other efficiency-related actions. These have taken us nowhere.

Thankfully, in recent times, the approach to this vexing problem is changing and the centrality of the teacher and the need to invest in their professional preparedness is being recognised. To those working on the ground with rural government schools for years, this acknowledgement is a welcome validation of the criticality of teacher education. This signals that sustained improvement in school quality will not come through fixing a few specific aspects but by addressing the core issue which is to create well-equipped, well-prepared teachers. There are no shortcuts, the path to a complete revamp of teacher education in the country will be long and arduous. How well we can reform teacher education, implement high quality four-year integrated teacher education programmes and create excellent institutions for teacher education will determine the fate of three hundred and seventy million children who will, in a few years, join India's adult population. Obviously, many parallel strands of radical reform in our education system need to be addressed simultaneously but teacher education is the most critical.

Perhaps one of the most crucial aspects within this that needs to be fixed is our very weak undergraduate education system that fails to equip teachers with subject-matter proficiency. For our teachers to be truly competent in their subjects, our Bachelor programmes ought to provide them with depth and breadth in their chosen disciplines. One cannot discuss quality in school education without acknowledging that the root cause is the abysmal quality of our undergraduate programmes.

The Kothari Commission report of 1966,[7] the National Education Policy of 1986,[8] and the National Curriculum

Framework of 2005[9] are milestones in India's quest for equitable quality in education. The next National Education Policy may well prove to be one of the most important documents with radical suggestions to transform public education in India. If it can provide clear recommendations on teacher education, the need to invest in teacher preparation and the accompanying systemic and structural reforms, it will go a long way in strengthening our public education system. The reality is, that for at least 60 per cent of our children, the government school is the only lifeline. It is only when the children who are completely dependent on government schools, receive equitable quality of education that we can hope to progress towards the ideals enshrined in our Constitution.

1

THE HEAD TEACHER AS CEO

Rural government schools have the odds stacked against them. The most socio-economically disadvantaged children go to these schools. Around 50 per cent of these children are first generation learners whose parents are daily-wage earners. It is in these circumstances that government school head teachers have to demonstrate that their schools are good; that the children are well cared for; and, are learning well. They have to not only revitalise and sustain the relationship with the community but also manage a bundle of diverse issues and constantly look out for resources. Viewed in this context, these head teachers perform a role akin to that of a CEO of an institution.

During my visits, I discovered that the head teachers considered community relations and winning back enrolment from private schools as one of their main responsibilities. They consider this so crucial that they do not delegate this to their colleagues and personally lead all communications and actions involving the community. The dynamic head teachers have a clear three-pronged communication strategy.

One, articulate a clear vision of the school and its goals; two, visit and meet parents and community members individually and in groups to explain this commitment; and three, conduct visible time-bound actions that demonstrate their commitment to the safety and learning of children. Invariably, the community begins to respond positively to such efforts. Once this initial boost is received, the head teacher consolidates and ensures other actions for continuous and sustained improvement in every aspect of the school's functioning. All along, transparent communication with the community is maintained, expenditure statements are shared and visible improvements are showcased to garner their confidence and trust.

While parents may be barely literate, they have a basic desire to educate their children and a keen perception of whether the school is doing its work well or not. An assurance that it is indeed doing well leads to a significant improvement in attendance. Despite pressures of sibling care, migration of families for livelihood, and seasonal help to be extended on farms and during festivals that lead to absenteeism, committed head teachers have created a culture of regular attendance. The head teacher and other teachers often have mobile phone numbers of every parent and call them up if a child is absent from school. This not only works as a gentle reminder to parents to send their children regularly but also substantiates the fact that the school is an ally, a partner equally invested in their childrens' development.

Some months ago, at a seminar in a university, when I was asked to list the key elements of such committed leadership, I placed the following before them:

- Many schools may have well-articulated goals, but in these schools (that also feature in this section), the goals are not merely expressed on notice boards or in conversations but are firmly ingrained in the detailed plans and actions of every single day. As a result of this commitment to make this vision a reality, one can see a perceptible impact on the attitude and work of teachers.

- Every head teacher is aware of the importance of good relations with the community but the distinguishing feature of effective leaders is their ability to communicate and present their efforts and children's learning and development visibly. So, events such as *Bal Mela*, Annual Day and Independence Day are celebrated in a manner that reflects the school's commitment to all-round development of children and showcases their learning and talent. These head teachers have a clear metric to assess the impact of such a rapport—an increase in enrolment by winning back students from private schools.
- With regard to planning and preparation, I noticed that they have a rhythm for specific, periodic and long-term actions. One can see this in the manner in which they identify priorities, implement actions, and then set new priorities as a natural progression towards the attainment of their goals.
- From hands-on daily management of the school to keeping a keen eye on critical school processes such as the morning assembly, maintenance and use of the library, meticulous preparation and effective use of children's learning portfolios and regular reviews with teachers, these head teachers have their tasks cut out. But going beyond regular duties and demonstrating extraordinary drive and leadership, they assume complete ownership of their schools through how they care for the infrastructure, ensure safety and hygiene;

attempt to mobilise funds from the community, gram panchayat, block office and also contribute from their own pockets; focus on children's learning; and put in extra efforts for identified children. In larger schools, conscious of the criticality of their teachers, the head teachers also provide supervision and encourage teachers to attend development programmes for continuous improvement.

'Going the extra mile' might have become an oft-used cliché but regains its salience when used for these head teachers whose resilience and courage help them to either ignore constraints or overcome them with bold, ingenious solutions.

'Sangharsh karo!'

KRISHNA KUMAR SHARMA

**Government Primary School, Ravindra Nagar
Rudrapur Block, Udham Singh Nagar District, Uttarakhand**

Rudrapur is comparatively more urban than many other district headquarters. It has, in recent years, become an industrial hub because of the SIIDCUL industrial area in Pantnagar where several leading companies have set up factories.* As a result, a number of skilled and semi-skilled workmen and labourers from Uttar Pradesh, Bihar and Orissa have found employment here and made Rudrapur their home. Ravindra Nagar in Rudrapur is a basti (hamlet) which is home to most of this industrial workforce. As it often happens in such cases, such a mohalla also becomes the source of livelihood and home to the

---

*State Infrastructure and Industrial Development Corporation of Uttarakhand Ltd, a Government of Uttarakhand Enterprise

tea/momo/pakoda vendors. There is a seamy underside to this mohalla, with drinking, gambling, drugs and the undercurrent of small-town violence and bullying.

This background is essential to understand the context and work being carried out at the Government Primary School (GPS), Ravindra Nagar. The challenges that this school faces are quite different from those of other government schools but the goal is the same—to provide quality education to every child. The school is not very old, established in 2008 with an enrolment of around a hundred children and two teachers. One among them was a Shiksha Mitra (para-teacher) earlier. Shortly after the school was established, Kirti Nidhi Sharma (KNS) was appointed to this school. His professional background included administration of a management institute and a medical college. Qualified with an MA (Sociology) and BEd, KNS was quick to recognise the very grim conditions and challenges that faced him. As the acting head teacher, he tried his best to make the school reasonably functional. And though the enrolment went up to one hundred and fifty-six in 2011, a number of boys in the primary-school age group were not enrolled. They were supplementing their family incomes by going to work and worse, were involved in petty crimes, assisting the local gang lords—including a lady don who is active even today.

KNS knew his limitations; while he was a good administrator and a sincere teacher, he did not have the force of personality to demand more facilities for the school nor could he count on the support of the community. He realised what the school needed was an assertive and courageous leader. It so happened that at one of the district-level meetings, he heard of and met Krishna Kumar Sharma (KKS), a teacher from Gadarpur, who seemed like an antithesis of himself in many ways—forthright, in-your-face and astute. KKS had been like this ever since he joined the education department in 1993. 'Sangharsh karo and the truth will win,' he says, somewhat dramatically. After spending six years (2007-13) in a primary school in Gadarpur, KKS was transferred to a small school and overlooked for promotion. He challenged this and won a promotion to Ravindra Nagar as the head teacher. The authorities thought they had 'punished' KKS by transferring him from his Gadarpur base to Rudrapur and that he would be inconvenienced and chastised but they did not know that KNS had invited him to Ravindra Nagar. With a wink, KKS says, '*Lekin unko nahin pata ki mera ghar Rudrapur mein hai. Aur upar se* promotion *bhi mil gaya!*' *(*But they did not know that Rudrapur was my hometown. What's more, I even got promoted!)

Once he arrived in Ravindra Nagar, both the teachers took stock of the school. KKS knew that the challenge he had on hand called for daring and innovation, something he thrived on. As the first step, he decided to mobilise resources and people to upgrade school facilities. He identified large-hearted industrial benefactors and with their help had a compound wall built to prevent the school from being inundated as it used to be during floods when the river gushed dangerously. Toilets and a kitchen were also built.

KKS then communicated a bold, clear statement to everyone, 'Children who come to this school should not worry whether there are adequate teachers or infrastructure. Nor should they worry about being first-generation learners. Their goal should be to come here to learn. It is *our* responsibility to ensure that every child gets a good education.' KKS and KNS made rounds of the basti combing it for unenrolled children to bring them to school. At one point, they were threatened by the local gang lords. 'You are unnecessarily interfering and inviting trouble by pulling these boys back into school when we are using them for our work,' a local don warned them but KKS remained undeterred. He began running regular street theatre in the basti to create awareness about the evils of drugs, liquor and domestic violence. How else could he convey that school was serious business? In his dramatic style, he talked to parents and told them that he would only admit those children whose parents were serious; the rest could go to other schools. In a subtle way, he had shifted the ground rules—from cajoling parents to send their children to his school, he was telling them that there was no place in his school for their children if they were not serious.

Inside the school, both KKS and KNS were completely considerate to the children, keenly aware of the difficult domestic circumstances that they came from. In the meanwhile, KKS had also managed to get the Shiksha Mitra, Rajkumari, regularised as an Assistant Teacher and another teacher, Geeta, on deputation from a nearby school. Even when the enrolment in 2017 rose to one hundred and eighty-seven (one hundred and ten girls and seventy-seven boys), KKS' only thought was, 'There are still a number of boys who are working as child labourers and I have to draw them in.'

The focus inside this school is on learning and both Sharmas are clear that come what may, they will not let their students succumb to the malaise of rote learning. KKS says, 'I admit that in the traditional exams our children may only get average scores because these exams test how well students have memorised and reproduced. But we want our children to develop conceptual understanding and express that in their own words.' He adds, 'Our children must ask questions; if they don't, it means we are not teaching them well; it means our schooling process is failing.'

The teachers maintain a painstakingly detailed portfolio of every child's learning. Going through these reports, it is clear that the teachers have a real challenge in ensuring that every child is learning. The portfolios also reflect the honesty of the teachers' assessments. These are not portfolios meant to impress others. KNS says, 'The average attendance is around 75 per cent. During the festival and wedding seasons, it drops even further as the children go to their native places for long periods.' KKS adds, 'They must learn to like studies; they must like to read books and develop curiosity. What do we want? We are realistic, we want these children to develop enough interest to continue their studies. I want the girls to continue their education. So, both of us personally take children who complete Class V to get them admitted to Class VI in the upper primary schools.'

KKS has an interesting association with the Foundation. When the Foundation first began work in Udham Singh Nagar during the days of the Learning Guarantee Programme (LGP, see glossary), KKS was the President of the Bajpur Block Teachers' Union. He was apprehensive of the intentions of the Foundation and it was only after he moved to Gadarpur in 2007 that he saw the manner in which the programme was introducing assessment reform and was convinced. He felt that he had been unnecessarily biased and resigned from the teachers' union to get completely involved with the work of the programme. The BEO of Gadarpur at that time was a gentleman named Bharadwaj, whom KKS considers his mentor. Together, they started an initiative to make the Block Resource Centre (BRC) a vibrant hub for academic discussions among teachers.

'In those days there was no WhatsApp, so we would have to phone each teacher whenever we scheduled a meeting at the BRC. The teachers began coming. All meetings were held after school hours. The teachers' union opposed this. But we kept at it even after Anup Datta, the ABRC (Assistant Block Resource Coordinator) and Bharadwaj, the BEO were transferred,' recalls KKS giving us an insight into those early efforts. Much later, when the VTF began in Gadarpur, KKS became an active member participating regularly and leading the discussions on topics of his interest. 'The VTF has taken root,' he says, and adds, 'Many teachers have begun assembling at TLCs close to their homes. This is a good initiative that encourages participation. We have good attendance. We have also started a programme called *Inse Miliye* in which we ask the more accomplished teachers to share their experiences.'

KKS has attended both the summer and winter workshops on Language teaching and acknowledges the value that a fine facilitator brings. His colleague, KNS attended the School Leadership Development Programme (SLDP, see glossary) and the English Language Teaching Workshop at the Foundation's Dineshpur facilities. When the Foundation's district institute at Udham Singh Nagar decided to create a compilation on language learning based on articles contributed by teachers, KKS was at the forefront of the initiative. *Koshish Jaari Hai* (the name of the compilation) according to him, gives voice to the work and identity of a good teacher.

These two teachers share such a close association with each other that it was KNS's father, a retired school principal and Sanskrit teacher, who released *Koshish Jaari Hai* at a function held at the district institute. We learnt from some of the local people that invariably, both the teachers contribute around Rs 2,000 each, every month from their salaries for some or the other material that the children require at school. When we bring this up, both brush it aside as something of little consequence and say, 'This is nothing. Just look at the much larger contributions of generous well-wishers like the doctor at the local hospital (the doctor contributes regularly to the school). That is the kind of contribution that you must recognise.'

'Is my school good? Well, my children study here!'

AYUB KHAN

Government Higher Primary School, Kolur M, Shahpur Block, Yadgir District, Karnataka

Ayub Khan, forty-seven years old, a veteran with over twenty-five years of experience, joined the education service in 1992 at the Government Higher Primary School (GHPS), Yadgir. After many years as a much-respected teacher, he became head teacher of GHPS, Kannelli in the Surpur block in 2009. Four years later he was transferred to GHPS, Kolur as head teacher but before I narrate what he has achieved at Kolur, I must describe his previous stint at GHPS, Kannelli.

Kannelli is a large village and a complex political cauldron. No head teacher has ever wanted to go to GHPS, Kannelli for not only was it a large school with six hundred and twenty children but also because there was no support forthcoming from the community. The environment was hostile, teaching and classes were not taken seriously and the midday meal programme was being run erratically. There was disillusionment among the teachers as they could not work effectively and had to face transfers or worse, suspension. Ayub Khan took over such a school and in the four years that he was there, left an imprint of which he can justifiably be proud. Ayub set things right, one by one. He knew it would be slow and arduous but that was the only way to begin any kind of redemption for GHPS, Kannelli. Meticulously, he planned and held meetings with individuals, small groups, teachers and the community. He demonstrated his faith in Kannelli by shifting his home there, moving his family and admitting his own children to the school. By 2010, Ayub was focusing on getting at least some of the children from his school admitted to the Adarsha Vidyalaya (see glossary). He motivated eighteen students to apply and qualify for admissions to the Morarji schools. He also identified one exceptional student for admission to the Navodaya school. He repeated these efforts in subsequent years. Ayub's reputation travelled fast and he received the state government's 'Janamechida Shikshakara' award.* By 2011, his school was also recognised as among the exemplary schools under the Child-Friendly School Initiative (CFSI). The improvement that he was able to bring about in the school environment was such that the school won the 'Parasaramitra' award in March 2012.**

When Ayub arrived at GHPS, Kolur in July 2013, the school just had three teachers. With five hundred students, the pupil-teacher ratio (PTR) presented a daunting situation. The sorry state of affairs became clearer when he saw that the average attendance was a pathetic 30 per cent, with only one hundred and sixty out of four hundred and ninety-four children enrolled attending school regularly. Ayub knew that here too, the first thing that he had to do was to establish a

---

*Literally, teachers who are appreciated by the people. Award instituted by the Government of Karnataka to recognise and reward outstanding teachers.

**Literally, 'friend of the environment'.

direct connection with the community and a bond with his teachers. Once again, in a demonstration of his commitment to Kolur, he moved his family there and admitted his two children to GHPS, Kolur. In this challenging assignment, Ayub knew he needed trustworthy allies and ensured he got a couple of key people on his side. Siddharam, an old colleague and a loyal lieutenant was one of them; the other was Mallikarjun, a teacher at Kolur since 2002 who had also studied at the school. Ayub could see the emotional bond that Mallikarjun had with the school and quickly co-opted this young man into his mission to turn around GHPS, Kolur's fortunes.

Ayub identified some key things to do to create energy in the school and earn the faith of the community. He knew of the power of school melas to galvanise the community and so he organised a mela on the Constitution of India. Ayub asked his teachers to contact parents and request them to contribute funds according to their capacity. It was a major communication exercise and they were able to collect nearly Rs 55,000. The mela brought teachers, students and the community together and the school could demonstrate its commitment to the learning and progress of their children. The Zila Panchayat president and the MLA from the Surpur block were also in attendance. All visitors, including the parents, were proud to see how well the school had been able to organise the event. Ayub had achieved his first goal—the school had united the community.

Ayub held meetings with teachers to analyse learning levels achieved by the children, their attendance patterns and if they had support at home. The teachers took their responsibilities seriously. Ayub was also able to get teachers from Doddaballapur and Mandya to come to his school because he felt that they could help coach the children better for admissions to Navodaya, Adarsha and Morarji schools. They conducted many sessions with numerous sets of multiple-choice questions (MCQs) and mental ability tests that are a standard feature of the admission tests. There was meaning and purpose behind this drill and practice routine. Mallikarjun, the teacher, told us, 'Earlier the school had sorely lacked leadership and coordination. But now there was urgency and purpose.' Ayub organised the teachers into a cohesive and dynamic team. He scheduled routine teacher review meetings; periodic student progress reviews; informal but daily assessment of students. The parents were encouraged to take interest in their children's education and provided regular progress updates. The morning assembly became an important part of the school day. Held on time, it presented an opportunity to all children to participate actively.

Ayub was one of the most conscientious teachers when the CFSI was being run in Surpur. He acknowledges that during the years he was at Kannelli, he learnt a number of aspects of school management as well as the potential of Nali-Kali if implemented in the manner that it was designed to be (for more details on Nali-Kali, see glossary). After attending the SLDP, Ayub, as part of his project work for the course, created an effective school library and also designed a remedial teaching programme for students.

Constantly navigating the problematic, politically volatile community, Ayub repeatedly told them, 'In a clash between the community and the school, the ones who will suffer will be your children. Please do not bring politics into the school. Trust us, your children will do well.' Ayub ensured that all the school finances were transparent and he shared photocopies of the school's bank passbook and cheques issued with the community so they knew how the school was spending its money. Ayub was also astute in pressing all the right buttons.

Given the large presence of the Valmiki community, he organised Valmiki Jayanti, cleaning and sprucing up the school for the occasion. The community appreciated the gesture. He also organised a public event to honour the teachers who had completed twelve years in the school and did this in great style by also inviting their spouses.

The attendance in the school has gradually risen from one hundred and sixty in 2013 to upwards of three hundred and fifty in 2017. Students who had earlier quit the school (taken transfer certificates) have started coming back. Ayub feels that in the last few years, he has become more confident and fearless; he assumes complete ownership of the school and has forged a good team. In 2016, Ayub received the district 'Uttamashikshaka Puraskar' award.* The reputation of GHPS, Kolur and the story of its impressive turnaround has spread beyond Surpur. So much so that the BEO of the neighbouring block has asked the head teachers in his block to visit GHPS, Kolur to observe Ayub and the manner in which he leads the school. GHPS, Kolur is now a Model School.

'We may not have nursery classes but please bring your younger siblings too!'

SARITA
Adarsh Primary School, Barkot, Naugaon Block, Uttarkashi District, Uttarakhand

Gangotri and Yamunotri are two of the four 'chaar dham' (Badrinath and Kedarnath being the other two) that devout Hindus consider as among their holiest pilgrimages. To visit

---

*Literally, 'best teacher award'.

these places where the holy rivers of Ganga and Yamuna originate is for millions of people a life fulfilling experience. While the journey to Gangotri begins from the town of Uttarkashi in the Ganga valley, the pilgrimage to Yamunotri begins from the town of Barkot in the Yamuna valley.

Bang in the middle of Barkot town in Naugaon block, surrounded by many private schools, is the Adarsh Primary School. In 2015, it just had fifty-one children, which is not surprising considering that parents were opting for private schools for reasons described below. It was around this time that the school was chosen to be an Adarsh Vidyalaya after the education department decided to create one Adarsh or Model Primary School (for Classes I to V) and one Model Upper Primary School (for Classes VI to VIII) in every block of the state's thirteen districts. The criteria for selection are not always clear but the selected schools are resourced with sufficient teachers to ensure a favourable pupil-teacher ratio (PTR) and a teacher for every subject. So, the first good thing to happen at Barkot was the appointment of a head teacher and the allocation of a sufficient number of subject teachers. The appointment of teachers to a Model School is on the basis of a written test and interview. That is how the head teacher, Sarita, joined this school in 2015. Within a year, three more teachers were appointed to the school.

Head teacher Sarita began her career in 1998 at a remote village school in the Mori block. After four years there, she moved to the Sukhan Primary School in the Naugaon block where she taught till 2015. Here at Barkot, her new colleagues are much younger. Vinod Methani (MSc [Mathematics] and BEd) joined the department in 2012; Yashpal Singh (MA [English] and BEd) has been teaching for the past three years and Punita Rana who teaches Hindi, joined the school in

2016. All three of them wrote the test, qualified and got the 'coveted' appointment to the Adarsh Primary School. The school has good facilities—an adequate number of rooms, a longish open courtyard for assembly and games, a neat corridor for dining and an audio set, to name a few.

Sarita is a clear-thinking leader. It helps her set goals and the direction for all efforts. Her first task as the head teacher was to let the community know that the school was now a designated 'Model School' with adequate resources and teachers for every subject, including English. She had to attract the parents back to the school, which meant meeting them frequently, inviting them to not just see the school and its facilities but to also have them interact with her young and bright colleagues and observe their engagement with the children that was positively impacting learning. These efforts were well-directed and the community saw that the school was indeed vibrant. Convinced, they began sending their children to the school and by July 2017, enrolment had jumped up from fifty-one to ninety-six, with many children being pulled out from private schools to be enrolled at the Adarsh Primary, Barkot.

Sarita realised that private schools had an advantage in enrolment because they admitted children at ages three and four in nursery and KG classes, unlike the government schools that only admit children to Class I. Once a child enters KG or nursery in a private school, it is difficult to attract that child to the government school. Sarita decided to overcome this problem by asking her students to bring along their three and four-year-old siblings to school with them. These younger siblings sit with the older children, observe, assimilate, participate in the daily assembly and games and in this manner, develop a bond with the school. Sarita believes that this 'informal' strategy will ensure consistent year-on-year enrolment numbers for the school.

High on her priority list is the morning assembly. Within a year, the excellence of the school's morning assembly was being widely commended. Sarita has organised the children into three houses and each house conducts the assembly for two days in a week. The children ensure that each one of them gets to participate in one or the other activity—prarthana (prayer), pledge, samooha gaan (group song), news and newspaper headline reading, followed by five to six questions on topics of general interest. Each day, the children are exposed to ten English words or phrases and poetry. The morning assembly closes with the national anthem. Sarita is convinced that the assembly is one of the best platforms for learning and confidence-building, one that offers an equal opportunity to every child to exhibit their talent.

With Yashpal, Vinod and Punita in her team, Sarita is assured that the children's learning will be of high quality. There is a regular meeting of these teachers to gather a shared understanding of children and their learning levels. Like most conscientious teachers, they invest a couple of hours after school each day to provide additional support and guidance to children who need it. The teachers are also very well organised. For instance, they have set aside Saturdays for weekly updation of profiles and progress reports of children. It is also the day they sit together to plan for the upcoming week. Teamwork is a given and Sarita drives it with a light touch. Yashpal and Vinod are young and idealistic, and her gentle steering enables them to see where they need to combine realism and idealism without losing that burning desire to provide quality education to these disadvantaged children. The result of such teamwork and organised planning is reflected in the quality of the children's portfolios which the teachers maintain and share with parents during monthly meetings. There are detailed comments in each child's portfolio, which reflect the teachers' deep understanding of the child's learning. At this school, one can see that the implementation of CCE is a regular and integral part of the teaching process.

Yashpal and Vinod are eager and regular participants at the TLC and the VTF. They see the discussion forums and workshops as platforms for both expressing their views and for absorbing the wisdom of the more experienced teachers. With their youthful energy, both actively contribute to the workshops. They are also active on the block's teacher WhatsApp group.

These are early days for the school but all the good signs are visible. It is these teachers who will make the Adarsh Primary School, Barkot a Model School. The children may be too young to realise their good fortune now, but in the years to come, they will look back at their education in this school with gratitude.

'Aapko kaisa school chahiye?'

HARISH CHANDRA SINGH RAWAT

Government Model Primary School, Shivlalpur Dallu Kashipur, Block, Udham Singh Nagar District, Uttarakhand

Some schools perform well primarily because of the dynamism and competence of head teachers whose imprint can be seen in every facet of their existence and operation. The flip side is that these schools are also more vulnerable because if the leader leaves, there is a danger of collapsing into mediocrity. While this caveat might well apply to a number of schools I visited, I thought I would mention it here because this account of the Model Primary School, Shivlalpur Dallu as a vibrant, thriving school is based entirely on the vision and work of its head teacher.

Harish Chandra Singh Rawat, a native of Almora, joined the education department in 1996, after completing his Intermediate and certification in Physical Education. After six years in Bageshwar district, Harish worked at the Barkhedapande Primary School till 2013. It was a very large school—typical of Udham Singh Nagar schools—with six hundred and fifty children. People from the Foundation cannot easily forget that school because when it participated in the LGP, the district authorities had to commission multiple teams of evaluators to conduct oral assessments. Harish was also selected as a member of a team of evaluators that went to various schools in the block to conduct these assessments.

In 2013, Harish was transferred to Shivlalpur Dallu as head teacher. This school was much smaller with seventy children and two teachers. The first thing that he did upon taking charge was to strengthen the School Management Committee (SMC) by briefing members about their responsibilities and making them aware of their crucial role in the improvement and effectiveness of the school. Harish then convened a meeting of all parents and community members and explained to them the goals of the school and how he would be able to realise these with their support. 'Only when parents, teachers and children come together, can a school run well,' is his dictum.

His next step was to make the morning assembly a distinctly superior and useful exercise. 'Assembly is something that is visible and, in many ways, sets the tone for things that happen inside a school,' explains Harish. He made children take responsibility for it and encouraged parents to visit and observe the assembly. Harish believes that these two initiatives were enough to make some parents shift their children from private schools to the government primary school. By 2014, one hundred and twenty-eight students were enrolled. Meanwhile, the need for additional teachers was acute. The department has an odd rule—more teachers are posted in disadvantaged areas called 'durgam,' even if the PTR there is already favourable and fewer teachers are posted in places perceived to be favourable or 'sugam', even if there is a dire need for teachers there. However, the department is also pragmatic in its operations and sends teachers on need-based deputation from 'durgam' to 'sugam' schools. That is how two teachers joined Harish's school in 2014-15.

In 2014, Harish decided to conduct an Annual Day function at the school for the first time. It was the twentieth year of the school's existence and Harish decided that it would be a theme-based event around the animals of Uttarakhand with the Corbett National Park as the central theme. The idea was to involve all children, to have them study and create projects. The children created models of a lion's den, a bear's lair, a gaushala, a hill and even a running river and displayed these in what was an educational mela. Harish gave children the opportunity to set up food stalls to enjoy the experience of entrepreneurship. Very consciously, he too put up a stall to be one among them. It was an event that required funds. Harish contributed Rs 10,000 from his own pocket and his colleagues also chipped in with their contributions. The teachers explain it thus, 'We are able to provide a good life for our own children because of this job. If we spend a little money on our students who are not well off, we are not doing anything out of the ordinary.' Harish, whose relationship with the Foundation has remained strong since the days of the LGP, told us, 'Sanjay Yadav and Harendra Bisht of the Foundation helped us plan and execute the entire event. They brought their experience of the Bal-Shodh Melas to our Annual Day.' Harish described how the event spread such a lot of goodwill and positive energy among the community that the school has never looked back since. The school held a grand Annual Day function the following year too with a different theme. They managed the stage and the lights differently and invited a local industrialist as the chief guest. The ground was packed with members from the community.

With renewed confidence, Harish reached out to parents to ask them, '*Aapko kaisa vidyalaya chaahiye?*' The parents said they wanted their children to dress like 'convent school students' and for the school to be clean. The education department provides funds for uniforms of only the children from the SC, ST communities and girls. So, Harish contacted the principal of the neighbouring Guru Nanak College and obtained funds that enabled him to provide uniforms for every child. 'I am very transparent and share everything with officials, as well as, the community. When trust is established, it enables me to take the initiative. We only had two classrooms and I could go to the Gram Pradhan and my block functionaries and demand support.' The Block Resource Person came forward to mobilise some funds to enable the construction of an additional classroom while the Gram Pradhan agreed to construct toilets. SSA funds also came in handy and Harish got the playground levelled and started setting up a garden.

In 2015, GPS, Shivlalpur Dallu was selected as a Model School and immediately, two additional teachers were appointed. Harish now had teachers for English and maths which the school had sorely needed. When it was admission time in 2017, Harish was delighted to see that forty more parents came forward and enrolled their children, shifting them from private schools, to his school. The school now has one hundred and sixty-eight children. Two private schools in the vicinity of Shivlalpur Dallu have since closed down.

Insufficient classrooms remain an issue as there are only three rooms but Harish and his four colleagues have recently pooled in Rs 60,000 from their own pockets to construct a tin-roofed annexure that can serve as the fourth.

The teachers and the head teacher are familiar with each and every child's learning levels. They also share this information among themselves, so if one were to talk to the English teacher, she would also know the child's competence in maths. Child-wise portfolios and progress reports are maintained with great care. These are shared with parents during monthly PTMs, that are a serious affair. With an entire day devoted to PTMs, the teachers show parents samples of their children's work, subject-wise answer papers, project papers and artwork.

In the morning assembly, in addition to the everyday prayer, group song, storytelling and poetry recitation, the school has added a five-minute play to provide the children with an opportunity to express their creativity. Different groups of children take turns to participate in these events. Every teacher, without fail, is present in school before the start of the assembly. Since it is a Model School, it has been provided with a whiteboard, aluminium topped dining tables for midday meals, a harmonium, drums and sports equipment including dumbbells and lezim sets. As a result of these provisions, the teachers are able to enrich the activities and include music, PT and games in the timetable. The children from this school, in the past two years, have won cluster and block level competitions and have reached the district finals in sprints (sports), painting, poetry and storytelling competitions.

It bothered Harish that while the children in private schools could go on excursions, the children in his school had no such opportunity. So, he and his colleagues pooled some funds and took the children of Class V on an educational tour of the Nainital district where they saw a dam, a barrage, a water mill and observed the basic principles of hydroelectric power generation. They also climbed a hill to visit one of the oldest temples in the district. Harish derived a huge sense of fulfilment from this tour. 'Our school has been selected as a Model School, not because of the existing infrastructure or facilities, which everyone knows are inadequate. They must have heard about our work from some of the senior functionaries who have visited our school.'

Harish attaches great importance to visibility. He believes that the self-esteem of the children and their parents is as important as the quality of learning and educational experiences. So, he has provided an ID card, a belt and a tie for every child, just as the private schools do. He also recognises the fact that he must continuously engage with the community, not taking the relationship with them for granted. Recently, at a community meeting, he played the game of Chinese Whispers with the parents starting with the innocuous sentence, *'Maine kela khaya.'* When the round ended, the last person spoke the sentence which, by then, had totally changed. Harish did this to drive home the point about how information gets distorted and that it is unwise to rely on hearsay. 'Come and check directly with me about anything pertaining to the school,' he advised the parents.

What I have said so far may give the impression that Harish concentrates only on school administration and relationships. The fact is that he is also deeply invested in teaching—not only does he teach EVS, he also stays current on the subject, both in terms of content and pedagogy. He is an active member of the Kashipur VTF and leads discussions during meetings. He has been co-opted into the district's capacity-building workshops on EVS and is currently developing a resource book on the subject that will be of immense help to teachers in the district.

Through all the pressing priorities of running the school, Harish has also found the time to complete his BA and MA degrees by correspondence, another indication of his commitment to his own professional development. He is now fifty years old and looks forward to strengthening GMPS, Shivlalpur Dallu during the remaining years of his service. His own children are well-settled—an older son is an engineer in Delhi, a younger son is studying Hotel Management, an older daughter is married, and a younger one is a qualified nurse employed in a Kashipur hospital. Harish has enormous amounts of energy and passion. Any visitor to the school is bound to spend more time than intended because the head teacher has so many facets of the school's operations to show them. He will also have his colleagues share the children's portfolios, that make for a compelling read. At the core of this head teacher's success is his clear vision of a vibrant school that provides learning experiences that are invaluable to children.

'I will bring the boy: girl ratio in the school to 50:50. I don't want girls to drop out of school at any cost.'

SANGAIAH

Government Higher Primary School, Gedhalamari, Surpur Block, Yadgir District, Karnataka

---

Head teacher Sangaiah is a fascinating man. He joined the education department in 1992 after completing his PUC and ITC (Instructor Training Course, a teacher training certification). His first posting was at Government Lower

Primary School (GLPS), Hanumasagara. After six years, in 1998, he moved to GHPS, Balashettihalli and was there for eleven years. Since 2010, he is at GHPS, Gedhalamari as the head teacher. Over the years, his work has been recognised and rewarded. He received the 'Best Teacher in the District' award in 2010, followed by the 'Best Teacher in Karnataka' award in 2015. He was among the eight teachers nominated by the state to present their experiences at the National Teachers Conference organised by the Ministry of Human Resource Development (MHRD) in Bhubaneswar.

Gedhalamari is a largish village with around two thousand people, with most of the population belonging to Scheduled Caste (SC) and Scheduled Tribe (ST) communities. GHPS, Gedhalamari has three hundred and forty-one children—one hundred and thirty-seven girls and two hundred and four boys. Like many villages in this region, Gedhalamari is beset with social issues such as the prevalence of child marriages and the impact of sibling care on the schooling of girls. The ratio of girls and boys is nearly the same till Class IV, but around the age of nine, girls start dropping out.

The attendance in school is 90 per cent on most days and one of the ways Sangaiah drives this is by entrusting his teachers with the task of personally following up with parents if a child is absent. Sangaiah has ensured that all teachers have mobile phone numbers of all parents. Teachers call up parents if a child is absent, followed up with the class teacher and the physical education teacher visiting the child's home and also informing the School Development and Monitoring Committee (SDMC) president. In the early days at GHPS, Gedhalamari, life for Sangaiah revolved around the school 24x7. Sangaiah set the example for punctuality and regularity by coming to school every day at 9.15 a.m. sharp and leaving only at 6 p.m. His home is fifteen kilometres away, a distance he covers on his motorcycle.

Teacher Renuka who has been at the school since 2004 knows that Sangaiah has come here with a goal. She says that it is only since his arrival that positive changes have taken place. She lists these—better infrastructure; refurbished classrooms; rebuilding of the stage that was on the verge of collapse; and, a culture of absolute punctuality, firmly established. The reconstructed building is of an excellent quality, set up under Sangaiah's eagle eye. The progressive BEO of Surpur block during those years, Santha Gowda, having seen that, sanctioned four more rooms for this school.

Sangaiah wants his school to become a model school and has identified key aspects that he will concentrate on—good infrastructure, an attractive garden, maximum attendance, punctuality of teachers and achievement of all-around learning levels of children. While significant improvement in infrastructure has been achieved, Sangaiah feels good that there are also signs that learning levels are improving. 'Around fifty children have been selected for Morarji schools in the last seven years since I came here. Every year, around three children also qualify for Navodaya schools,' he informs us. All these achievements and improvements are visible to the community and as a result, parents have responded by moving their children from the nearby Bhoruka Steel Private School to this government school. 'It is very important that we demonstrate the quality of our school and the capability of our teachers and children to the BEO and the community. I did this by organising a learning mela, taking forward the idea of the school mela that has been popularised by CFSI. The support of the SDMC is very critical in these efforts.' Even parents from neighbouring villages have noticed how well GHPS,

Gedhalamari is functioning and have moved their children to it.

With Sangaiah as the driving force behind the transformation of this school, a noteworthy team spirit has also been inculcated among the five teachers. Mallappa, the PT teacher and Manjunath who teaches the junior classes, both joined the school in 2010. Renuka the longest-serving teacher here, works closely with Manjunath in teaching Classes I-III, both teachers use the Nali-Kali methodology. Ambarish, who teaches Classes VI-VIII joined the school in 2016 while Manjunath D has been at this school since 2008 and teaches Class V-VI. These five teachers are indispensable in order for Sangaiah to realise his ambitious plans.

Sangaiah's deep interest in learning and pedagogy is reflected in how whole-heartedly he participated in the Nali-Kali training programme when this multi-grade, multi-level teaching pedagogy was implemented as part of CFSI in Surpur. As a result of CFSI, Sangaiah has also attended almost all the key school leadership programmes conducted in Surpur. Sangaiah is particular that he and his teachers constantly learn and grow. So, one will find the teachers of GHPS, Gedhalamari regularly attending meetings of the VTF and visiting the TLC. The school has a functioning science lab and relevant teaching-learning material, much of which has come from the teachers' participation at the TLC and VTF. In fact, Sangaiah's school has hosted four meetings of the VTF in eighteen months. It is interesting to observe Gedhalamari's teachers play badminton with the children after school (from four-thirty to six in the evening). The importance given to physical education is evident from the fact that GHPS, Gedhalamari qualifies and participates at district level competitions in kho-kho, throwball and kolaata.

Sangaiah tells us, 'On Saturdays, I concentrate on the administrative stuff—data collation and paperwork. I don't find it difficult or tedious because my colleagues share these administrative responsibilities, which also enables me to get the time to teach science and Kannada in Classes V-VII.' The only difficulty that he faces is the adverse PTR because vacancies created by transfers of teachers have not been filled.

The school that he was earlier in, had also participated in the LGP but could not qualify for an award. The enrolment was huge but they had inadequate teaching staff. However, in Gedhalamari, Sangaiah says the picture is already different. When the recent Karnataka School Quality Assessment and Accreditation Council (KSQAAC) assessment was conducted, the external observer told Sangaiah that he had not seen such an environment or such responses from children. This outcome, according to Sangaiah is due to the emphasis that is laid on foundational learning in Classes I-III, which is critical. 'In our school, by Class III, every child is able to read and write and I think we use Nali-Kali in the best possible manner. I also think our thirty-minute morning assembly plays a vital role. The quiz is a major feature of the daily assembly.' Those who have had the opportunity to observe the assembly at GHPS, Gedhalamari will agree. Each class takes turns to conduct it and there is an effort to ensure that every child has the opportunity to participate, be it reading from a textbook or newspaper or answering questions. The quiz on Friday is special with three prizes sponsored by the community.

Sangaiah is very understated and matter-of-fact when he discusses his work but one realises how inspirational he is when one hears other head teachers in the Surpur block say that they want to emulate what Sangaiah has achieved. In the immediate vicinity of Gedhalamari, around four to five schools have sent their teachers to observe and learn from this school. When these visitors ask Sangaiah and his colleagues for advice, their suggestions are simple. One, focus on the basics: infrastructure, attendance, punctuality and learning; two, work as a team keeping the quality of education at the core of everything, and three, be completely transparent and clean in every transaction, spending every paisa scrupulously. Sangaiah's parting words as we take leave, are full of resolve, 'I am confident my school will be among the top ten in Surpur taluk. I do not want the girls to drop out at any cost. The ratio is 35:65; I will bring it to 50:50 in a few years. This is a remote and disadvantaged area, but we will make this a model school.'

> **'The children coming to our school are really vulnerable. Only teachers can help them.'**
>
> **DUNDAPPA KOLKAR**
> Government Model Primary School, Hunusigi (Town),
> Surpur Block, Yadgir District, Karnataka

Dundappa Kolkar, the head teacher of the Government Model Primary School (GMPS), Hunusigi is a fifty-five-year-old veteran who joined the education department in 1982. A native of Vijayapura district, he has spent his entire career in the Surpur taluk across three schools—GHPS, Yedalabhavi (1983-2006) where he was also the head teacher; as a Cluster Resource Person (CRP) (2006-2012) and at GHPS, Devatkal (from 2012-2016) as head teacher. And now, in what might well be his last posting before retirement, he is the head teacher at GMPS, Hunusigi.

During his twenty-three years at Yedalabhavi, Dundappa became a legendary figure among the local community. When he arrived there in 1983, the school was only in name with no physical infrastructure. He started the school in a temple with about ten children. The school register was kept in the custody of the village Gowder, the agricultural landlord. For the next five years, till 1988, this is how the Yedalabhavi school was run. In 1988, the Gowder, impressed by Dundappa's dedication, donated land for the school and the Mandal Panchayat sanctioned funds for the construction of a 1200 square feet school building. When the children started coming, a second teacher was appointed. Soon around sixty children from the forty-five households in the village were enrolled and regularly attended school. The Tehsildar sanctioned more land for the school and the villagers agreed to the housing land being used for what they came to understand as a good cause, a school building for their children.

This piece of land was rocky with boulders jutting out. The villagers were very poor and all they could contribute was physical labour—'shram-daan' as Dundappa puts it—to help level the land and build the compound wall. Dundappa planted trees around the school at different stages of its development, from the time the Gowder had first given the piece of land. It is very interesting to see the trees today at different heights that indicate the stages of the growth of the school. As the school got on a steady footing with the two teachers able to ensure that the children were learning well, they also started focusing on sports. Soon, the children of Yedalabhavi became so competent at kabaddi and kho-kho that they qualified through cluster and block level inter-school competitions to reach the district level.

In 1992, the school added Classes VI and VII to become an upper primary school. The six to seven tribal hamlets in the vicinity also started sending their children to the school and by 2002, there were two hundred and twenty children at GHPS,

Yedalabhavi. When we ask Dundappa to review the early days and how he could create a thriving upper primary school, starting as he did with a ten-pupil school in a temple, he puts it very simply, 'I think there were two primary reasons. One was the relationship and trust established with the community; the other reason was the visible effect of our teaching on the children. The parents were illiterate but they could see that their children were learning. They always saw me at the school from 8 a.m. to 7 p.m. and also the activities and sports that I conducted every evening for the children. I would bring artists and musicians to the school. The school became a cultural hub and the children were learning other things in addition to their classroom lessons.'

After he left in 2006 to become a Cluster Resource Person (CRP), his replacement turned out to be a leader of lesser mettle. Several unfortunate events involving violence took place in the school, including a clash between the community and the teachers, and very quickly, the spirit of GHPS, Yedalabhavi was broken. After many years, I hear that a committed teacher who joined the school in 2015 is trying to rebuild this school.

Dundappa, now in-charge of GMPS, Hunusigi for just over a year, also inherited a run-down school and a hostile community. The earlier head teacher had left the place in desperation. Dundappa reviewed the situation—the school had enough space, also a building, although old and derelict. The community was engulfed in divisive politics and the school premises were being used not only for social events like marriages and for parking tractors but also by anti-social elements. These adverse circumstances only strengthened his resolve to set things right.

When he got down to work, his first step was to invite the top boss of the district education department, the Deputy

Director of Public Instructions (DDPI), to visit the school and see for himself the condition of the school and manner in which the school premises were being misused. He also made sure some key people from the community were present during the DDPI's visit. Throughout the visit, Dundappa stressed the importance of the school which had started way back in 1943 and how the community ought to take pride in owning such an old school instead of being ashamed of the pathetic state it was in. The school had some unused funds in its account and he got the DDPI to sanction those and built a gate as a sign that people could not just enter the school premises and use it as their personal property. His next step was to mobilise support and funds to demolish the dilapidated building and construct a new one with a sufficient number of rooms. For this, he received the support not only from the DDPI and the BEO but also from the Zila Panchayat and the Public Works Department (PWD).

While Dundappa was elated that he had succeeded in obtaining funds, he was also aware that in the preceding ten years, the school had neither utilised the allocated funds nor maintained proper records of the expenditure. They had, in fact, allowed around six lakh rupees of the sanctioned funds to lapse even as the facilities fell into ruin.

Dundappa knew it was now or never. He wasted no time in constructing a fine new building, and also ensured that all accounts—inflows and expenditure—were available for scrutiny to all members of the community. It was this transparency that helped him develop a powerful bond of trust.

Having built this trust, Dundappa called for a meeting of the parents and encouraged them to elect members to create a new SDMC. He successfully staved off the attempts by the MLA and the Gram Panchayat to plant their nominees and chartered a three-year plan with the newly-formed SDMC, which he placed before the community with a request for funds to construct toilets, repair the compound wall and put up a name board for the school. During all this, Dundappa was firm that on no account would anyone bring politics inside the school. It is interesting to note that the composition of the three hundred and seventy children at this school includes one hundred and forty from the Scheduled Caste (SC) and Scheduled Tribe (ST), forty-eight Muslims and around fifty children from the Other Backward Castes (OBC) category but none from the Lingayat community that comprises a large portion of the community and whose children study in the ten to twelve private schools in town.

Having set in motion actions to address the infrastructure, Dundappa turned his attention to getting additional teachers for the school and had remarkable success. Four teachers were appointed and three guest teachers were also deputed to the school. Only one vacancy remains to be filled now. With ten teachers in his team and a PTR of around 35:1, Dundappa began to concentrate on improving the quality of learning in his school. He believes that foundational learning in the early years determines how well children learn and develop in the later years. He, therefore, supervises Classes I-III very closely and is planning to add a fourth section so he can distribute the children of the three classes into four sections.

Dundappa has instituted a system of formal monthly meetings of teachers to discuss and reflect on their experiences. Key issues faced and possible solutions are discussed and agreed upon in these meetings. He holds formal reviews with teachers to discuss how lesson plans are executed; which portions take more time; and which topics or aspects are difficult for the children. With help from his teachers, Dundappa has created a format for them to fill in all these details so that these can be discussed with the objective of improving the quality of teaching. He has even been able to persuade teachers to do one 'demonstration' class every month—one of them teaches while the others observe and provide feedback.

Dundappa recalls that he had only a nodding association with the Foundation when the LGP was launched in northeast Karnataka and it was only after the CFSI was launched in 2004 that the association became stronger. He has attended every major SLDP. Being a hands-on teacher and one who places great emphasis on foundational learning in lower classes, Dundappa has also attended the Nali-Kali training. He is candid when he says that he can still focus only on achieving competencies in reading, writing, comprehension and numbers. Some children, even in Classes VI to VIII, are not able to read and write or do basic arithmetic. He identifies such children and runs a special remedial teaching programme during the summer holidays, which he has named, 'Parihara Bodhana Summer Camp.' He wants to start special classes during the school term too to provide additional support to children who need it. These efforts are perhaps the most important for him, 'The children coming to our school are really vulnerable and it is our duty to focus on them; only we can help them.'

Like most head teachers, Dundappa wants his school performance in the KSQAAC assessment to improve but he realises, 'Even more important is our own self-assessment. We must be able to see for ourselves that our processes are effective and meaningful throughout the year rather than just once a year in an external assessment like the KSQAAC.'

He does not leave for home before 7.30 p.m. and spends the time after school (4.30 p.m. onward) to compile and update all administrative information. A visitor observing Dundappa during an entire school day will notice that this man, in a starched white dhoti and Gandhi cap, is on his feet all the time, doing rounds of classrooms—a friendly pat here or a word of support there. For all his dynamism and the pressure that he exerts on his teachers, Dundappa is not inconsiderate. Without being judgmental, he says, 'Of the ten teachers in my school, two or three are low on energy. But my job is to encourage them, build their morale and take them along.'

'From fourteen students to becoming a Model school'—the go-getter leader

TAPANSHIL
Government Model Primary School, Chandeli, Khatima Block, Udham Singh Nagar District, Pantnagar, Uttarakhand

Tapanshil joined GMPS, Chandeli in 2008 when it had just fourteen children on its rolls. It was his first posting since joining the education department. He had earlier worked as a volunteer and then as a Block Coordinator during 2005-07, when the Foundation, in partnership with the state government, ran the LGP. Tapanshil was always a go-getter and at Chandeli, he has been no different. By 2010, the enrolment had gone up to sixty-four and in the following three years, it touched one hundred. A private school in the vicinity is on the verge of closure as many children from that school have moved to this government school.

Tapanshil's defining characteristic is his energy. Meet him any time of the day in the school and one will find him briskly handling at least two to three tasks simultaneously, often directing and guiding colleagues to possibilities that they have overlooked. He is a solution finder. When he came to the school in 2008, he tells me, he had decided, '*Vibhaag ka sehyog chahiye, community ko involve karna hai.*' (We need support from the department, we must involve the community). In the Gram Pradhan he found an ally, genuinely interested in the children's education. He spent substantial time with him and they decided to work as a team in talking to the community. Together, they established the SMC and then met all four hundred and sixty residents of the village. This population is largely composed of people from the SC/ST community and despite their modest means, many of them were sending their children to a private school, spending a good part of their hard-earned wages on fees. When Tapanshil asked them the reason, they replied that the private school had more facilities and a dedicated teacher for each class. Tapanshil appealed to them to give the government school a chance. Confident of his own capabilities, he proposed to them, 'If you have two children in the private school, will you send one child to my school?'

Tapanshil then pooled in money from the Gram Pradhan, a few benefactors, and adding his own to it, used this kitty to hire an English teacher. In 2009, when the enrolment was completed, he had seventeen children. He spotted potential in one of them and personally coached the child for the entrance examination for the Navodaya Vidyalaya. The child qualified and Tapanshil felt a huge sense of satisfaction. 'I remember as a child, my classmate got into Navodaya school but I could not as there was no one to guide me. I was determined that when I got an opportunity, I would be there to guide and prepare my students for admission to Navodaya Vidyalayas.' This achievement did not go unnoticed. The community was watching Tapanshil's efforts and the following year, forty-seven children were shifted from the private school to the government school. That year, Tapanshil coached and prepared fourteen children for the Navodaya entrance examination. He could do this because, as a head teacher, Tapanshil says, he had ample freedom to try new things; to experiment. So, when the academic year began, he held regular classes in the school for five periods and used the remaining three periods in a manner that was most optimal for preparing the fourteen children for the entrance exam while the rest of the students concentrated on sports. Tapanshil and his colleagues, Rajeev Singh and Vipin, divided their responsibilities. Tapanshil taught maths, Rajeev taught Hindi and Vipin taught the students how to attempt the mental aptitude section of the exam. Their efforts paid off. While a few of the fourteen children qualified and have joined the Navodaya school, the others too had built a strong foundation to be able to do well in upper primary classes. The emphasis on sports paid off too and the Chandeli sports teams became a name to reckon with in kho-kho and kabaddi. While the kabaddi team participated at the district level, the kho-kho team went on to win the cluster, block and district level competitions and played at the state level. In athletics too, the school produced winners in the 50 and 100-metre sprints.

In 2016, when the state government initiated the 'Adarsh Vidyalaya' concept, Tapanshil went to the district officials to press the case for his school to be nominated as one of the model schools. Once it was nominated, the school got three additional teachers. Among the teachers who joined the school in 2017 was Maurya—a thoughtful, soft-spoken person who looks much younger than his forty-five years. Maurya with an MA and BEd had joined the education department in 2009 and when the vacancy for a social science/EVS teacher in Model School, Chandeli came up, he cleared the qualifying exam and was appointed. A very analytical person, it was easy to get some sharp and clear insights into the working of the school from Maurya. He believes that the school has enough staff and resources and the community is completely behind the school because it has seen how things have improved dramatically in the last seven years. There is excellent cooperation among the SMC members and village politics remains outside the school gates. The community recognises the part head teacher Tapanshil played in convincing the block authorities to get the school nominated as a Model School. Maurya adds that there was no need for Tapanshil to have done this as running a Model School means assuming greater responsibilities. But all that the head teacher saw was the opportunity to build a fine school. Maurya acknowledges that parents are very involved in the progress of their children; they attend school meetings and take teachers' suggestions seriously. The teachers, on their part, remain in direct touch with the parents. He says, 'I talk to parents of Class III children over phone till 9 p.m. and then with parents of children of Class V till 10 p.m. I consider this as my basic duty. At school, sometimes, the children do not open up but when I talk to them on the phone when they are in their homes, they are more relaxed and forthcoming. All of us have the names and phone numbers of every parent. We, teachers, are a united team and share Tapanshil's vision of creating a fine school here. Good teamwork is critical to it. Our teaching is based on paying attention to every child. Each teacher here knows every child's learning level and their areas of difficulty in various subjects. Among ourselves, we share and plan how to tackle these.'

Maurya has been a participant in the various capacity-building programmes conducted by the Foundation since he joined the education department in 2009. He is a regular participant in the VTF and also of the various workshops and discussion groups at the TLC at Khatima. 'We discuss issues around pedagogy, classroom processes and the creation of learning resources that are central to our profession. At these meetings and workshops, the experience sharing is rich. Because of their experience, the faculty is able to help us build a perspective and critical understanding which enable us to be more creative and proactive in the classroom and to develop alternate methods and implement these in a practical manner.' Maurya also finds the TLC rich in resources and the library stocked with good reading material. Maurya's eight-year-old son also studies in the government school. With a smile, Maurya says that his son is also a regular visitor to the TLC as there are a lot of interesting books for children in the library.

Attendance at Chandeli is invariably over 95 per cent. The school has a welcoming environment that can be felt by anyone stepping in. There are four classrooms, and the veranda is used as the fifth one. The room for Class IV also houses the library. There is a small garden just outside the school which also serves as a playground for kabaddi and kho-kho. The local MLA contributed two lakh rupees for the furniture while the Gram Pradhan contributed money to build the school compound wall. A Zila Panchayat member contributed towards the cement flooring of the school and the BEO provided an electricity pole close to the school. As Tapanshil says, 'Once we showed we were serious and that the children were learning, it was easy to pull all these elected representatives and key community leaders into our efforts. The guardians are also benefited greatly. Instead of spending money on private schools, they now get quality education for their children for free. They reciprocate by contributing part of their savings towards the school because they realise that this school belongs to them.' Maurya's parting words as we leave are, 'Children are so innocent and honest; to get to spend my time with them and to live among them is the best thing that could have happened to me.'

'I will quit if the school does not get a filtered drinking water unit.'

BASAVAGOWDA
Government Higher Primary School, Hunasugi Camp, Surpur Block, Yadgir District, Karnataka

This is a story of incorruptibility, determination and courage. Basavagowda Chowdhary is forty-seven years old and joined the education department in 1997 at GHPS, Halepet in the Shahpur block of what was then Gulbarga district. The initial years in that school were a period of immense learning for him. In 2002, Basavagowda became the acting head teacher at the same school. Halepet comprised of poor people from mostly the Muslim community. It was at Halepet in those early years that Basavagowda realised the importance of working closely with the community and also the necessity of showing them what their children were learning at school.

After twelve years at Halepet, when he came to GHPS, Hunasugi in 2009, Basavagowda was immediately faced with a series of exigent challenges. There were four hundred students in seven classes with eight teachers. There were four vacancies. The school was poorly managed and he was quick to notice that the staff was lazy. The environment was hostile with a disgruntled colleague also plotting to trip him up.

The challenge before him was enormous but Basavagowda decided to take it head on. Step one of his strategy was to move his home close to the school. This enabled him to be at the school every morning by 8 a.m. to confront the problems of absenteeism, irregularity, poorly managed assembly, and the staff's complete disinterest in the functioning of the school. He insisted that every teacher be present at the morning assembly. The next thing he knew, there was a formal complaint registered against him for embezzlement of funds meant for the school and midday meals. He had to face the ignominy of the police coming to school to question him. Basava told the police to go to his house and search it in his absence. It was his way of telling them that he was innocent and being framed. Once he got a clean chit from the police, he did not let this pass. He insisted that they investigate those who had complained against him and sought a DDPI-level inquiry into the incident. In November 2009, it was established that the disgruntled teachers had made the mischievous and completely baseless complaint against him and they were transferred. New teachers were appointed in their place.

The community now saw through the politics that was being played by the earlier set of teachers and how the children were the ones who had suffered; it was their education that had been affected. They realised that Basavagowda meant well and everything that he was doing was to get the quality of education in the school back on track. They also saw him as a courageous and upright man who meant business and backed him in improving the school. Having earned the community's support, Basava proceeded to the next stage of his school improvement plan. He obtained a drinking water facility—a tank with 2000-litre storage—through the Panchayat. He got the rooms that were being used as dump yards for old and useless furniture, cleared out so they could be used as classrooms. He then added more classrooms with the available budget. As a result of these additions, he could use one of the rooms for the midday meal. He also had functional toilets constructed.

Having improved basic infrastructure and shown the community that their trust was well-placed, Basavagowda decided to address the issue of political interference in the running of the school. Hitherto, local political leaders had nominated the SDMC president but Basavagowda put his foot down and insisted that only parents could elect this officer. This was a crucial challenge but he won the round because of the goodwill and trust he had earned in the community.

Basavagowda now set his sights on the quality of children's learning. With clear expectations and suggestions, he organised his teachers to ensure that they give maximum attention to learning in their classrooms. The learning levels improved and we could see this clearly in the manner in which they responded, asked questions and came up with interesting observations while talking with us. From our discussions in the classrooms, it was evident that they held no fear of exams. Basavagowda has prepared motivational videos to show his students how children who started quite poorly have become competent and capable. He has set up a library in the school and the children are encouraged to borrow books, read and share their thoughts in the school assembly. He has organised his classes in a manner that the Keli-Kali radio programme (see glossary) is used effectively. The teachers maintain a progress portfolio of each child and assign projects to students to encourage them to explore and learn from their local environment. Every year, at least ten students from this school clear the entrance examination for the Morarji School. Basavagowda who tracks the students who pass out from his school tells us that the SSLC (Class X Board examination) toppers of the taluk and the district have passed out of GHPS, Hunasugi.

The all-round development of the children is a goal Basavagowda has been devoted to. He says, 'Just a day spent observing the children closely is enough to spot some talent in each child. It is the duty of the school to nurture a child's talent to its full potential.' It is with this spirit that GHPS, Hunasugi prepares its children and participates in state education department-run events such as 'Pratibha Karanji' (see glossary), 'Kalikotsava' (see glossary) and sports. In all these, GHPS, Hunasugi has qualified right up to the district finals. The school has also received the 'Parisara Snehi' award for its efforts towards environmental protection.*

Basavagowda credits all these achievements to his teachers, 'I am very happy with my teachers. They are extremely conscientious. For example, Irakka, the teacher responsible for Nali-Kali provides an excellent language and comprehension foundation for children in Classes I to III. Sunitha, the science teacher; Suvarna, the social science teacher; Geetha, the language teacher, are all doing a fine job.' He has instituted a system of regular teacher meetings. When he first established this process, he had insisted on meetings every week, now he has eased this to fortnightly meetings. Professionally conducted, these meetings have a clear agenda, a review of the previous meeting and documentation of the minutes, actions and next steps. I had the opportunity to peruse the register that the school maintains and it is obvious that the diligence and seriousness of these meetings are being maintained. The teachers as a group, review lesson plans and exam preparations. They hold bi-monthly meetings with parents to apprise them of their children's progress.

---

*Literally, 'environment-loving' school.

In the past few years, the school has also organised a series of melas to demonstrate to the community the abilities of their children. An 'environment mela' was followed by a 'science mela' with the whole-hearted participation and involvement of the community. Some of the members were so astonished to see the children from their village demonstrate such acuity in describing concepts that they asked if the children had been brought from the nearby private schools for the mela! The school's achievements and activities are now also discussed in the Panchayat.

The current strength at GHPS, Hunasugi is four hundred and sixty-two and there are thirteen teachers. The average attendance on most days is more than 85 per cent. The private schools in the vicinity of this school are shutting down as parents are shifting their children here. Basavagowda is currently pushing for a filtered drinking water unit for the school and is threatening to quit if the community and the Panchayat do not accede to this request!

Amidst all this, Basavagowda has also remained a continuous learner. Having become computer literate, he has encouraged three of his teachers to also learn and become proficient in the use of computers. He has attended the SLDP conducted by the Foundation and found it very helpful. His teachers too have followed in his footsteps and are all active participants in the VTF and workshops conducted by the Foundation. They are regular visitors to the TLC at Kakkera where they receive suggestions and ideas for creating suitable materials for classroom transactions. As a result of their regular interactions at the TLC, they also avail the various materials, books and equipment available there. Irakka, the teacher who uses the Nali-Kali pedagogy in Classes I to III was adjudged the 'Best Nali-Kali Teacher' in Surpur in 2011.

Full of energy and ideas, Basavagowda is now also embarking on a personal initiative to begin an 'unofficial' LKG and UKG with exposure to English for the children of the village. He is putting his own money into this for a stunningly simple reason that he shares with me. He too came from abject poverty wearing patched clothes till high school but education helped him climb out of that poverty and he wants the children of Hunasugi to have the opportunity to defeat the dire circumstances they are born into. Hence, this 'pre-Class I' initiative for children to get into the school-going habit early. He tells us that he started on a monthly salary of Rs 1,100, which has now risen to Rs 35,000. He feels he has enough and can spare some of his earnings towards this initiative. He also has ten to twelve acres of farmland to augment his income, which is all the more reason, he says for him to give.

Basavagowda says that the one thing that rankles is that the school got a B+ rating in the KSQAAC assessment of 2016. Not happy with it, he says, 'My ambition is to make Hunasugi GHPS a Model School.' This is the next goal of this determined and indomitable school head.

'To hell with the syllabus! Let us teach the children fundamentals.'

RAMESH CHANDRA PAL

Government Utkrusht Upper Primary School, Meethan, Reodhar Block, Sirohi District, Rajasthan

---

The village of Meethan in the Reodhar block is a drive of over sixty kilometres from Sirohi town, the district headquarters. The nearest town is Abu Road which is over thirty kilometres from the village. Like much of the drive through the cultivated areas of the Sirohi district, one crosses large fields of 'arandi' (castor beans) on the route to Meethan. Twisting and turning through the village road, one arrives at the Government Utkrusht Upper Primary School. 'Utkrusht School' is Rajasthan's equivalent of a 'Model/Adarsh Vidyalaya'. The education department conducts an evaluation of schools and then selects (and names) one primary and one upper primary school in every gram panchayat as an 'Utkrusht school'. It is more of an honorific as one may not always find any special facilities provided by the department to such schools. Clearly, there are variances in programmes and implementation across states and sometimes even across districts in the same state.

We arrived just as the children of the eight classes were organising themselves into lines for the morning assembly. It was a buzzing, humming time but not chaotic; it was well-organised and quick. A mike set and a band were at the front with a small group of students who were in charge of conducting the activities. Also, in the front was the head teacher of the school, a short, bespectacled man in his mid-fifties. He was clearly unwell but obviously determined to participate and work through the day. All eight teachers and two hundred out of the two hundred and fifty-four students were present. In addition to the customary songs, the group conducting the assembly engaged the students in current affairs and encouraged them to narrate poems and stories. At the end of the assembly, as the children went into their respective classrooms—the school has a classroom for each of the eight classes—the head teacher moved to his office. I had been told by my colleagues that a meeting with him would be the highlight of our visit. They were right. Ramesh Chandra Pal settled into his chair and after a round of introductions, for the next few hours, we talked to him and his colleague, Ramraj

Gujjar and gathered a fascinating insight into the history and evolution of Meethan's Upper Primary School. We also spent time with the children, observing and interacting with them in the classrooms.

The first thing that strikes a visitor to the school is a large banyan tree in the middle of the compound with its aerial roots. This majestic tree is like a magnet that draws students and teachers to congregate under it. We soon learnt the reason for this as Ramesh Chandra Pal began to narrate the history of the school. 'Established in 1956, the school had no classrooms or building; the lessons were held under this banyan tree.' Over time, classrooms were added one by one. In 2005, the school was extended to Class VIII to make this a proper Upper Primary or Middle School. 'I came to this school in 2009 on promotion. The enrolment at that time was one hundred and twenty students but only eighty to eighty-five students attended. In the previous year, none of the students of Class VIII had passed the Board exam. When I came here, the first thing that landed on my table was a court case asking why the school had a zero result in the Class VIII Board exams.'

What have I landed into, Ramesh asked himself when he saw that his teachers were busy going to court to defend the school which had been hauled up for its 'hundred percent failure' in the Board examination. But he also asked himself the crucial question, what should I do? Ramesh was living in the town and realised that the daily commute to Meethan would not be sustainable. He decided to shift to the village. He had a history of ill-health (more about that later) and his family felt Ramesh was taking a huge risk. But Ramesh was determined to change things at the school which he did not think could be done if he did not live close by. He started coming to school early, setting the bar for punctuality. Gradually, the teachers began coming to school on time too. He started talking to every child and spending time in the classrooms. By November 2009, 50-60 per cent of the 'syllabus' was completed but the understanding and comprehension of the children, in his words, was 'zero.' He called his teachers and said, 'What is the use of completing the syllabus if the learning is zero? Course *aur* syllabus *ko maaro goli; bacchon ko* fundamentals *sikhao!*' (To hell with the syllabus! Let us teach the children fundamentals.) Ramesh was clear that they had to begin with teaching basic literacy and numeracy as this was the door to reading, writing and comprehension. With this clear direction, the teachers began to create their own timetables and concentrated not on meaningless completion of topics but in ensuring that the children were following and learning the basics. Ramesh also recognised that there was no one to teach Sanskrit and though he had never taught the subject before, decided to take up the responsibility.

He then called a meeting of the village folk. He recalls, 'I said to them with folded hands, please send your children to school daily, punctually. I will make this school work.' Ramesh followed this up by visiting parents in their homes along with his teachers. He asked parents to spend a few minutes every evening to check their children's classwork and homework. 'I asked them for feedback. They realised my home was open twenty-four hours for the children to come and clear their doubts. Some children began to visit my home on Sundays too. The community began to develop trust and we built a bond.' The quality of teaching and learning began to show visible improvement with regular attendance and motivated teachers. Ramesh supervised the efforts closely, spending as much time in Class I as in Class VIII. He would informally assess the children's learning and development. At the same time, he provided freedom to his teachers to develop their own methods and pedagogy.

Ramesh is a native of Kanpur in Uttar Pradesh. At the end of the first school academic year, while he was on a well-earned vacation to his native place, he got the news that all twenty-three children of Class VIII in his school had cleared the Board exam. When he returned, the BEO, the DEO and the community came to ask how this remarkable turnaround had been achieved. 'It is teamwork. Parents supported and believed in us. Our teachers were sincere and hardworking. Good results had to come,' he told them. This success had a huge bearing on the events that followed. The community stopped sending their children to private schools. '*Wahan se nikal liya aur hamare* school *mein bharti kar diya,*' *(*They removed the children from private schools and admitted them here.) Ramesh recalls with visible pride. Enrolment jumped from one hundred and twenty to two hundred by 2010. The community saved the money that they previously spent on the fee, bus charges and other expenses in private schools and started contributing part of it to this school. Speaking to us that day, Ramesh was running a high fever, coughing and sneezing, but his energy was unfaltering. He got up to take us to the board in the corridor that lists all public benefactors of the school. They are called 'Bhaamashah' in this region. 'See the names, these are only from the year 2010, all the facilities here are built from their contributions.'

After about an hour, when Ramesh said to us, '*Yeh junoon hai*, (this is an obsession) I have left my native place and come here. I must create something for these children who come from extremely disadvantaged backgrounds,' it did not sound hollow. We were able to observe his easy interaction with teachers and the respect and space he gave them. He told us that he has always insisted that he is their colleague and if they suggest any improvement for the school, he would try and implement it. Some children came into the room as we were talking, asking for some papers. Calmly handing the papers to the children, Ramesh took a minute to inquire about a child who had been unwell. The rapport with children seemed natural and we pointed it to him. 'It has to be natural and genuine. They can sit on my lap, I will hold their hands but they must study, they must be regular. We celebrate their birthdays and I invite their parents to school.' Ramesh recognises the need of a good diet for the children and has asked the community to contribute. 'We teachers also contribute so we have fruits in the menu. We got the walls painted, and added a swing and a slide. When children come to school happily and go back home happy, learning is not a burden.'

Ramesh's father was never in favour of his taking up teaching as a career. 'He wanted me to be a policeman or patwari (revenue officer) but I wanted to be a teacher. I taught in a private school on an ad-hoc basis for five years before landing the job in the education department.' Ramesh has built his reputation over the years. Around twenty years ago, he was deeply involved in the adult literacy programme. The illiterate ladies whom he taught during that period, still remember him. Ramesh does not take any casual leave and when he was ill some years ago (a paralytic attack because of which he now walks slowly) he insisted on attending a head teachers' training workshop. He told the DEO that he would go with his wife, who he said, 'Is my right hand. She is the inspiration for all the work I do.'

Since 2010, the school has had a 100 per cent pass rate and the enrolment numbers are sustained year after year. The community support has only improved and the school has been able to add lights, computers, a few laptops and a laser printer. The school's SDMC has received the 'Best SDMC' award and in 2015, the district nominated the school for the 'Utkrusht School' recognition. Ramesh has won the 'Best Teacher in the District' award which is not only a recognition of what he has achieved at Meethan but of the work that he has done for over twenty years.

As we were walking around the school, Ramesh received an invitation to attend the wedding of his former student's son. Showing the invitation to us, Ramesh smiled and said, 'I attended Govardhan's wedding and it is time already to attend his son's!'

We had come to the classroom where Ramraj Gujjar was teaching. We had been told that our visit would not be complete without spending time with him. Ramraj has been at the Meethan School since 2010. He teaches Hindi to the primary and Sanskrit to the upper primary classes. We sat engrossed as Ramraj taught the little children. Time took wings till teacher and students suddenly realised that the period was over. Ramraj had a smile throughout the lesson and every child was participating, although it was not always easy for us to follow the Marwari dialect. After the class, Ramraj told us, 'In the years before Ramesh joined as head teacher, the school was in shambles. Two teachers had fought so bitterly that one of them committed suicide. It was a sad place and it was no surprise that the parents were opting for private schools. It is a completely different, happy and peaceful place now.' Quite succinctly, he brought us up-to-date with the situation, 'The children's mother tongue is Marwari, so I learnt Marwari to be able to teach them. I teach Classes I and II by speaking, singing, adding poetry and story-telling. The trick is to encourage them to speak freely. So, they are free to add Marwari words wherever they cannot readily think of the corresponding word in Hindi. In Class II, I begin helping them to write. All the children are from the Bhil tribal community whose economic condition is tough. Their parents work as labourers in quarry mines or at construction sites in Reodhar. Ninety per cent of the menfolk drink heavily. Whether their children have warm clothing or not, the men must have their liquor. Health is a matter of concern and some people also suffer from AIDS.'

However, he adds that the SDMC is well-chosen and committed. He believes that as a result of the better quality of education these children are receiving, Meethan's next generation of adults will have better habits and will be more responsible citizens. Slowly, the level of literacy among the parents is also rising, and only 30 per cent are 'angootha chhaap' (illiterate). Seventy per cent of Meethan's alumni have continued their studies although the girls discontinue for reasons of marriage or other domestic responsibilities.

Ramraj reflected on his own growth and development as a teacher. 'Earlier, I was the traditional "ka-kha-ga" teacher. We used to ask children to copy and memorise mechanically. But I have learnt the advantages of the "whole word" language teaching method and the superior meaning-making and expression abilities through it. I have learnt to use stories as a means of developing children's language abilities.'

When we stepped out again, the children were washing their plates after their meal; and, games around the majestic banyan tree were in full swing. The teachers looked on indulgently while some of the students came up to ask us the distance from Meethan to Bengaluru. 'Will you go by road to Bengaluru?' they asked. 'No, by hawai jahaz (aeroplane),' we told them. As we left, one of them called out, 'When will you come back again?'

2

REFLECTIVE PRACTITIONERS: A COMMITMENT TO LIFELONG LEARNING

'My attitude and approach to teaching have changed. I now love teaching the lower primary as much as the upper primary. When I went for a programme to the Centre for Learning near Bengaluru, I saw highly qualified PhDs teaching Class IV and V with such passion that it changed me completely and I promised myself that I would teach each class with the same passion.' I heard this from a teacher in the early days of my travels and it has stayed with me. Building one's content and pedagogic ability in a subject is something we expect of a committed teacher, but this kind of attitudinal change is rare and difficult. Here was a teacher whose open mind, receptive to new experiences and inputs had changed him. In my interactions with nearly three hundred teachers—and these are admittedly the good teachers I had sought out—I heard many of them talk of how they have changed as a result of this quest to become better in their profession.

An oft-used phrase to describe a capable and thinking teacher is 'reflective practitioner'. The teachers I feature in this compendium bring this phrase to life. These are teachers who are always thinking about their intellectually and ethically demanding profession in a meaningful way and connecting what they do with how children think, feel and learn. I had a difficult time choosing just a handful for this section from among the many 'reflective' teachers I met.

When I complimented a teacher after observing her class, she tried to downplay her accomplishment by saying, 'You should have seen me ten years ago, I would mechanically transact the syllabus. I was a traditional teacher...' Teacher after teacher narrated how they learnt and developed into better teachers. They acknowledged the many training programmes and workshops they benefited from and told us how they tried some of the ideas they picked up and attempted projects in their schools. The libraries—so critical in helping children develop the reading habit—in many of these schools were often the result of an 'aha' moment in workshops that discussed children's language abilities.

Often, in these kind of conversations, one can get carried away by polite generalities. Only if a training programme has been truly worthwhile would a teacher remember it. Therefore, we would always ask teachers to tell us specifically the name of a few such programmes, their contents and how they were helpful. Many teachers could accurately recall the title of the programme and many also remembered the facilitators' names with gratitude. They showed us the materials they had developed and explained the practices that had emerged out of the workshops. They illustrated with examples how they built their content and pedagogic capability in subjects, like how the workshop on the use of maps opened their minds to making social science more interesting or to use home-grown experiments to explain a scientific phenomenon to children. As one of the teachers explained, 'The science and mathematics workshops have been two of the best initiatives in the capacity-building of teachers. All the charts and material we are using are a result of these workshops.' What gives more credence to their commendation is that they are also forthright in naming the programmes that were either too esoteric or had no practical use for them.

One of the milestones in their journey of self-development was when they learnt to exercise greater autonomy in their timetables, pedagogy, methods of assessment and in the overall conduct of school activities. As one of the teachers told us, 'I came back liberated from the workshop. I realised I was no longer a slave of the syllabus or textbooks. Rather, I was the master.' Above all, many of them spoke about how, in this quest to become better teachers, their understanding of the aims of education, the role of the curriculum, their belief in the principles of fairness and equity and the connection between education and a better society were sharpened. Central to this transformation was the conviction they developed that every child could learn, that equity in the classroom defines the ethos of any school.

It is a sad fact that in our country people with great scholastic or academic achievements seldom choose school teaching as a profession. Those with ordinary academic abilities become school teachers, a choice that may not always be their first career option. So, it is remarkable to see these ordinarily endowed people having become teachers resolutely strive to become better at their profession. The complexities and scale of our education system are such that it fails to adequately support our teachers with in-service professional development. Teachers in rural postings often fend for themselves. Some find this daunting but those who have the grit, stay the course. They seek out opportunities to learn, in both formal settings and in informal and voluntary groups. Voluntary Teacher Forums have been formed to encourage teachers to raise and discuss academic and pedagogic issues. Teachers also attend residential summer and winter workshops, willingly sacrificing their vacations. Many teachers narrated their interactions at VTFs and TLCs (also known as Learning Resource Centres in some districts) showing the immense value these hold for them. Teachers invest time after school hours to participate in these. Over time, this keen desire to improve has become a lifelong habit. Perhaps, this is what makes them reflect on a daily basis, writing a daily journal of what went well and what could have been done better in their classroom. Fifteen years ago, the practice of writing a daily diary was negligible among teachers, even general reading was limited, but now, more teachers are inculcating this habit.

There are other winds of change. In the feudal districts of Rajasthan, the number of lady teachers who attend residential programmes is slowly increasing. It is as much a revelation of changing gender norms in families as of the teachers' commitment to their self-development. Some of the senior teachers who joined the department after their Class XII have since acquired their undergraduate and even postgraduate degrees while in service. The younger teachers who are more tech-savvy, find the computers at the TLC quite useful for browsing and sourcing material that they can use in their classrooms. A few of them have bought laptops for personal use.

In recent years, WhatsApp groups have become a major source of academic support for teachers. While only around 15-20 per cent of teachers may regularly attend VTFs, a much larger number are members of their local block or district WhatsApp groups. There are subject-wise groups in which they discuss issues and offer solutions to one another. These are early days but reticent or diffident teachers derive benefit from this platform as their peers discuss issues that are equally relevant to them. The one subject that all teachers struggle with is English. But they hope to find their way through it with the help of smartphones and the internet.

On a rainy day, this teacher wades through waist-deep water to reach her school, always on time.

MADHULIKA THAPLIYAL
Primary School, Gamdidgaon, Bhatwari Block,
Uttarkashi District, Uttarakhand

Gamdidgaon is a gently winding uphill trek of around two kilometres from the main road. On a rain-swept day, clouds can be seen gliding slowly over the roof of the school building. The village's population of around five hundred people is spread across a cluster of two to three bastis (settlements). Twenty boys and nineteen girls in the age group of six to eleven years are enrolled in the Gamdidgaon Primary School. Around ten to twelve children attend a private school. The Gamdidgaon Primary School has three classrooms. Madhulika Thapliyal is the head teacher, assisted by Pavitra Rawat. The two ladies teach all the classes and have divided the subjects between themselves.

Madhulika has an MA in Hindi and the BTC (Basic Teaching Certificate). She started her career as a teacher in 1993 at the Primary School, Mushiksaur in the same block of Bhatwari and was there for thirteen years. It is now nearly eleven years since she moved to Gamdidgaon. Her imprint on Mushiksaur is evident from the fact that it is now one of the Model Primary Schools in the block. At Gamdidgaon, Madhulika has built a deep and lasting relationship with the community and the SDMC. The president of the SDMC is Sharad Singh Negi and chances are that if he is not working on his farm, he will be at the school. He was instrumental in persuading the NGO, Goonj, to donate a desktop computer to the school so that children could get acquainted with computers. The SDMC has engaged a young volunteer from the village to teach the basic uses of computers to children of Classes IV and V. Whatever may be the merits of this initiative, the important thing to note is the extent of the involvement of the SDMC president in the affairs of the school and his willingness to bring into the school, for the benefit of the children of his village, facilities that are outside the system.

This support is a form of reciprocation that Madhulika has received from the community for her deep commitment towards the children of Gamdidgaon. Madhulika lives in far-away Kutchidevi. Her day begins at 4 a.m. with the preparation of meals for her family. By 6.45 a.m., she is at the bus stand to take a bus to the stop nearest to Gamdidgaon from where she takes an auto (spending around Rs 2,000 every month on it) to the foot of the hill and then climbs the two-kilometre foot trail that leads to the village. By 7.45 a.m., Madhulika is at the school. On rainy days, this trudge up the hill has to be experienced to understand the ordeal. More than once every season, Madhulika finds herself waist deep in slush at some point in her trek. Sometimes, a tree branch that she can hold to haul herself up and proceed is all she can count upon but come what may, she is at school on time, every single day. This is not the only reason that has endeared Madhulika to the community.

Madhulika is a modest person and if you ask what makes her such a fine teacher, she will gently brush the compliment aside by saying, 'I am not doing anything special.' Observing her at work, however, one will notice a person who cares for every child and a teacher who is immensely competent. There is a focus and energy with which she moves around the classroom to ensure that every child is engaged. One can also see how completely at ease the children are in her classroom. Even on the rainiest days, thirty-six of the thirty-nine children will be at the school in time for the morning assembly. They love to come to school and will not miss it for anything. Many of the children are siblings and Madhulika believes that too is a factor that adds to their daily attendance.

In 2010, the education department of Uttarakhand sent around twenty teachers from each district to observe and learn the acclaimed multi-grade, multi-level (MGML) pedagogy developed at the Rishi Valley Institute for Education Resources (RIVER) in Madanapalle, Andhra Pradesh. The Government had high hopes that this activity-based learning methodology would be absorbed and integrated over time but sadly, it did not take root. Only a handful of teachers came back with a sound understanding and a resolve to attempt this pedagogy in their own classrooms. Madhulika was one of them. She says that this exposure had a deep impact on her. Earlier, she was aware that despite her best efforts some children would disengage and fall behind in her Class. Returning from her training at Rishi Valley, she tried the pedagogy and observed that her students were able to learn at their own pace and also importantly, sustain their interest as they moved ahead. She saw that in this way, the entire class was engaged. The children, she observed, were motivated to put in efforts when they saw that their classmates were also trying to learn. This, she believes, was the key to the children becoming independent learners and, in a way, take charge of their own learning. For a teacher, this methodology, perhaps calls for greater skill and more work but most importantly, it needs a keen eye, an alert mind and even physical agility to move from group to group.

Often, in lonely outposts like Gamdidgaon, the learning achievements of these first-generation learners are only an incidental indicator of their actual learning. Their ability to discuss issues freely with their teacher is a more nuanced indicator, something we saw here. Another remarkable pointer is the way in which children from Classes IV and V take turns to write the 'News of the Day' on the blackboard in the courtyard reserved for this activity. That rain-swept morning on the board we read, 'Shivraj's father is coming from Dehradun today', indicating the importance of the event for the village folk. Below this, written in another child's handwriting was, 'Pankaj's great-grandmother is very ill', which demonstrated their care and concern for each other. For Madhulika, what features on this school news bulletin is an important marker of the children's ability to express themselves and of the social values they are developing in her school.

The members of the Foundation's field institute at Uttarkashi have had a long-standing relationship with the teachers of the district since 2005 when almost half the total number of primary schools participated in the LGP. That is how they have developed a close relationship with the Primary School, Gamdidgaon. Madhulika takes an active part in various events and capacity-building workshops and is a regular participant at the TLC. Despite all her domestic responsibilities after school hours, she attends the meetings and says that it is worth the effort because these interactions have further strengthened her competence.

In the education department, it takes some sustained effort or luck for word to get around and for good work and people to get noticed. Madhulika's work earlier at Mushiksaur had probably got her the nomination to the Rishi Valley training programme. And now, the Primary School, Gamdidgaon is gaining the reputation of a school where children are learning well. The Deputy BEO, having heard this, visited the school to see for himself what Madhulika and her colleague, Pavitra were doing for the children of Gamdidgaon. It was a momentous occasion for the villagers, for no senior officer of the department had ever visited the school before.

'We must learn to come out of our comfort zones.'

RAGHUVENDRA SINGH

Government Primary School, Tilpuri No.1, Gadarpur Block, Udham Singh Nagar District, Uttarakhand

---

'Sanchar aur yaatayat ke saadhan'—this topic about the means of communication and transport is part of the EVS syllabus of Class IV and teaching this is Raghuvendra Singh, the head teacher of GPS, Tilpuri No.1. There is an air of expectancy in the classroom because the children know that their teacher, as he always does, will introduce something interesting in the lesson. Raghuvendra asks each child to draw an item of their choice, name it, list its uses and also recall when they first saw it. Keeping all the children engaged, managing the enthusiasm of some, and coaxing the shy ones to speak up, he soon has a long, tabular list on the blackboard.

Raghuvendra has been a teacher for over twenty-five years. He had just passed his Intermediate in 1991 when his father, who was a government school teacher in the Jaspur block, passed away and as a dependent member, Raghuvendra was given his job. It seems like a long time ago to Raghuvendra, who, after serving at Jaspur for over twelve years, was posted to the Ramjivanpur Primary School in the Gadarpur block and ten years later, in 2013, came to GPS, Tilpuri No.1.

Raghuvendra believes that his greatest strength is his open mind and keenness to continuously learn. He acquired his BA and MA (sociology) degrees through correspondence, while in service. Quite candidly, he tells us that he was initially a very ordinary and conformist teacher but has grown and evolved, absorbing and learning from the numerous teacher development workshops over the years. Self-development gives him fulfilment, he tells us. 'For example, after many years in service, when I was in the Ramjivanpur school, the department sought the voluntary participation of schools in the LGP. My school participated and as a result of that, I understood how we could move from rote learning and mugged-up answers to designing questions that give the children the opportunity to think and write. There were several workshops conducted at that time and I tried to apply what I learnt there in my classroom and slowly my approach changed, my processes changed.'

People who know Raghuvendra from those days, say that he is being modest because even during those years, he would bring a lot of ingenuity to his language lessons. Apparently, the department records show that Ramjivanpur was assessed as the 'best school' in language among the schools of Gadarpur in the school assessment conducted during the LGP. Another old and valuable practice that Raghuvendra maintains is a daily register of his students' responses and learning. What is remarkable is that he manages to update this register in the classroom itself. He says that this enables him to bring a lot more value to the concept of CCE. 'The formats provided by the department are limited and their value, over time, can diminish unless I enrich those with my daily observations.' One simple measure that Raghuvendra applies in assessing his own teaching, is the attendance. He does not want to hide behind the ruse of difficulties in the communities or the lack of interest among parents. So, at Tilpuri No. 1, the attendance which was only around 65 per cent when he arrived, has risen to a consistent 85 per cent. He shares the attendance data with the community, knowing this will gently keep the pressure on the parents to send their children regularly to school. The people of Tilpuri and surrounding areas belong to the Buksa tribe and bring their own dialect and culture to the school. 'I have absorbed a lot from this exposure,' says this teacher. 'Nothing has changed in the children's circumstances but we are teaching and interacting with them in a manner that they feel respected and welcome. People, too often, say that these children cannot learn or will not learn. My mission is simple; I want to prove them wrong. Every child can learn. And purposefully, I make this known to everyone—colleagues, parents and education functionaries—because when they are convinced, it influences their beliefs and practices.'

When we discussed the teaching of Environmental Studies (EVS) with him, Raghuvendra asserted that language is at the core of learning. '*Agar bhaasha mein unki kshamta aur abhivyakti ban sakti hai,* (if they become competent in language and express themselves well) then other things will follow. It makes the children's learning enjoyable.' He refers to his own learning and development as a reason behind this, as also, the reason why he is always looking for a child's language development in the EVS class as a means of assessing the child's overall learning.

Many years after the LGP, when the VTF was initiated, it was only natural that Raghuvendra would be a core member of the initiative. In fact, much earlier, when the district education functionaries mooted the idea of making BRCs as active hubs for teachers and calling these, 'Vibrant Resource Centres', Raghuvendra had championed the proposal with a lot of enthusiasm. He still feels sad that this promising initiative did not take off because some influential teacher union leaders felt threatened that the teachers leading the initiative might themselves become union leaders and office bearers. But he is happy that VTF and TLC that are in many ways, a new avatar of the original proposal, have given the initiative a fresh lease of life. 'The one thing teachers must guard against is complacency. These forums and interactions keep them alert and also help them learn new things. We must learn to come out of our comfort zones. But the urge to learn has to come from within. We must be willing to sacrifice time and put in efforts to learn.' Perhaps among all the teachers we met in Udham Singh Nagar, this teacher best articulated the scope of the VTF and did not mince words in explaining why 'voluntary' participation reflects the teachers' genuine desire to learn.

School, administration and planning take up a lot of Raghuvendra's time but he makes light of it. Thoroughly self-motivated, he is also a person of initiative who did not hesitate to approach the top brass of the nearby Dabur India Ltd. factory to ask them to contribute a part of their CSR fund for the infrastructure that his school was in such dire need of. As a result, a much-needed toilet for girls was built with the active help of a local women's self-help group. The wall of the new toilet speaks of the importance of hygiene and cleanliness. A board at the entrance of Tilpuri No.1 provides a public commitment of the key goals that the school has set for itself. Raghavendra believes that this enables the community to know the quality of schooling that they aim to provide and also invites public scrutiny of their work, which he welcomes.

'Every child from my school must complete high school.'

ANITA RAWAT

Government Upper Primary School, Chaukuni, Rudrapur Block, Udham Singh Nagar District, Uttarakhand

The Upper Primary, Chaukuni has a picture-perfect appearance with a garden and potted plants that the students look after and maintain. The other thing that will strike visitors is the cooperative groupwork that students do without supervision and the manner in which they engage in independent study, seeking help from each other. Such transformations do not happen on their own and here at Chaukuni, they have come about as a result of the gentle guidance from the head teacher, Anita Rawat.

The school has sixty-one children—forty-one boys and twenty girls. The number of girls was even lower in the previous years because they were being sent to an all-girls' school near the village. After Anita spoke to the parents and explained that the Chaukuni school too had good facilities, including a clean functioning toilet, parents were persuaded. Moreover, since the boys were already coming to Chaukuni, it made better sense for siblings to study in the same school. Anita is confident of a further increase in the enrolment of girls in the coming years.

Anita comes from a family of teachers. Her father was in the Army Education Corps who after retirement, taught English in a government-aided school. Her elder sister is a head teacher at a government primary school in Sitargunj and her brother, also a teacher, is a respected academic resource person in the district. Anita joined the education department in 1998 after completing her MA in sociology and BTC, the teacher certification. Later, while in service, she also obtained a BEd degree. She started her career at the Primary School, Malsi in the Rudrapur block and came to the Upper Primary, Chaukuni in 2010 on promotion as head teacher.

Anita is deeply interested in learning and growing in her profession. Like every good teacher, she looks at each day as a fresh experience and constantly seeks avenues where she can build new capabilities. She and her brother have both been involved with the LGP when it was launched in 2005. Her school (at that time, the Primary School, Malsi) participated and in the process, she was also selected to be part of the block's school evaluation team. She says, 'This LGP experience helped me move from textbook-based questions and rote learning to creating a variety of questions that test a student's understanding.' The exposure changed her teaching process as she began to give primacy to understanding and allowed students to express themselves in their own words and not merely reproduce memorised text. 'The wisdom to accept children's expression in their own words enables a teacher to know whether they have understood,' says Anita, who has been an active participant in the various workshops and capacity-building programmes organised in the district. She has attended both the summer and the winter science workshops conducted by the Foundation. 'I liked and valued the biology programme because that is the subject I was least confident in. The course was very practical and I learnt to use a microscope. The manner in which the modules on Light and Electricity in physics; and on Mixtures and Compounds in chemistry were taught, enabled us to visualise how we could teach these topics to the children of Classes VI and VIII. Content is one thing, but we learnt how to develop a topic going from simple to complex concepts—from simple reflection and plane mirrors to reflection off concave and convex mirrors.'

A regular at VTF and TLC, Anita says that the interactive nature of the discussions at these forums have benefits beyond the obvious. She is now able to move from rigid timetables to flexible schedules without losing sight of the syllabus. She has understood the autonomy that is available to teachers and is now in a position to use it. When we talked to her about the continuous assessment of children as an integral part of pedagogy, Anita said that the workshop conducted on CCE provided her with an understanding to develop her own framework of assessment. Instead of being a mechanical exercise, it has now acquired meaning and value. Children's projects in various subjects are now related and connected and that is how she builds each child's learning portfolio.

Anita is a member of a large, ten-member joint family that lives in Rudrapur town. Her husband who was earlier employed in a factory in Gajraula, is now an agriculturist with a twenty-five-acre farm. Her day begins at 4.30 a.m. with a morning walk with her husband. Back home, she prepares breakfast for the large family before leaving for school which is twelve kilometres away, on a Scooty. She does not take work home; it is not a practical proposition for her. Instead, Anita ensures that important tasks such as checking of students' workbooks, lesson-planning for the next day, organising her teaching material and tasks for the children are all completed at school before she leaves for home. Professional work at home constitutes only internet research and exchanges with the teacher community on WhatsApp groups.

Considering the circumstances, Anita feels that the quality of learning in her school is good. She makes it a point to emphasise that apart from acquiring sound conceptual knowledge in subjects, what pleases her more is the all-round development of the children and the manner in which they have developed a socially-responsible and caring attitude. She tells us, 'I keep a close watch on every child to make sure they are well-adjusted and interact with others. If I give them an independent assignment and they are able to do it in a responsible manner, it is an important indicator of their interest in learning. For example, I always ask them to sit in small groups to solve question papers on subjects of their interest. They can take up the subjects in any sequence. They have the freedom; they know we trust them and, so they have to reciprocate with their own commitment.'

Sports is one area where she feels the school has not progressed. Going forward, it is a priority, she says but without much conviction. The children are from economically weak backgrounds and find it difficult to continue through to high school. The community comprises unskilled labourers in cardboard factories, masons, farm labourers and brick-kiln workers. The costs entailed in high school education, the distance to the high school and the need to earn and augment family income is a crushing combination that compels these children to drop out of school. Anita hopes that the situation will improve but irrespective of that, she is focused on the goal she has set for herself—that every child from the Upper Primary School, Chaukuni completes high school.

'I am the master of the syllabus and the textbook.'

SHIKHA GANGWAR

Government Primary School, Maharajpur, Rudrapur Block, Udham Singh Nagar District, Uttarakhand

Shikha Gangwar is candid about her journey as a teacher, sharing where she started from and what she is striving to achieve. One could argue that Shikha was very frank and open because I was accompanied by a person whom she had known professionally for years. But by the end of my visit I was convinced that frankness is her trait and Shikha would have been equally forthcoming even if I had met her by myself.

Shikha completed her MA and BEd and since her husband had a job as a math instructor at the inter-college in Dineshpur, decided to stay in Rudrapur to look after her ailing mother-in-law and work as a teacher in a local private school. For many years, Shikha says that teaching meant completing the syllabus mechanically, being a 'prisoner of the textbook'. In 2006, she completed her Vishisht BTC* and joined the government education department. Three years later, she was posted to this primary school at Maharajpur. Since Maharajpur is at quite a distance from Rudrapur, she quickly concluded that a daily commute by bus, followed by a two-kilometre walk to reach the school would not be a sustainable option. So, at the age of forty, Shikha Gangwar learnt to drive a Scooty.

Maharajpur is a largish village with over one thousand families. Like everywhere else, the well-off folks send their children to private schools while the poor—the ones who eke out a meagre living as farm labourers, factory workers and daily

---

*A qualification required to teach primary classes.

wagers—send their children to the government school. It is a spacious and neat school; has four classrooms, a veranda, and an office-cum-staff room. The library is housed in the room where the children of Class I study. 'It is a good village—parents support the school and appreciate our efforts,' Shikha tells us. There are one hundred and sixty children enrolled, ninety girls and seventy boys. Including the head teacher, there are four teachers. Shikha teaches all subjects in Class III and EVS in Class IV. 'One of the best things here is the understanding and teamwork among us. However, the PTR is a disadvantage and we also have our share of non-academic responsibilities,' she says.

The turning point in her journey as a teacher, that is, when Shikha became aware of a completely different approach to teaching, came a few years ago when the Cluster Resource Coordinator and the Foundation's representative, Amit, asked Shikha to attend a workshop on maths and EVS that was being organised at Rudrapur. 'The workshop opened my eyes. I realised teaching is not a one-way process. I understood that the syllabus and textbook are not my masters, rather I am their master.,' says Shikha. 'Give us an example,' we ask. Shikha responds, 'Earlier, if it was a topic like, "My Family" or "My Home", I would write it on the blackboard and the students would copy it. They would prepare and write down the answers to a set of standard questions. But now, I link every topic with their lives and encourage them to build on their existing knowledge and expression.' So now, topics like "My Family" and "My Home" have become an opportunity for students to do a survey of sorts by talking to family members and relatives; to construct sentences and make illustrations to express themselves. 'Creative expression gets seamlessly built into the process as I also now ask them to complete stories by giving them a few sentences,' adds Shikha. This, obviously, translates into more work for her but it is also clear that she doesn't mind it.

For Shikha, with this changed approach, the lesson plan has become crucial. She invests time on preparing it because she is aware of the diversity in her classroom. 'I have to plan challenging assignments for the quick children even as I build the basics patiently with the others. I realise my methods have to be different and flexible for various topics.' She can see the difference and so can a visitor to her school. The children are at ease with understanding and solving word problems, which is an important indicator that the children have grasped the language of mathematics. *'Ibarti sawal* hamare liye bahut* important *hai*,' is how Shikha summarises this aspect of learning. The children are also able to converse freely with everyone and can explain their comprehension of a topic without hesitation. When we mention these striking aspects about the children to Shikha, she replies, 'We have no need to show or demonstrate our children's achievements to outsiders. We know it and see it daily in the classroom. This is our grip on the CCE. It is a fact that around thirty to thirty-five of the hundred and sixty children are irregular and their learning suffers as a consequence. But what really makes me uneasy is that despite all our efforts, some children, even when they attend school regularly, struggle. I look at this as a failure on my part and I want to come with fresh energy each day to try and give my best.'

Visiting the Primary School, Maharajpur, observing her work and talking to Shikha, provides us with a precious window into the thinking and application of progressive methods of

---

*An arithmetic problem in words.

a dedicated teacher with a genuine interest in continuously improving her own capabilities.

'My students realise the beauty of an equal society through logic and reason.'

CHANDRABHUSHAN BIJLAWAN
Upper Primary School, Sunali, Purola Block,
Uttarkashi District, Uttarakhand

There are two ways of enjoying a visit to a good school. One is to be the proverbial fly on the wall, melt into the crowd to take in everything that happens in the school. Observe how the children come in and take up duties such as cleaning the school, watering plants—smoothly organising and owning responsibilities. Watch how teachers keep a close eye and yet remain unobtrusive as daily activities are carried out. Sit quietly in the classrooms and understand the manner in which the teachers introduce a topic or a theme; how they encourage children to ask questions and develop understanding; the way they use group work, peer learning and teaching-learning materials. One can form an opinion whether there is freedom in the classroom for the children to ask questions, to enquire, explore and develop their understanding of a topic. One can see how children resolve their daily fights and arguments. One can observe the midday meal and also spot teachers gather at the end of the day for an informal briefing session to share observations and insights; and, then as they leave, catch a few laughs on their way out. That kind of a day can be fascinating.

Occasionally, one might also enjoy an equally fantastic day in a school just by sitting with the teachers and having a long, free-wheeling and uninhibited conversation even as time seems to take flight. For the teachers in our remote government schools, these opportunities for long conversations with interested visitors are extremely rare so they too relax and enjoy these thoroughly. Our visit to the Upper Primary School, Sunali, turned out to be one such experience. It was not planned this way but the Annual Sports Festival at the block was on and more than half the students and most teachers were away, participating in it. We were at this school because we had heard that this was not only one of Purola's 'good' schools but a school which had a legendary head teacher, Satyapal Singh from 2000 till he retired in 2015. In fact, if one were to ask teachers from the other schools in the block to name an inspirational head teacher, chances are that they would name Satyapal Singh. But these teachers, as well as those who work closely with schools in Purola would also add that Satyapal Singh was supported by a couple of fine colleagues who worked shoulder to shoulder with him to create this reputation for him and the school. One of them is Chandrabhushan Bijlawan and this is his story, constructed from a day of riveting conversations that covered a range of subjects related to teaching, learning, curriculum and the overall aim of education.

Chandrabhushan, a native of Purola, joined the education service in 1985 after completing his BA in Hindi, political science and sociology. He also has a BTC. After twenty years in Barkot in the Naugaon block, during which time, he also got an MA degree through correspondence, Chandrabhushan came to the Upper Primary School, Sunali in 2005. The school had seventy-eight students in Classes VI, VII and VIII during those years but after another government upper primary school opened nearby, the enrolment in this school went down to thirty-three students. There are four teachers including the current head teacher, Sriram Singh Chauhan. Chandrabhushan teaches science and maths. The other two teachers are Bhajan Singh Rawat, who is in the school since 2002, teaching social science, Hindi and Sanskrit and Sarojini Rawat, who came to the school two years ago and teaches English.

Chandrabhushan is talkative but not garrulous. He is an articulate, thinking person. Without sounding disparaging to anyone, he lets us know, 'These opportunities for conversations on education with visitors are so rare that I get carried away. And it is a fact that such conversations do not take place with "adhikaris" (officers) when they visit the school.'

On children, and how children learn, Bijlawan had a great deal to say. He explained why it is important to understand students, the knowledge they bring to the classroom and give them the opportunity to show and use that knowledge. He says, 'Child-friendly and "bhaya-mukt vaatavaran" (fear-free environment) depends on how much space we give to the children's existing knowledge.' Textbooks are meant to guide one through a curriculum and syllabus but it is for the teacher to know when the textbook is enough and when it is not. 'When I teach science, my laboratory and resource materials become very precious; when I am teaching biology and nature, I must have the freedom to take my students out of the classroom. Teaching EVS from textbooks is hardly comparable to drawing lessons and applications from our daily lives.'

Chandrabhushan's aim is to help his students make connections between textbooks and the world. *'Zindagi se jodna,'* he says pointing to the baanj tree (oak) that abounds in the Yamuna valley and adding that his children have dug the mud around the tree and found water. So, they know that a place with baanj trees means there is plentiful water. He is of the opinion that we cram too much content into the syllabus and would do better with less content and more foundational and conceptual understanding. His reasoning is that if the foundation is strong, children will develop the ability to absorb more and become independent, lifelong learners. This approach is central to Chandrabhushan's pedagogy. As a teacher of maths, it is extremely refreshing to hear him say that a good foundation of maths is built on an understanding of the language of the subject. He says, 'For my students to move from the mechanical learning of algorithms to be able to understand various operations conceptually, to move from the concrete to the abstract, will depend upon my ability as a teacher.' Like all teachers who understand learning, he finds that the teaching of language, mathematics and science is in actual practice, seamless and inseparable. 'We must teach our children English and applications on computers,' he says with as much emphasis as he attaches to it.

A visit to the resource room at Sunali and spending time going over the various material and resources that Chandrabhushan has painstakingly built over the years is perhaps the best tribute one can pay this teacher. Many years ago—perhaps in 2007—he was given the district award for the 'Best teaching-learning material' in maths.

Like other committed teachers, Chandrabhushan too has grown and learnt over the past thirty and more years. A little ruefully, he recalls, 'In the first fifteen years, I taught mechanically. Then somehow, I realised I was not doing things properly. I wanted to really teach maths better.' Bijlawan bought books, read and practised. As his own knowledge improved, he could see it reflect in the soundness of fundamentals and concepts that his students gained. He says, 'Children realise this difference in the quality of their learning and they too respect it.' He says, teachers must read, observe and learn; try different approaches in the classroom and the best indicator that the methods of teaching are effective is when children demonstrate signs that they are becoming self-reliant, capable and confident. Perhaps this inner drive to learn and improve is one of the reasons that Chandrabhushan attends every meeting and academic discussion organised by the Foundation, VTF meetings and subject workshops. Some of these have had a profound impact on him and he recalls both the summer and winter workshops for maths as important in building his capabilities. He shows us the material he has developed as a result of these workshops. For Chandrabhushan, application in the classroom is paramount.

This attitude of self-regulation carries over to other aspects as well—he comes to school early every day to provide additional teaching to the children who need such support. He also identifies ten to fifteen children with an aptitude for science and helps them prepare projects for the Rashtriya Bal Vigyan Congress (see glossary); and in the evenings, after school, he spends time with children who live in Purola town where his home is. He says with a smile that there is self-interest in these actions too. 'You see, I learn from these children every day.'

But with all this focus on learning and teaching, Chandrabhushan is not a unidimensional person. His weekends are spent trekking. 'I have trekked every hill and mountain of Purola. I videograph everything on these treks and I use these in my classroom. There is learning for the children in these. For example, do you know that however well-off a person from the SC community is, they will not wear gold? Or that because of some crazy superstition, no milk is offered to the people of this community? My students learn to shed superstition and in a very natural way, realise the beauty of an equal society. They do not learn to recognise what is wrong or immoral by merely listening to sermons and speeches. They understand this by learning to appreciate reason and logical explanations. They learn to express their views.' Bijlawan then narrated an episode of which he is inordinately proud. A couple of years ago, when the District Magistrate visited Sunali, a student of Class VII, Preeti, submitted a list of things that Sunali Gaon required. The student stunned the DM when she told him, 'We need a good road to the village,' even as the elders hesitated to speak before the senior official. To Chandrabhushan, Preeti's ability to speak without fear and to speak for her people is perhaps the biggest vindication that Upper Primary School, Sunali is providing a good education. He has been able to achieve this within his family too. One of his daughters is studying medicine in Dehradun, and his elder son and another daughter have both completed their engineering degrees. For Chandrabhushan, however, the more important thing in this is that all three children chose their own careers and lived independently in Dehradun.

Chandrabhushan also writes regularly and expresses himself in academic articles for the DIET publication and in other popular publications, such as *Yuvavani* and *Dainik Jagran* on issues of public interest. That he is a thinking, reflective person can also be seen in his postings on the vibrant WhatsApp group formed by teachers in the Uttarkashi district. As our wonderful conversation comes to an end, his words are full of grace, 'I am extremely lucky to be a teacher. It is only in this profession that there is giving and sharing without any expectation in return.'

'The challenge is to learn and improve everyday.'

REKHA CHAMOLI

Primary School, Ganeshpur, Bhatwari Block,
Uttarkashi District, Uttarakhand

The Primary School, Ganeshpur is located quite close to the main town of Uttarkashi and unlike many other schools in the hilly district, is easily accessible as it is adjacent to the road running through the area. In that sense, the school is an 'advantageous' posting as it is not difficult for teachers to reach it and some may even call it a 'coveted' posting. Interestingly, teachers also hesitate to take a posting here because supervising education functionaries too find it convenient to visit and 'inspect' the school more frequently.

The Bhatwari block, of which Ganeshpur is a part, is not particularly prosperous. But Ganeshpur which supplies milk and vegetables to Uttarkashi town and its surrounding areas is a thriving village. It has recovered from the massive earthquake of 1991 and was spared by the 2013 floods. A local perennial river, a tributary of the Bhagirathi, is perhaps also a reason for the village's prosperity.

The Primary School, Ganeshpur has forty-one children enrolled in five classes and has always been a two-teacher school except for a short period, some years ago. There are three classrooms, an office room and a small two-hundred square feet courtyard for the assembly and children's activities. Both the teachers at the school are women—Rekha Chamoli, feisty, self-assured and articulate, and Manju Rana, quiet, unassuming, and a supportive team player.

Among the students enrolled, 65 per cent are girls and only 35 per cent are boys. And the reason for this, as it is in many other parts of the country, is that the parents send their boys to the three private schools in the vicinity and in the Uttarkashi bazaar area shelling out a monthly fee of around Rs 1,000 plus another Rs 1,000 for transportation. The girls are sent to the government school. During the monsoons, when the rains disrupt normal life, attendance can come down to around thirty pupils (around 75 per cent) but during the rest of the year, attendance is well over 95 per cent. In an indictment of the manner in which parents pamper boys and give them preferential treatment, Rekha Chamoli says, 'Even on days when there are heavy rains, it is the girls who come to school while the boys are allowed to stay warm and dry at home. The girls, even when they are seven and eight years old, help their mothers with the cooking, while the boys do not even pick up their plates after meals. All this must change and good education at school must inculcate a sense of equality and fairness among the boys and free us from the grip of patriarchy and male dominance.'

Rekha joined the education department in 2004 with a BSc degree in botany, zoology and chemistry, as well as a BTC. She has been at the Primary School, Ganeshpur since 2009. Between the two of them, Rekha and Manju have divided the subjects and teach all classes from I to V. Manju is elder to Rekha by five years and also her senior in the service. But it is Rekha who is the de-facto leader. Manju is comfortable with this and supports Rekha wholeheartedly. Uttarakhand has a system of rating schools on the basis of a combination of quality of infrastructure and learning parameters. Since the school has a sufficient number of classrooms and a functional toilet—two key components of infrastructure—the school has been rated 'A'. On the learning outcomes, it is rated 'A' or 'B' in the subjects assessed.

Rekha is particular that the education of the children in her school goes beyond learning achievements based on subjects and syllabus. The real learning outcomes, according to her, include having respect for all members of the society, building self-respect and self-confidence. She keeps track of every child who passes out of the school. The children, in turn, also keep in touch with her and share every little detail with her—their progress in studies, the goings on in their families and the community, and other titbits. 'The most satisfying aspect for me is the way in which they have developed self-respect and have gained the respect and trust of their parents and the community. Our motivation does not come from the praise or recognition of the adhikaris but from the people who understand our work,' says Rekha. The self-confidence that she talks about is apparent in the manner in which the children interact with us; in how they read and write trying to comprehend the text that is new to them; and, tackle the arithmetic problems that are outside of their textbooks.

For Rekha, being a reflective practitioner translates into a fairly detailed daily introspection of her work—a diary in which she records her reflections and emotional outpourings. 'For teachers, the challenge is to keep learning and growing. I must remember where I began in 2004; where I was five years later; and, how I have developed to where I am now. I must find the energy to learn every day.' It is no surprise, therefore, that a person with such an attitude finds the various workshops and discussion forums at Uttarkashi a valuable source of personal development. An avid and regular participant in all the teacher development workshops organised in Uttarkashi, Rekha is also a regular participant at VTF and TLC. That evening, we witnessed a VTF in Uttarkashi where around twenty teachers had gathered to discuss the role of poetry in building children's language capabilities. We saw Rekha express herself clearly and without inhibition in this forum and make a valuable contribution to the topic being discussed. At a young age, Rekha had developed a deep interest in poetry and some years ago, published a book of poems, titled *Ped bani stree* (A woman who turned into a tree). Much of the poetry in it is about the feelings and angst of a woman living in a patriarchal, male-dominated society. Rekha's husband is a patwari at Bhatwari, a government servant known to be a kind and conscientious officer and though he may not share the literary inclinations of his wife, is fully supportive of this remarkably forthright and committed school teacher.

How well she expresses herself can be gauged by these lines, 'The real issues of a thinking, working woman can be illustrated by the fact that if a lady teacher reads at home, she is considered as having an "attitude" but if she were to watch TV or knit a sweater or go shopping, it is considered normal behaviour. The restrictions by themselves are not as oppressive as the fact that everything that a girl does is tied to their family's prestige. Girls are brought up with restrictions that conclude with the incontestable *"naak kat jaayegi"* (the family will lose its honour).' For lady teachers who want to learn and grow, challenges manifest themselves in many ways. A male teacher can decide to travel and attend seminars whenever they want but lady teachers have to plan work-related visits months in advance and prepare the ground for the family to accept the travel plan. Often, the men are not interested in the professional lives of the lady teachers in their families. Not having to deal with interference and obstacles is in itself considered 'support' by many lady teachers.

'Children are not empty pots into which I have to pour information.'

SHRISHAILA

Government Lower Primary School, Karadkal Camp,
Surpur Block, Yadgir District, Karnataka

The Surpur taluk can be seen as three contiguous areas—the area in and around Surpur, Narayanpet and Kembhavi. In Kembhavi is a small hamlet called Karadkal Camp which essentially has a mix of SC and Muslim population with a small percentage of the dominant caste Reddy community. It has a lower primary school that caters to the children in the age group of six to eleven years. Being a small hamlet, the school, established in 2004, has only forty-two children in Classes I to V.

Shrishaila joined the school at about the same time that it was established. A native of Vijayapura, young Shrishaila had just completed his pre-university and the TCH (Teacher Certificate Higher) when he was appointed to this school. When he joined the GLPS, Karadkal Camp, the school was a one-room unit and Shrishaila and his colleague (also newly appointed) went around the village and enrolled twenty children in Class I. Step by step, year-on-year, they added classes. Working closely with a very supportive SDMC president, they also built an additional room. The SDMC president personally contributed Rs 4,000 and the two teachers added Rs 2,000 each from their salaries and with this money, purchased basic equipment for the school.

Today, when one visits GLPS, Karadkal Camp, one cannot but appreciate how amazingly well-kept the school is with a neat garden and functioning, clean toilets. This has not happened overnight. Shrishaila has toiled hard for twelve years to create and maintain this school. He has established a great rapport with both the SDMC and the community. The relationship with parents is based on mutual trust. When he first began work, Shrishaila had to visit every home to plead with parents to send their children to school; he had to visit each SDMC member's house to request them to attend meetings. Today, an intimation is enough to summon them all for school-related work and meetings. The relationships are so enduring that the alumni of the school visit regularly. The day we were there, two former students, currently studying at a Morarji school, had dropped by to greet Shrishaila.

By a coincidence, the following day was the 8th Annual Day of the school and we got to talk a bit about the event. The first Annual Day was held in 2009 when the first batch of the school 'graduated' from Class V. Over subsequent years, the alumni of the school have involved themselves completely in organising this event and making sure that it is a grand success. The community too contributes funds for the event. It has also become a tradition that every student who graduates from GLPS, Karadkal Camp is given a gift by the school—a dictionary or a book.

The quality of education that the school provides is evident from the learning levels of the children. Every year, four of nine students from Class V clear the entrance tests to join Morarji schools. Shrishaila and his colleague invest time and extra efforts each day to prepare the children of Class V for the qualifying examination. The school has also received the 'Best Child-Friendly School' award while Shrishaila has received the 'Best Nali-Kali Teacher' award. The community is highly appreciative of how far the school has come since it opened in 2004. They realise that this is a remarkable achievement for a remote village, like theirs. It has instilled in them a pride for their school and a great affection for its heroic teacher.

Shrishaila's home is in Kembhavi town, a ten-kilometre drive that he covers on a motorbike. From 9.30 a.m. to 4.30 p.m., Shrishaila dedicates himself completely to the school and deeply engages with the children. To meet the challenges of multi-grade teaching, he has devised his own methodologies. He has all the autonomy he wants since no block education functionary has visited his school since 2007. He makes and manages the school's schedule smartly and flexibly so that he and his colleague are able to devote appropriate time to each topic. Shrishaila finds the education department's radio programme, *Keli-Kali*, relevant and useful, and uses it unfailingly for the children of Classes IV and V. One fine example of his initiative and farsightedness is that he has established a community library where some of the educated members encourage children to inculcate the habit of reading.

The school has a cabinet with responsibilities assigned to children. These include looking after the garden; ensuring all facilities are well-maintained; and, organising the morning assembly. There are no altercations among the children; they conscientiously avoid physical fights with each other. 'The children have good relations among themselves and resolve all their conflicts by talking and negotiating,' Shrishaila tells us. He is also very pleased and rightfully so, about the fact that right from the time he joined the school in 2004, and much before the RTE came into effect, there has not been a single incident of corporal punishment in his school.

Aware of his strengths, Shrishaila clearly identifies these as: self-confidence to accomplish that which he takes up; investing his own resources and earnings in what he believes will be useful for the children; continuing his studies and acquiring his

BA, MA and BEd degrees through correspondence from the Karnataka University; and, the desire to contribute and commit himself to the community. Self-development and continuously upgrading his own capabilities are of utmost importance to Shrishaila. He regularly attends VTF organised at the TLC at Kembhavi. At the TLC, Shrishaila also plays badminton and volleyball with fellow teachers and has started learning to use the computer. This attitude to constantly better himself is perhaps an inherent trait. As a young, newly-appointed teacher in a small school where he also doubled up as the acting head teacher, he absorbed all the learning he could from the ten-day head teachers' training conducted in 2004 and filed every single nugget of learning, adapting and applying it sensibly and practically in his school. In fact, Shrishaila is one of the teachers in Surpur who has been associated with the Foundation ever since the inception of the CFSI. This association enabled his participation in M.N. Baig's* head teachers' training programme and in a rare, large-group head teachers' workshop conducted by Sunny Tharappan.**

He acknowledges that his understanding of the nature of social science and its pedagogy have been greatly informed by the summer workshop on the subject. 'Perspective on social science using the content of map reading, hunters and gatherers,' he tells us, recalling the title accurately.

---

*M.N. Baig, retired Director in the Karnataka Education Department, led the Nali Kali programme when it was launched in the State in early 2000. He led the Child-Friendly School Initiative (CFSI) in Surpur from 2004 to 2007.

**Sunny Tharappan is a Mangalore based Human Resource Development trainer who conducts large-scale leadership development programmes for school principals and leaders in social sector organisations.

Shrishaila believes that these continuous capacity-building workshops have helped broaden his understanding of the aims of education and changed his beliefs about teaching and the way children learn. He explains, 'I am aware that children are not empty pots into which I have to pour information. I would rather use worksheets, discuss concepts and let my children deliberate in groups and build their own understanding.' He adds, 'I now completely understand what people mean when they say children learn in a fearless environment. The classroom is not just a space for joyful learning, rather it is a space for children to work things out by themselves; where they have the freedom to ask questions. In fact, this is also a reason why my children do well, both in traditional exams and also in the entrance test for the Morarji school.' His clear articulation explains how well he has absorbed the essence and spirit of Nali-Kali. While he gives credit to the inputs that he received from the CFSI for his growth and development as a thinking teacher, those who have seen him over the years maintain that the credit belongs entirely to Shrishaila due to his attitude towards learning.

Keen on sports in his school days, Shrishaila wanted to become a policeman, but after he secured good grades in the pre-university examination (equivalent to Class XII), he decided to do a teachers' training course and become a teacher. 'The best decision of my life,' he will tell anyone who asks him.

Three young teachers—their vision, will, energy and efforts

GOVIND PRAJAPAT, MANSAURBAI CHAUDHARY, KALURAM YADAV

Government Primary School, Rawta, Deoli Block, Tonk District, Rajasthan

The Deoli block is in the southwest part of Tonk district. When the government decided to build the Bisalpur Dam on the river Banas in this region to supply water for irrigation to Sawai Madhopur and Tonk districts and drinking water to Ajmer, Jaipur and Tonk districts, the people of the block protested against displacement and difficulties caused by the project. At the height of the conflict, I have heard that Medha Patkar too was there. All that seemed like a long time ago as we drove to the village of Rawta. There were residential quarters on both sides of the road that the government had built for the displaced. The village of Rawta is very close to where the dam has been constructed and when we met people here, they asked us to go see the Bisalpur Dam. It has now become a tourist attraction.

My colleagues were hesitant while recommending the Primary School, Rawta for my visit. They felt that the school's minimal infrastructure and unattractive appearance might be a dampener. But as I have said elsewhere in this narrative, sometimes, many fine attributes can lie hidden behind a poor appearance. Truth be told, the infrastructure was not bad. There were three classrooms and three teachers for the seventy-two children in Classes I to V. The school had a functional toilet although no running water. Water has to be carried in a bucket from the only tap in the school.

All three teachers were immersed in their lessons when we arrived at the school. Spending enough time there, we were able to observe them in their classes; interact with the children; observe the midday meal; and, we also had some time left for a chat with the teachers. Throughout our time there, we could feel the school buzzing with energy and this evidently was because of the three young teachers. Classes IV and V are held in one room, Class III in another and Classes I and II in the third classroom. Kaluram Yadav teaches English, Mansaurbai Chaudhary teaches Hindi and EVS and Govind Prajapat teaches maths.

Our first stop was Govind's maths class for the children of Classes I and II. Teacher and students were sitting in a circle as Govind taught them about numbers. Within minutes, it became clear that here was a bright teacher bringing some rare innovation to his class. Usually, teachers use pebbles or twine with coloured beads to teach the concept of numbers. However, here, Govind had given each child a few small wooden blocks—cubes of an inch, cuboids of two inches—and it was fascinating to watch the children use these to count, add, subtract and create numbers, following the teacher's instructions. Later, we asked Govind about the use of the wooden blocks. 'I realised that pebbles could be used only for counting and at times, could cause injury too. In my village, there is a furniture maker who has a lot of leftover teak pieces that are useless for him. So, I asked him to chop those into small blocks. I now use these for the numbers theme and also to help children understand operations like multiplication; patterns, shapes; and, to build the most stable constructions.' Even as we were speaking, two children could be seen building towers with the wood pieces. Govind showed us how he uses the wood blocks to create multiplication tables. Govind is very young—twenty-six years old and joined the education department in 2017 after clearing the REET (Rajasthan Eligibility Examination for Teachers). He did his BSTC (Basic School Training Certificate), the teaching diploma after school and plans to complete his BA through correspondence. His father is a tailor in the village but many of his close relatives are teachers, and he was motivated to become one too.

'I got the 168th rank in the state and the 5th in Tonk district in REET,' Govind says with evident pride. He is enjoying every minute of his life as a teacher and acknowledges that the work of his predecessor at the school has been indispensable. *'Ghanshyam sir ne bacchon ko itna accha padhaya ki unke* concepts *bilkul* clear *hain.* He has gone away on promotion and it is my responsibility that I maintain the high standards that he has set.' We asked him about the challenging aspects of being a teacher and what efforts he has taken to overcome them. Govind's response was quick, 'Because I found it difficult to teach fractions, the children found it difficult to understand. The responsibility was entirely mine. When I attended the maths training workshop conducted by Hanuman of the Foundation, I was able to understand how the use of puzzle blocks, cards and fraction wall would help me explain the concept to the children. It was a breakthrough learning for me.'

Bright and inquisitive, Govind also downloads material on his smartphone. We noticed that everything he told us was accompanied by a display of the material and a demonstration of its application. For example, he showed us a YouTube download of the concept of two-digit addition with carryover. With a broad grin, he says, he is now improving his English. 'Now-a-days, there are so many new words being used in the news on TV. I am keen to learn and understand words like impeachment, auxiliary, amendment ... I am building my own dictionary.' Govind looks slim and fit and when I compliment him on his agility, he immediately demonstrates how he can stand up, from sitting cross-legged on the floor, balancing himself on one leg. This child-like pleasure in simple things is going to be the secret to this man's enduring energy and inquisitiveness.

In the next classroom was Mansaurbai, teaching children the uses and applications of clay and mud. It is a continuation of an earlier class on the topic and the children are helping her construct a table of items made of clay and their applications. As the table is being constructed, there are some useful nuggets that Mansaurbai discusses with the children—why is water cool in a mud pot and not in a steel vessel? Why should a potter run the fine mud through a sieve before adding water to make the putty? Why is firing a clay object important? But the best part of the class, according to us, was when the children trooped out into the courtyard to make objects with clay. Mansaurbai and a few children sieved a large basin of mud, mixed this with water and distributed the dough to children in small groups. Since they had done this exercise earlier, some of the children brought what they had made in the previous class. A diya, a vessel, a pot with a lid and stunningly, even an intricate Shivalinga in a base with a small Parvati beside it. They had even fired these items in an oven. A routine class had turned into an adventure. We asked Mansaurbai whether this kind of 'project work' slowed her down in completing the syllabus. 'Not at all,' the teacher's reply was unambiguous. 'If we plan well and pick and choose themes for such work, not only will children build concepts that will remain with them lifelong, they will also develop the interest to try things out by themselves. Syllabus complete *karne mein koi dikkat nahi* (no problem with completing the syllabus),' she states with confidence. At thirty, she is the eldest among the trio at PS, Rawta. She lives five kilometres from Rawta and has a three-year-old child at home who is looked after by her husband while she is at school. She commutes on a Scooty and has an air of confidence that is quite pleasing. She joined the education department in the Deoli block in 2015 and taught maths in her previous school before coming to Rawta in 2017. With a BA and BEd, Mansaurbai is a 'Level 2' teacher, which means, she is qualified to teach the upper primary classes. One feels that if she gets an opportunity to teach upper primary classes, she would take it even though she is enjoying her time with the primary classes in Rawta. If she moves away, the children of Rawta will miss her sorely.

Kaluram Yadav was teaching grammar—the use of articles 'a', 'an', and 'the' in the English language. He seemed like a very organised teacher. One could gather that he had the lesson planned meticulously with clear examples, a set of tasks for the children, a method for engaging every child and a clear means of testing the understanding of the children before proceeding with the lesson. By the end of the lesson, he was reasonably confident that the children had learnt when to use which article. We loved the way he explained why 'an' is used before the words, 'hour' and 'honest.' Kaluram wrote all the vowels and words in Hindi which immediately enabled the children to grasp the concept that the consonant sound in some English words beginning with it is silent. So phonetically, the words begin with the vowel sound that follows it. As he put the chalk away, it was time for the midday meal.

After their midday meal, the children spent some time in the open compound that serves as a playground before quickly assembling in their classrooms. Independently, they formed groups and were quickly engaged in work. There was rumble and chatter as they settled down but the teachers at Rawta are not overbearing or insistent on silence and such kind of 'discipline'.

Kaluram is twenty-eight and he joined the education department in 2012 with a posting in Barmer district where he taught in a single-teacher school till 2015. But he wanted to come back to his native district of Tonk so he resigned from service and wrote the teacher selection examination again to get a better rank that would enable him to get a posting in Tonk. That is how Kaluram came to this school at Rawta in 2015. When he joined the service, he had only completed his schooling followed by a diploma in teaching, but in the ensuing five years, Kaluram has also obtained a BA degree through correspondence.

All three teachers are young, energetic and bright and this must be one of the best teams of teachers in the Tonk district. They have marked out some clear goals for the near future. One among them is that at least some of their Class V students should write and clear the Navodaya exam. 'It is difficult but we think four to five children have the potential to clear it. Last year, of the seventeen children who wrote the Rajasthan Board Class V exams, thirteen got an A+ grade which is awarded to those who score more than 91 per cent.'

The teachers would like the community to take more interest in the school and their children's education. But they are so hard-pressed for time—both parents working as daily wage labourers who leave home early and return late—they cannot even cursorily check what their children are learning at school. Most of them belong to the Kahar (OBC) community while a few are from the Mali community whose occupation is growing or selling vegetables. Most people in this village and surrounding ones lost their land when the Bisalpur Dam was constructed. As we leave, Kaluram says, 'Although they received compensation for the land that they lost, they are no longer farmers. They have become mazdoors.'

The ringing tones of '*Ekai, dahai, saikda, hazaar*'

KAMALCHAND MALI

Government Primary School, Damodarpura, Diggi Panchayat, Malpura Block, Tonk District

---

Generally, if one is planning to visit a school in the morning, it is good to reach in time for the assembly. That early winter morning, we reached the Primary School at Damodarpura at 9.15 a.m., a good twenty-five minutes before the start of the school day. Wondering how we would pass the time before school started, we walked in hesitantly, only to be greeted by a noisy bunch of three- to eleven-year-old children. The school is a long straight building with three rooms and a veranda. On either side of the steps leading to the veranda, we counted thirty-four pairs of tiny footwear neatly lined up. Wow!

The children of Classes I and II had already deposited their school bags in their classroom and were engaged in animated discussions in the courtyard. Their seniors, the children of Classes III, IV and V were quieter and still inside their classroom. The room in the middle was the anganwadi and nine of the fifteen tiny-tots had already arrived and seemed quite comfortable amidst the older children, some of who must be their siblings. The enrolment at the school is forty-eight and thirty-four children were already present.

In the courtyard, Kamalchand Mali, one of the two teachers at Damodarpura, had also arrived and was engrossed in a conversation with a group of older children. We came to know that these seven children were the alumni of PS, Damodarpura, currently studying in the Upper Primary School, Diggi, about two kilometres away. Apparently, they are so attached to their primary school and teachers that they make it a point to spend a few minutes here every morning.

The remaining fourteen children and the second teacher, Radheyshyam Chaudhary also arrived by 9.25 a.m. and the school was ready for the morning assembly fifteen minutes ahead of schedule. It was being conducted that day in one of the classrooms rather than in the open because the mid-November morning already carried a sharp nip in the air. Sitting cross-legged among the children in the last row, we reflected on this daily routine, called 'Prarthana' in our rural schools. Eyes closed, reciting sometimes in tune but often off-key, slokas in Sanskrit, the Saraswati Vandana, the national pledge and some Hindi poems and couplets that invoke 'prem ki ganga' and 'prem ka sagar'—do the children internalise any of this? Is it just a hollow routine? But looking at the young, earnest faces, one wants to believe that it creates some gentleness, some virtues of sharing and caring in the hearts of these children. Perhaps, it prepares them for the day's work at school. Even as we reflect on this, the children move on to other activities. A Class IV boy narrates a story about friendship in Hindi which has words in English, such as *ducks, pond, friends* and *rabbit* that every child understands. Three girls from Class III recite a poem and the rest of the assembly joins in the chorus. The poem is about the rain and how precious water is. Another rhyme follows and then some general awareness questions were asked. There were hands raised for almost all the questions. Next, Kamalchand asked the children some maths and language questions. Most children attempted an answer. The wrong answers too were accepted with equanimity. Kamalchand wrote '5555' on the board and asked if each of the '5s' has the same value since it is the same digit. The children knew the concept of place value well and one of them explained, 'Sir, *har paanch alag* seat *par baitha hai is liye uski* value *bhi alag hai.*' (Every five is in a different place and hence their values are different.) After which children called out the place values and their chorus of '*Ekai, dahai, saikda, hazaar*' (units, tens, hundreds, thousands) resounded across the room. Apparently, the assembly begins early each day so that they are able to get an extra fifteen minutes for these activities.

While Radheshyam went with the children of Classes I and II to their classroom, Kamalchand and the children of Classes III, IV and V stayed back in the same room and organised themselves for the maths class. Kamalchand assigned a task to children from Classes IV and V that looked very interesting. They were divided into smaller groups and each group had a chart with a number of coloured circles, like polka dots, and each of these had a value in units, tens, hundreds or thousands. Each group was also given a bangle that they had to spin on the chart. When the bangle stopped spinning and came to rest encircling some of the dots, the children had to count these dots and calculate their assigned values. Class III children had been told to go out, identify and count the different kinds of trees and shrubs in the premises and then compile a table with the names of the trees in one column and their numbers in descending order in a corresponding column.

Since the children were engrossed in their projects, Kamalchand could talk to us while keeping an eye on them. Forty-eight-year-old Kamalchand, a native of Diggi, completed his BA in 1996 and taught at a private school for two years before becoming a para teacher (contract teacher) at the

Upper Primary School, Malidani, not far from his home. He remained a para teacher till 2008 when he finally became a formal teacher in the education department and was posted to the Primary School, Damodarpura which is five kilometres from his home. He has an eight-year-old daughter who studies in a private school near his home. 'Why not at your school?' we asked. Kamalchand gave us a reason that touched us. He explained that he comes to school either on foot or riding pillion on any scooter coming this way. 'Till 2008, my salary was just Rs 1,200. Only now, have I saved enough to buy a motorcycle. From next year, when I come to the school on my bike, my daughter will come with me and join this school in Class III.' Kamalchand is part of a large joint family, with two brothers farming their 'nau-bigha zameen' (nine bighas of land) and a third, who runs a vegetable shop. They belong to the Mali community known for their skills in cultivating vegetables and fruits. The joint family is a robust and thriving institution in these parts and Kamalchand explains, '*Sab ka kitchen alag hai,*' (everyone has their own kitchen—indicating a certain separateness and a sense of private space amidst their togetherness) almost hinting that it is the reason the system of joint family has sustained. When it comes to family functions, all the brothers pool in the resources and no one looks at the amount each one has contributed.

Coming back to Kamalchand, the teacher, we told him we liked the way he explained the concepts of ascending and descending numbers, the application of graphs and tables and of course the innovative manner of explaining place value. Taking time to reflect, Kamalchand replied, 'What you saw in my classroom today was completely absent ten years ago. I had a very mechanical "talk and chalk" manner of teaching. I might have been sincere and hardworking but that was not enough.

I began attending the VTF in 2009 when it started and I think I owe a lot of my growth as a teacher to what I learnt at the various workshops. I learnt a new way of looking at the organisation of a lesson, the classroom and the pedagogy.'

Without a hint of hyperbole, he asserts that he has not missed a single meeting of VTF because he finds great value in the interactions and the topics discussed. 'I connect these directly with the manner in which I have grown as a teacher and built my skills. I especially remember a workshop on fractions conducted at Malpura in 2010. Till then, I had little confidence in teaching fractions but that workshop provided me with the understanding that I needed.' Reflecting some more, Kamalchand said that the Learning Resource Centre (LRC) with its rich stock of books and material is a great help for teachers like him. The kind of teaching learning-material that he has developed—such as the one we saw for place value—has enabled him to ensure that most children grasp the concept thoroughly. He is a serious person when it comes to his work. 'My only focus is my work—what I must do in school today, what my children should learn, what kind of exercises I must prepare so that every child is engaged. Most of the parents these days take interest and know if homework is given or not. The elder siblings are all literate and therefore now there is a learning environment at home too.'

Kamalchand has an interesting way of explaining how well his children are learning. He says, 'When the children join us in Class I and I begin teaching them, I feel that about six out of ten will go on to complete graduation. By the time they reach Class V, I am confident all ten of them will complete graduation.' It was perhaps the first time in our many school visits that we had heard such an analysis. Incidentally, Kamalchand's confidence seems well-placed because their Class

V Board exam results show that six of the seven children that year had received an A+ grade. The neighbouring villages, as well as the education department authorities, also acknowledge that PS, Damodarpura is one of the better schools in the block. The District Collector heard of it and visited the school.

Head teacher Radheyshyam has been at the school since the time it started in a temple one kilometre down the road. He was the sole teacher till 2006. He and Kamalchand make a good team. Radheyshyam is outgoing, charming and an easy conversationalist. He tells us that the catchment area for his school is the Diggi panchayat with a population of five hundred. Except for two children who go to a private school, all the others attend PS, Damodarpura. The community comprises of people from the Jat, Gujjar, Bhil (ST) and Bhopa communities. While the Jats and the Gujjars are farmers, the Bhils are labourers and the Bhopa community earns its livelihood by rearing and selling animals. 'We make it a point to meet the parents socially outside school hours. Kamal and I exercise complete autonomy in the way we plan our lessons and timetable, so we have almost an hour for assembly, as you saw today and then a full hour for the midday meal and some rest for children at noon,' Radheshyam tells us. As we prepare to leave, he comes along with us to show us the temple where the school began. From there to where it is today, for the two teachers in this small village, the school represents a lifetime's work and achievement.

3

EQUITY AND QUALITY: THEY BEGIN IN THE CLASSROOM

Equity and quality in rural schools is an abstract aspiration. I understood how this plays out in practice years ago when I walked into a primary school in the hamlet of Alluru Vaddarahatti in the Ballari district of Karnataka. Alluru's population was almost entirely made up of people from the ST community; most adults were illiterate and eked out meagre livelihoods as agricultural labourers. In such a setting, the head teacher and his colleague ran a school with a simple and straight yardstick of equity and quality. The two teachers, year after year, prepared every child so well that when the children passed out of the school, each was competent and determined to complete Class XII. This might seem a narrow goal but for children from very disadvantaged backgrounds, completing high school is an orbit-shifting opportunity.

That is why in my current study of good schools, I consciously looked for such evidence in classrooms. Is the last child included? Is the effort on the last child as much as it is on the others? This was the affirmation I sought. In most of the schools I visited, I saw teachers completely involved with their children, trying to engage every child; challenging the quick ones and supporting those struggling. It was clear to me that the children in these schools were learning better from the manner in which they were following the topic in the classroom; responding to or asking questions; the way in which they were interacting with each other; in their ability to read and write texts independently; the manner in which they were attempting maths problems or trying to explain scientific phenomena.

Why are the children learning better in these schools? What are the belief systems of these teachers that are reflected in their classrooms?

If I summarise the core beliefs and pedagogic practices that we saw in these classrooms, the foremost would be the teachers' belief that 'every child can learn; the responsibility is ours.' These teachers try to make the learning experience interesting for each child and respect the existing knowledge they bring to the classroom, using it to build new knowledge. These teachers believe that children develop understanding when they are encouraged to ask questions, are inquisitive, and express themselves without fear. We are the masters of the syllabus, the textbooks and the timetable, not the other way around, teacher after teacher told us. These teachers help children connect concepts with the world around them. The learning of language, maths and science occurs seamlessly together and the boundaries between these subjects often disappear. These teachers recognise the fact that a good grasp on language supports the understanding of mathematical concepts and scientific phenomena.

It is important to note that these teachers try and make up for any inadequacies in their subject knowledge through hard work—painstakingly preparing lesson plans and a variety of worksheets in anticipation of the children's learning responses;

and creating activities, materials and experiments to facilitate learning. An integral and distinctive part of their pedagogy is the manner in which they strive to implement the CCE in true spirit. Many go beyond prescribed formats to record rich observations in individual child portfolios. These are shared with parents in PTMs and among the teachers themselves to plan additional support for identified children. Such support includes personal attention in the classroom, extra classes and customised worksheets.

When one talks to teachers about the quality of teaching and learning in their classrooms, they may often talk about learning achievements and scholastic abilities around subjects. That might mislead us into thinking that they may not have a larger appreciation of the aims of education. Quite the contrary. I observed in many of their processes and practices, a deep appreciation of what they do for the all-round development of a child. These teachers understand that every child has some talent and it is their responsibility to create opportunities for them to express and cultivate it. They believe that good education is not limited to academics but should enable children to develop socially-responsible behaviour and learn to be kind and helpful.

Many of these teachers have created a vibrant and functional library in their schools and appreciate the books and technical expertise offered by organisations such as Room to Read (see glossary). The teachers encourage children to not only borrow and read books but to also narrate what they have read in their own words, in the morning assembly. Teachers believe this develops children's power of expression in addition to widening their worldview. Many schools do not have the luxury of a separate room for the library, so they house it within one of the classrooms. In much the same vein, the morning assembly too is regarded as an important platform that helps children develop the confidence to express themselves in public and to present their talents. Illustratively, a vibrant morning assembly includes storytelling, mastery of multiplication tables, introduction to new English words and phrases, public speaking, questions on general knowledge and current affairs, and music.

At almost every school, the teachers contribute money from their own pockets for stationery, books, worksheets, teaching material, even for uniforms and the upkeep of school facilities. If we probe this, they are embarrassed and brush it aside as a matter of little consequence. Many schools and teachers keep track of what their alumni are doing. A few have the names and records of every old student. Some also have a record of how well their students have performed in Board examinations. For us, an indication of the teachers' relationship with the students is the manner in which the alumni participate and contribute to the Annual Day, Independence Day and other school events.

I must end this introduction by sharing an illustration of the impact of such pedagogy and classroom processes on children's learning. For the children from very disadvantaged backgrounds, admission to the government's Navodaya, Morarji, Adarsh or Rani Channamma schools is a life-changing opportunity. During our school visits, when conversations turned to the question of students' learning, teachers would invariably talk about the preparations for these entrance tests in their schools. Within a block, only around two hundred seats are available every year in these schools so only a fraction of the students who seek admission, get it. But as a result of this diligent preparation, the children are in an excellent position to pursue education in the higher classes. From among the thirty schools that I visited in Surpur, two hundred and thirty-five

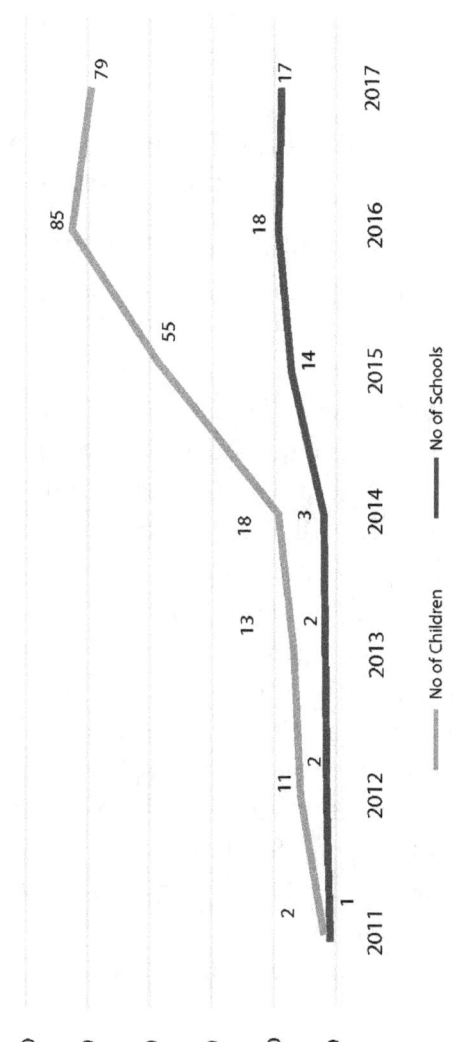

children had qualified for admissions to these schools in the last three years. (see graph 3) It is a remarkable testimony to the teachers' efforts and irrefutable evidence of the children's learning.

The infectious enthusiasm of a wonderful science teacher

SHOORVIR SINGH KHAROLA
Model Upper Primary School, Laata, Bhatwari Block, Uttarkashi District, Uttarakhand

The Model Upper Primary School in the village of Laata, perched high in the serene hills of the Bhatwari block, is special. It has thirty-nine children enrolled in Classes VI, VII and VIII. Of these, twenty-three are girls and sixteen, boys. Because it is a designated Model School, it is also well-resourced with an adequate number of rooms, reasonably-good infrastructure, a good-sized playground (a rarity in the hills) and five teachers. The five teachers form a competent team—the head teacher, Chandramohan Singh, who is just two years away from retirement; the English teacher, Narendra Singh Chauhan at fifty, another veteran; Kushlaprasad Bhat, who teaches Hindi and Sanskrit; Balwant Singh Bisht who teaches social science; and the maths and science teacher, Shoorvir Singh Kharola.

There is not a person in Uttarkashi's education network who has not heard of Kharola. The head teacher and the other teachers know that Kharola is among the finest maths and science teachers in the district and have the wisdom to come together as a cohesive team to complement Kharola. Kharola is almost sixty but since he was awarded the 'Rajya Shikshak

Puraskar' in 2004, he qualified for a two-year extension of service.*

Shoorvir Singh Kharola is a short, broad-built, soft-spoken man whose age sits lightly on him. His enthusiasm for scientific phenomena and his sense of wonder at the world around him can only be described as 'seriously contagious'. His inventiveness and ability to use anything and everything around him—cardboard, calendars, old wedding invitation cards—to convey scientific concepts or mathematical principles makes learning an adventure into the unknown for his students. Even after spending an entire day with Kharola, one is reluctant to leave because he still has so much more to show and share. The subjects he teaches his three classes may be maths and science but his approach and influence on the children and other teachers are not limited to these. For the children, therefore, the three years at this school are a special learning experience, something that those who have opted for private schools shall miss.

When Kharola discusses maths and science education with visitors to the school, he is most comfortable walking them around so he can point to all the things that he connects the science curriculum with. Mushrooms, frogs, moss, lichen, berries, gourds and birds in the surroundings augment the textbooks as he takes the children through the designated syllabus. In the room where he has collected precious teaching resources over decades—geo-boards for shapes and areas, a prime number gameboard and a fraction wall—his joy is akin to that of a child in a toy shop. It is easy to see how the concept of fractions, highest common factor, lowest common multiple and prime numbers, all come alive for children in his class.

---

*State award to teachers for their exemplary work in the field of education.

Maths and science blend seamlessly together for the children of this school. On a bench is the cross section of a tree and a hint of mischief is clear on his face as Kharola asks us to estimate the age of the tree. When we flounder, he shows us the correct way to count the rings on the transverse section of the trunk and gives us another chance. 'I planted this tree and I was here when it was cut, so who but I should know the answer!' With a laugh, he puts us out of our discomfiture.

Lying on his table is a bird's nest. When a bird began building its nest in their school compound, Kharola co-opted his students into a project to study the nest from egg to flight. Research ethics were explained—no touching, no disturbing, just quiet observation and jotting down of notes. Among the fascinating things that the children learnt in this fourteen-day project was that the mother bird kept her nest clean by picking and throwing out with its beak all the baby birds' droppings. Kharola's students also recall how he explained the concept of light and its constituent colours by spraying water from the garden hose against the sun and creating a rainbow on a bright summer day. Recently, when the computer was stolen from the school, Kharola was distraught. But only for a short while. On a visit to Dehradun, when he saw a man selling a six by four-inch rectangular magnifying lens in a pink plastic frame for Rs 150, an idea struck him and he bought it in a flash. Today, to show a video to his students, he just places this pink-framed lens in front of his mobile phone screen for all of them to watch.

Kharola tells us that the science and mathematics workshops organised by the Foundation in Uttarkashi have been one of the best initiatives in the capacity-building of teachers. He points to a large chart with prime numbers and shows how he has also added other interesting aspects to the chart thanks to the practical tips provided by the facilitator. Kharola is a regular at VTF meetings at Uttarkashi, both as a participant absorbing new ideas and as a resource person contributing from his rich experience. Kharola's magnetic pull on his community of science and maths teachers is one of the major strengths for the district's continuing efforts to build academic and pedagogic capacity among teachers. He plays a significant role in leveraging the various WhatsApp groups that he is a part of—teachers of the block, science teachers of Uttarkashi, maths teachers of Uttarkashi—by regularly sharing inputs, insights and topical news. Within a year, there were over a hundred members in the maths group and over sixty in the science group. Their commitment to learning is such that on a rainy Sunday evening when few people would have left the comfort of their homes, one hundred and twenty-five teachers of Uttarkashi thronged a hall to listen to Devendra Mewadi, a well-known speaker, on the philosophy of science.

Kharola, who is perhaps one of the flag bearers among India's government school teachers devoted to developing scientific temper among children, is, ironically, not a science graduate. He began his journey as a teacher nearly thirty-six years ago on a salary of Rs 440 after completing his Intermediate and BTC. His first posting was to a remote village school of Sanglai in Tehri, which had forty children. As he started working with the children there, mysteriously, vegetables, milk, grains and cereal started arriving on his doorstep. It was the community's way of showing their gratitude. A year later, in March 1982, he officially joined the government education service as a teacher for the upper primary classes and was posted to the Bhatwari block of Uttarkashi district. As time went by, Kharola completed his BA and MA in Hindi and sociology through correspondence programmes. After the stint at the Sanglai school, Kharola taught for eight years at Dilsaur. It was in 2001 that Kharola was transferred to the Upper Primary School, Laata. Even as he now draws up to the end of what has been a most successful and fulfilling journey, Kharola's enthusiasm for science and maths shows no trace of waning.

Like all outstanding teachers, Kharola is a reflective practitioner and something that epitomises this is his daily diary. Writing a daily log has been an old habit and he shows it without hesitation. The first volume has over two hundred and fifty neatly-written daily notes, some as concise as two-hundred words, while others run into several pages. These are the reflections of his day at school, the joys and struggles of teaching. In simple Hindi, he has unfailingly recorded his experiences—from the fulfilment in watching his pupils learn about the lifecycle of birds from real experience; through his frustration at not being able to convincingly explain 'moss and ferns' to them; to an emotional essay on a sad and troubled new child in the school. Kharola's diary would be a precious educational resource for young teachers. Sometimes, he posts some of these diary jottings on the WhatsApp groups.

The National Education Policy and the National Curriculum Framework, for many decades, have emphasised the need to inculcate a scientific temper among children. But this remains confined to documents because of the vice-like grip of rote learning and the tyranny of admissions to higher education institutions based on examinations marks. To break free from this and create classrooms that encourage the spirit of enquiry is a mammoth, uphill task, even in city schools that are considered progressive and have all the necessary equipment at their disposal. Which is why people like Shoorvir Singh Kharola in remote rural schools are trailblazers. They may not have formal degrees in science or the access to sophisticated equipment but their methods are unarguably those that kindle scientific enquiry in the minds of children. When you see Kharola in action, you see hope.

'The ability to read, write, count or multiply without being responsible, cooperative and helpful means little.'

RAMESHWARI LINGWAL
Primary School, Gyansu, Bhatwari Block,
Uttarkashi District, Uttarakhand

Gyansu is a few kilometres away from Uttarkashi town and just a hundred metres from the main road is the Primary School, Gyansu. It is an old school, established in 1960 and in those days was the only school in the entire Gyansu territory. It has historically been a good school and even with the springing up of a number of private schools in the area, has managed to hold its own. PS, Gyansu has forty-one boys and twenty-nine girls on its rolls. It had two teachers till 2015 and has four now. Within its limited space, the school has four classrooms, a library, a toilet and a small courtyard for assembly. It has a good reputation too, for which the credit goes to Rameshwari Lingwal, the head teacher and her colleague, Darbeshwari Bahuguna.

Rameshwari's story is fascinating, with the person being as much so, as the teacher. She had a bit of a shaky start to her career with the education department when she joined in 2001 and was posted to a school in a remote village called Banaut in the Chinyali block. On the first day of her first job, Rameshwari left home in Uttarkashi town at 8 a.m. but reached the school only by 1 p.m. to be greeted by a locked gate. The other teacher at the school had not come! By the time she returned home, she was in tears. At around 11 p.m., someone knocked at her door. She opened it to find the other teacher standing outside. She had come to tell Rameshwari that she would take her along to the school the next day. That is how Rameshwari joined duty the next morning at 11 a.m. It was clear to her that the only way she could work there would be if she lived in the village. So Rameshwari found accommodation for herself and her two-month-old daughter with a family that had a home with some basic amenities like a toilet. For the next five years, she lived there, away from her husband and their large, joint family. Once in two months, she would visit them but was otherwise completely devoted to the school at Banaut. She would carry her infant to school and everywhere she went because she had no other option. In no time, Rameshwari had won the hearts of the people of the village.

In 2006, Rameshwari applied for a transfer to a school in Khand village in the Dunda block and was finally able to join her husband and the joint family in their home. Her sincerity and devotion in Banaut and Khand were recognised by the department and in 2010, she was transferred to this school at Gyansu. Her life has become relatively better organised after this move since the family home is not far from Gyansu. Her husband runs a shop in Uttarkashi which is a stable business. At home, she has her hands full with caring for her sister-in-law and ninety-year-old father-in-law. Only when their personal needs have been taken care of, does Rameshwari retire for the day. She gets up early to cook for the family and by 7 a.m., she is ready to leave for school.

Within minutes into a conversation with Rameshwari, one is struck by her optimism and good cheer. For the children in the school, it is wonderful that they have a teacher who is intent on spreading this cheer and energy among them. Rameshwari's ownership of PS, Gyansu is reflected in a number of ways and she credits this to her continuous learning and development. In 2010, she was among the teachers that the state government sent to the Rishi Valley Education Resource Centre to learn their MGML pedagogy. Not all teachers who received this opportunity brought the learning back into their classrooms. But Rameshwari not only found ways to adapt and use this in her classroom, but was also able to inspire interest in her colleague Darbeshwari who also learnt this pedagogy from her. PS, Gyansu, was thus, able to implement the Rishi Valley model of MGML pedagogy.

As the Foundation team in Uttarkashi established the district institute and began conducting workshops and cluster-level meetings of teachers to discuss the larger aims of education as also the specific aspects of pedagogy, subject knowledge and the running of a good school, Rameshwari began to interact closely with her peers and with the facilitators at these workshops. As a result, she says, her perspective and understanding grew significantly. She was always passionate about being a good teacher and these opportunities empowered her to become a more accomplished teacher.

Rameshwari maintains a daily diary and is convinced that this is one of the most important things that a teacher can do. She says, 'To reflect on what went well and what did not during a day is important in a teacher's life because every day is a fresh experience. How children learn, how they should be taught are complex issues that we need to think about constantly.'

Rameshwari credits learning outcomes of her children to their command over reading, writing and numeracy and this, she believes, can only be possible if they are able to express themselves and are not trapped in rote learning. To understand how she is able to translate this into action, one needs to observe her class. The lesson of the day was to learn to write a formal letter. In most schools, this is a mechanical process—representative of the ills of rote learning—of children memorising the standard application of leave to their head master either due to illness or to attend a wedding. In Rameshwari's class, the children began by discussing and understanding the concept of a letter. They, then, discussed why a formal letter is required, what kind of issues require a formal letter, who one addresses such letters to and so on. At the end of this brainstorming, nearly half a dozen situations were finalised and the children began to write letters on their own. One child wrote to the District Magistrate about the water problem his family faces, another to the authorities on the power cuts in her mohalla, and a third composed a letter to her teacher asking that her essay be published in the 'Deewar Patrika' (wall magazine) of the school!

Later in the afternoon, the topic was to understand herbivores and carnivores. Rameshwari decided that for this topic the children ought to bring their existing knowledge into the discussion. She set the fourteen children on the task of discussing the subject among themselves before they came back to her with their understanding. It is difficult for even mature adults to discuss any subject in a large group while giving space to each other but the children demonstrated remarkable maturity and perspicacity in this. They formed three sub-groups—two with five and one with four kids—for an initial discussion and then came together to discuss and synthesise their learning. Sitting ten yards away, with a cursory eye on them, Rameshwari could not have been more pleased. That evening, in her diary, the reflection of the day was on how her children had been able to organise themselves and manage a difficult task exceptionally well.

These examples are also evidence of another attribute of the school—high energy combined with space for each one. It is Rameshwari's constant attempt to ensure that every child is actively engaged; that children help each other and are cooperative. In this way, she combines the social development of the children with the syllabus that she has to transact. She says, 'The ability to read, write, count or multiply without being good, responsible, cooperative and helpful means little to me.' The children actively participate in the upkeep of their school and extracurricular activities like art, music and general awareness are as much a part of their timetables, as the lessons. They have won several cluster and block level competitions and have participated at the district level too. All their activities and achievements are shared with parents and the community who Rameshwari meets every month or even in a fortnight if she thinks it necessary. Parents attend the PTMs in good numbers. The SMC works smoothly and has won the 'Best SMC' award, a testimony of the trust the community has in the school.

In many government schools that I visited, I learnt how teachers support the economically and academically disadvantaged children. At PS, Gyansu, while the government provides free uniforms for all girls and all children from the SC community, there are some boys who cannot afford to buy uniforms and it is Rameshwari and Darbeshwari who fork out the money for this. They have also identified the children who need extra academic support. For Rameshwari, CCE was never a new concept. 'We know each child intimately; we know what a child learns each day and the kind of attention they require. In fact, our children do not even know that we are assessing their learning; it is such an integral part of the teaching-learning process at our school. Periodically, we identify children who are facing difficulties and give them personal attention.'

In 2015, Rameshwari was awarded the 'Rajya Shikshak Puraskar'. She remains modest as she tells us, 'This has always been a good school and the teachers here were always dedicated. PS, Gyansu's children have gone on to become teachers and engineers.' Perhaps it is this modesty and her insistence that she is only continuing the good work at the school that speaks the most about the outstanding person this primary school teacher is. At the end of a hectic day at school, Rameshwari was as buoyant as she was in the morning assembly; as though she could not wait to come back to school the next morning.

From winding transformers to transforming the lives of children

PARAMESHWARIAH HIREMATH
Government Higher Primary School, Yaligi, Surpur Block, Yadgir District, Karnataka

Parameshwariah Hiremath, forty-eight, is a man of few words. Solemn and serious, he has little time or inclination for small talk. He would rather spend time with his students. So, while observing him in a classroom interacting with children is a pleasure, to get him to spend a couple of hours talking about his school and work, is fascinating.

Parameshwariah began his career as an assistant librarian in a Navodaya school and later took up a job as an electrician. He spent three years winding transformers. In 1999, when he was around thirty, he joined the education department after obtaining a graduate degree and the ITC. His first posting as a teacher was in GLPS, Dadalapuri, Surpur taluk. In 2003, he was removed from service because the court ruled that the additional grace marks for 'rural reservation' that had been introduced by the previous state government were no longer valid. Many teachers in a similar predicament, affected by this overturning of the government order, appealed against it in the High Court. The High Court upheld the appeal and reinstated them. So, in 2004, Parameshwariah was posted to GLPS, Ektapur. Within a year, his capabilities were recognised and he was appointed as a BRP in which capacity he worked from 2005 to 2013.

After this long stint as a BRP, Parameshwariah joined GHPS, Yaligi, an old institution that was established in the mid-1950s. This is a large school with six hundred and seventy students in Classes I to VII and eleven teachers (against a sanctioned fifteen).

Parameshwariah teaches Class IV. There are ninety children enrolled in his class but only sixty attend school. The thirty other boys, who do not come to school, are sent by their parents for private coaching—a curious case of boys being enrolled in a government school but attending a private school, which is known as 'private coaching' in local parlance. Parameshwariah is, however, not fazed by this situation. When he joined the school in 2013, only fifteen students would come to class regularly but within a year, he had demonstrated how well his students were learning and many parents pulled their children out of private coaching and put them into Parameshwariah's class.

Yaligi is a village where internecine wars and violence among the rich communities are common. As a result, many parents are wary of coming to school to ask teachers questions about their children's education, fearing that they may complain to the rich and dominant leaders of the community. So, Parameshwariah encourages his students to talk about school at home. Indirectly, the parents get to know how much their children love going to school and enjoy his classes. Most parents are barely literate, nearly 60 per cent of them can only put their thumb impression on report cards.

Parameshwariah came to Yaligi with a strong reputation as a good teacher who follows a sound pedagogy and classroom processes. The head teacher does not interfere in his work and Parameshwariah is thankful. An introvert and a private person, Parameshwariah keeps to himself. His interactions with colleagues are only during tea and lunch time or when common teacher meetings are held. He does not offer them advice but without a trace of false modesty mentions that these teachers can see that what he is doing in his class is very effective but are either unwilling or unable to apply some of these same principles in their own classes.

His class, students and their learning are his single-minded focus and he is not interested in assuming academic support roles such as that of a CRP or BRP anymore. He is completely content with being in his classroom with his students. His only regret seems to be that when the children from his Class IV go to Class V, they miss out on the teaching practices that he has effectively evolved. He wishes that at least the Class V teachers would continue with some of these. Not disparagingly, but rather pragmatically, Parameshwariah mentions that only one in four teachers change. Citing his own example, he tells us that it was only when he went to see an ideal school in Kerala that his mind opened up to the many possibilities that he could try out in his classroom. He deeply desires to be the best teacher he can and does not look for external approbation or endorsement from colleagues or supervising functionaries.

Having been associated with the CFSI during his tenure as a BRP, Parameshwariah acknowledges that the worksheets, individual reading boards and various teaching-learning material from the programme are extremely useful in his classroom and have greatly informed his own teaching style and pedagogy. Parameshwariah was selected as one of the trainers for Nali-Kali from the district and is also a member of a group constituted by the DSERT to develop training modules on Nali-Kali. When the TLC was established in the Surpur block, Parameshwariah became an active visitor and participant, eager to learn from all the material that was available. He is also a regular participant in the VTF where his contributions to discussions on various topics are valued highly by other members. Parameshwariah tells us that the summer workshop on social science organised by the Foundation in HD Kote has helped him gain a deeper understanding of the subject. In a fine articulation of why and how we must teach history, he said, 'We must communicate that evidence and enquiry, rather than memorisation, are important in this subject. That is why I bring reason, some logic and interesting connections while discussing historical events. Once I do that, I find children also tend to remember better.'

While Parameshwariah may be completely focused on his own classroom and students, it does not imply that he keeps himself restricted to these. When he joined GHPS, Yaligi in 2013, he could see the poor learning levels of students across all classes and decided that his first project would be to address this. He identified forty-five children from Classes V, VI and VII whose learning levels were far below expected, and conducted special Classes for them. He did this purely as a personal commitment to help these children achieve some competence in reading, writing, comprehension and numeracy. Within six months, these children were doing remarkably well and had demonstrated that every child could learn. 'If only,' he emphasises, 'we teachers are willing to put in more effort, a lot more effort.' He tells us, 'The learning that I got from the Foundation's programme was very useful when I conducted the accelerated learning for those forty-five children. Children themselves become aware that they are learning and realise that the classroom can be interesting. I think this is the reason they are regular and return to school every year.' Parameshwariah is confident that his school will be among the top ones in the KSQAAC assessments. But he still rues the fact that 'six to eight of these sixty children are still not learning at all and I am concerned about them.'

Parameshwariah organises his classroom meticulously. He ensures that the children are engaged in activities continuously because according to him, 'If they are idle, then we will have a problem.' His class has a well-planned timetable that includes a daily assembly where every child participates in recitations, story-telling and a short review of what was taught the previous day. Very naturally and discreetly, he incorporates some useful discussion and reflection on values into it. He has organised a class cabinet that is responsible for the assembly. Every day, a different student leads the class in the 'chintana' (reflection) on values. He has also helped form Kannada and maths groups that organise small group activities on alternate Wednesdays that enable peer learning and peer mentoring in the classroom. By having different peer mentors from different castes, he is able to practically demonstrate and inculcate the spirit of equality.

An integral part of Parameshwariah's timetable is to take the children to nearby places for 'exposure visits' so that they can connect their classroom learning with things they see and observe in the world outside. In order to gain some experiential knowledge, children conduct simple, local surveys on relevant topics from the syllabus. Parameshwariah has also helped them create a children's bank with their small donations. They borrow from this bank to buy books and other material that they need and return the loan when they can. Parameshwariah himself contributes Rs 200 to this bank every month.

In June and July, the beginning of the new academic year, the focus is on assessing the learning levels of children and providing each one with the support they need to come up to a level where they are able to adapt and absorb the curriculum of their class. So, Parameshwariah begins the syllabus only in August but the foundation he builds in the initial two months is critical. Another window to the quality of his pedagogy is the way in which he records the work and progress of his students. He has individual files for every child with their work. The reasoning and analysis that Parameshwariah has painstakingly woven into each child's understanding of a concept is remarkable. This becomes evident as one examines the children's work in maths—tables, graphs, pie charts etc.—each of these assignments reflect the importance that the teacher places on the application of concepts. All children's portfolios are uniformly good. But what shines through is also the humility with which he shows these outstanding portfolios, as if to say that he is merely doing what is expected of a teacher.

Meanwhile, Parameshwariah has another mission—to identify children with potential, aspiring to study in the Navodaya and Morarji schools and prepare them for entrance examinations for these schools. He has been able to get a colleague to join him in this mission and together, they run a special two-hour coaching for the children of Class V. Three students each year, for the past three years, have qualified for Morarji schools and around two to three exceptional students each year also earn admission to the Navodaya school. His colleagues may not be able to emulate him but their appreciation for Parameshwariah is obvious. Apart from his commitment and concern regarding the learning of his students, they also admire his willingness to constantly try out new and various pedagogic and academic inputs. They also understand that any discussion with him can only be around the learning of children, educational content, material or pedagogy; no personal chit-chat!

When it is time for us to leave, there is a short and brisk goodbye. Even before we reach the door, Parameshwariah has turned back to the files and notes on his table. Immersed in those, he does not look up again.

'How we work with these children may well create life-changing opportunities for them.'

DHARMENDRA KUMAR

Government Model Primary School, Teela, Jaspur Block, Udham Singh Nagar District, Uttarakhand

---

In the largely hilly state of Uttarakhand is the district of Udham Singh Nagar which is as flat as land can be. On both sides of the road, as far as the eye can see, are vast fields. In winter, they are green with the early shoots of wheat and by late March, they are golden brown, ready for harvest. There are also quick turnaround crops—paddy, sugarcane, mustard and more. The block headquarters, by contrast, are urban clusters with busy towns, while Rudrapur and Pantnagar have been transformed in the last fifteen years because of the number of industries established under the state government's SIIDCUL enterprise. The district's entire southern border is bound by the state of Uttar Pradesh and a number of people, including teachers, travel across the two states for work on a daily basis.

Udham Singh Nagar has more in common with Uttar Pradesh than with the other districts of Uttarakhand.

The schools in this district are also starkly different. If the feature of the hills is small schools with fewer students, Udham Singh Nagar has schools more akin to those in Uttar Pradesh and Bihar. The student strength is mostly high, impossibly so in some and in quite a few large schools, the number of teachers assigned is inadequate. These teachers seem resigned to high PTRs and believe that administrators are helpless too. So, even though the schools in Udham Singh Nagar may have adequate rooms and infrastructure and their large playgrounds may be the envy of many other schools in the country, their adverse PTR is a major impediment to the quality of education.

It is helpful to bear the above in mind as we discuss the story of GMPS, Teela. It is a neat school with four classrooms housed in two blocks joint in an L-shape. They have a reasonably-sized open ground that is used for assembly, meetings, PT and sports. A compound wall runs around the school providing safety and security. There are one hundred and thirty children enrolled in Classes I to V and because it is a Model School, it has been provided with five teachers ensuring a conducive PTR too. One cannot belabour the point enough that a PTR of around 30:1 as stipulated in the RTE is crucial in enabling teachers to perform their roles of providing adequate personal attention to every child; know how each student is learning; and, make necessary efforts to provide additional support to those who need it.

Among the five teachers at GMPS, Teela is Dharmendra Kumar, the maths teacher. He comes from a family that has always valued education and believes that this has shaped his own passion for teaching. His father studied up to the intermediate level and though he was a farmer, took a keen interest in the education of his children. While his brothers studied at the G.B. Pant Agricultural University and chose to become veterinary doctors, Dharmendra became a maths teacher. When one talks to Dharmendra, one will immediately sense the satisfaction and fulfilment he gets from teaching maths to young children. He has been a teacher now for eighteen years. After completing his BSc, he did his BEd and began as a teacher in a private school. In 2005, he joined the government education service and was posted to this school. The thirty-nine-year-old teacher says, 'The children here come from very disadvantaged backgrounds. They have limited facilities and few opportunities. The school years will just fly by and they will soon find themselves in the rut of daily wage labour and poor habits. That is why we have to do our best for them; this is their only chance.'

He is clear that whatever he does has to be within the school premises; the oft-praised efforts of teachers going to children's homes is not for him. 'All my work is inside the school. I do not go to the village or to the children's homes. I do not want to get involved in their personal lives. If I require the parents to meet me, I call them to school.' Pragmatically, he points to the fact that his efforts with most of the children is to just help keep them apace and help in building a basic understanding of concepts. But with the few children who show promise, Dharmendra pulls out all the stops. That is when his passion for teaching maths takes on a higher aspiration. He says, 'If we see a spark in some students, it is our responsibility to maximise their potential. What we do, and how we work with these children may well create life-changing opportunities for them.'

How good is Dharmendra at this? Let's see. Dharmendra noticed a flair for mathematics in Raj, a student of Class V and started working with him, investing a lot of his personal time in preparing Raj for the district-level 'Maths Wizard' competition that is organised every year by the state education department. Raj won through the cluster and block competitions and went on to ace the district-level competition, as well. When we visited the school, Dharmendra was preparing Raj for the state-level finals in Dehradun, where he would pit his mathematical wits against the champions from twelve other districts of Uttarakhand. This achievement is all the more remarkable because Raj is a fatherless boy living in impoverished circumstances with his mother in his uncle's home.

In another effort at enabling students to maximise their opportunities, Dharmendra keeps a keen eye on the twenty-five students in Class V who have the potential to attempt the entrance examination for admission to Class VI in the Navodaya schools. 'It is easy for me to prepare these children because I know them from Class I. So, I am able to pick five or six of them who can be readied for this very demanding examination.' Dharmendra's preparation is rigorous and the children derive their aspirations and confidence from his persistence and determination. Each of them has been given a long and thick bound notebook by Dharmendra. In these 'registers', Dharmendra makes them practice maths and other subjects. Dharmendra has also purchased, with his own money, the 'Navodaya Examination', a practice book that is a compilation of the previous years' question papers. He is acutely embarrassed if one asks him how much he spends on these children from his own pocket and will brush the query aside, '*Chodiye sir, yeh kuch bhi nahin hai.* It is just a small part of my salary.' But ask him about preparations and he will open up. He does not think that practising from the model questions is limiting. Given the challenges that these children face—being first-generation learners and having no support at home—he believes the practice papers enable them to develop understanding and confidence. The quality of questions is progressively complex, testing a higher-order thinking ability. He is, therefore, able to structure the preparation in a very practical manner.

The children adore Dharmendra but also keep a certain distance. They know how much he is doing for them and in some way, they too feel a responsibility to give their best. Perhaps this explains the distance. The reason I mention this here is that we often form romantic impressions of a teacher-student relationship based on how free and uninhibited the children are with their teachers. This may not always be necessary. Let me explain with an example of how he is committed to ensure that every child is learning. If you enter his classroom on any morning, you will observe that he has written down an array of sums and problems on the blackboard. He does not begin that day's lessons until every child either individually or in a small group has solved these. He examines every notebook and makes a note of what he needs to do next. Because he is so well-organised, he also has the freedom to complete his lessons in a calm and unhurried manner. After observing his work, when we talk to him about his pedagogy and methods, Dharmendra acknowledges how he has benefited from the capacity-building workshops and programmes. He attends the residential summer and winter workshops in maths and brings his trademark seriousness to these. He is not effusive in his praise but is selective and precise, 'The workshop where I learnt to prepare specific teaching-learning material was important. At the same workshop I also realised the importance of using multiple methods to explain a concept. These inputs have made me more flexible in my approach.'

'I need to know each child's habits, moods, shortcomings and talents. I need to understand their psychology.'

RAJNI NEGI
Primary School, Badhangaon, Chinyali Block,
Uttarkashi District, Uttarakhand

Rajni Negi joined the education department as a teacher in 1998 in Mori block, which is among the more remote and inaccessible areas of the Uttarkashi district. After a year, she was transferred to the primary school at Bhadkot village in Chinyali block. She had a young child and for the first three years of her teaching life, Rajni carried her infant on her back as she climbed the hilly trail to her school each day. She had no other option because there was no one at home to take care of the child. The thought that this was tough never occurred to her. Rajni belongs to a family of teachers and always wanted to be one. Her father was a teacher in their native district of Tehri and four of her sisters are also teachers. After fourteen years at Bhadkot, Rajni was transferred to the Primary School, Badhangaon, in the same block.

The school caters to the children of two villages with a population of around eight hundred people whose livelihoods are based on agriculture, small businesses and *kirana* shops. The school at Badhangaon has forty children (twenty-five boys and fifteen girls). Even during the monsoons, when rains completely disrupt normal life, attendance in the school is never less than thirty-six. Rajni, of course, does not have to walk to the school anymore. For many years now, she rides a Scooty. Rajni maintains that the good attendance is not just because the children enjoy coming to school but because,

'This generation of parents who are in their thirties are more educated and quite particular about the education of their children.' She tells us that all parents, without exception, are invested in the education of their children, 'I do not agree that poor parents are not concerned. Their awareness and desire for a good education for their children are indisputable. If their child's homework notebook is not checked on a rare day, they will notice and point it out to us.'

Usually, the girls are more in number in government schools because the boys are sent to private schools. Badhangaon is different, 60 per cent of the students are boys. Rajni's analysis of this situation is that the villagers are convinced that the school is doing its job well and have taken the decision to send siblings to the same school instead of sending the boys to private schools elsewhere. Rajni adds that in her service so far, be it here or earlier in Bhadkot, she has been able to maintain her school's enrolment without losing a single child to private schools. She is rather pleased with this track record of hers. On their part, the community has also recognised her as an action-oriented leader. The three classrooms, the office room, the toilets and the small courtyard which is the venue for the morning assembly, games and meetings with parents are all spotlessly clean. 'I think clean toilets are an excellent indicator of how much I love my school. The toilets of my school are among the cleanest in the district. I personally ensure this and if required, I clean them myself.'

Rajni has taken the initiative to build the infrastructure of the school. When she arrived at the Badhangaon school, she saw that the school building was at a slightly raised level, right next to the road and since the school did not have a compound wall, there was a real danger of the children falling down on the road. She spoke to the president of the Zila Panchayat and had a peripheral wall constructed. Rajni seems to know who to approach for help. She says that the education department functionaries take time to respond to requests and when they come, they seem rushed. So, in this case, she appealed to the Zila Panchayat for a quicker response.

The Foundation has a close association with Rajni for some years now. Ever since it established the TLC in 2012, she has been a regular participant in all the workshops and academic discussions organised by the Uttarkashi field institute team. Rajni tells us, 'I have particularly befitted from the numerous subject-wise discussions, the training workshops, as well as the wide range of books and material that I can access at the TLC. Being a primary school teacher, I have to teach all the subjects to the children in their formative years. I need to be equally good in every subject. It is in this area that I have most benefited by attending the subject workshops.'

Rajni uses a term which is very interesting and perceptive. 'A good primary school teacher must have a "360-degree touch" with her children.' She goes on to explain this by saying that she has to be with the children throughout the day, making sure that each one of them is actively engaged, not only in terms of the subjects being taught but also for a continuous, hands-on assessment of their learning on a daily basis. 'I need to know each child's habits, moods, shortcomings and talents. I need to understand their psychology. There is invariably a breakthrough point during the lesson when a child is able to understand the concept. As a teacher, I must be able to spot that breakthrough moment for each child.' Motivating the children and creating a friendly, happy environment at school is central to Rajni's conception of a good school. Even as she explains this, she is honest and objective enough to acknowledge, '*Kabhi iss bhaymukt vaatavaran ke kaaran bacche apna* homework *bhi nahi karte.*' (But because of this fear-free environment, sometimes children do not do their homework.) This is no starry-eyed teacher deluding herself but someone consciously and continuously evaluating and calibrating her approach to work. This alertness is probably the key to why Rajni is vibrant and agile and it is not surprising that people in the region's academic circles call her a 'learning teacher'. Rajni believes that though each child may have their own limitations, they must each learn to speak, interact, behave well, socialise and be curious and active. She tries to include these aspects in her reflections in their individual portfolios as part of the CCE.

Creativity is another feature of Rajni's pedagogy because she does not want to fall into the boring trap of transacting from textbooks alone. Often, one will find Rajni in her element when she teaches 'bhasha' (language; Hindi in this case). She will create poems for the children on things from their daily lives. She will then encourage the children to attempt the same. When she provides an idea or theme for a story, her children are able to complete it, each one using their own imagination. This aspect of nurturing creativity and offering space to children to express themselves and give reign to their talent is best seen during the morning assembly. The thirty-minute morning assembly is replete with stories, poems and physical activity in which all children get to participate. The practical streak in Rajni's thinking is reflected in this too. She believes that an assembly of all the five classes is most important for the children of Classes I and II because by watching the older children assume responsibilities, cooperate and help each other, the younger children assimilate these qualities that are so important for them to grow up into socially well-adjusted and caring individuals.

Pravaah, a sixty-four-page magazine of the Foundation's Uttarakhand institute—it began as a simple twelve-page newsletter in 2006—has recognised the quality of the morning assembly at the Badhangaon school and featured it in an article in one of its issues. 'In a setting like the morning assembly, children learn things like counting, some English and simple norms in a very natural manner. It helps teachers in the classrooms because the children are able to connect better with new concepts as and when these are introduced. The confidence of the children goes up significantly and prepares them to become independent, lifelong learners,' Rajni sums up the reason for why the morning assembly is one of the most important elements of pedagogy at Badhangaon.

> ### 'I must learn if I have to ensure that my children learn.'
>
> **MAHENDRA KUMAR DHABI**
> Government Primary School, Todaphali,
> Abu Road Block, Sirohi, Rajasthan

In rural schools, a teacher often leads a lonely existence. Help and support from the system are scarce and when all the odds seem stacked up against one, it is easy to give in to frustration. From there it can be a quick slide down to desultory teaching. But there are teachers who, in such situations, can summon resolve and respond to a higher calling. They find in this a new purpose for a truly fulfilling and rewarding career.

Bespectacled, bearded and lean, Mahendra Kumar Dhabi is one such teacher. We reached his school a little late in the morning and did not have the heart to disturb him for the next two hours as he single-handedly managed sixty students from five classes across two rooms. Sometimes the energy in a class is palpable. The children in Mahendra's class seemed almost impatient as they waited for their teacher to take them up every stage of the concept he was teaching. He was clearly enjoying the process and there was a point when both the teacher and children spontaneously broke into laughter as they grasped the underlying beauty of the concept. It was a privilege to unobtrusively observe this teacher. We saw how he tries to bring the excitement for maths to every child. As he steps across the two rooms where he has distributed his students, there are a variety of exercises and activities happening in both. These are planned so skilfully that when he leaves one group of students to attend to the other, the students are completely engrossed in the activities assigned. Mahendra has a clear idea of the learning levels of his children, their cognitive abilities and the wide disparity in their abilities. On the blackboard are a set of problems that vary across difficulty levels as well as in the concepts covered. There is a three-digit addition, a three-digit subtraction with carryover and a place-value problem that is quite intricate.

In addition to this clarity of how he wishes to take forward a child's learning, he has also invested efforts and personal money to create a variety of learning materials. The walls of his classrooms are covered with inventively created material—boxes painted with designs into which his students can plug in numbers and symbols to generate various numerical functions, geometries and arithmetic puzzles; a question and answer section where children can express themselves in Hindi or English. As Mahendra winds down the morning session, the children rush out into the corridor laughing happily and are openly curious about the visitors.

GPS, Todaphali is in the Abu Road block of the Sirohi district. It is an economically disadvantaged village of indigent labourers and marginal farmers. Like most parents in recent times, the parents in Todaphali are also keen that their children get a good education. When Mahendra Kumar Dhabi, a BA graduate with a teacher's certification, cleared the Rajasthan state's test for selection of teachers in 2012, he was posted to this school. Mahendra is just twenty-nine-years old and before he joined this school, he had acquired three years of teaching experience at Shree Saijanand Secondary School, a private school in Mount Abu. He taught maths to Class X students and many of them aspired to become engineers. Mahendra found the students serious about their studies and responsive to his teaching. He also realised that a decent grasp of English and computer literacy was a big help to them. As he narrated this to us, he also paused introspectively to say, 'I could clear the Rajasthan CET only in my second attempt. My first attempt was in 2008 before I joined the private school. I was a good student and my concepts have always been strong but I failed the first time because my English was poor. However, after joining the private school in 2009, I worked on it and maybe this helped me clear the qualifying exam in 2012.'

When Mahendra came to Todaphali it had just one para-teacher, who still continues at the school, but it is Mahendra who shoulders the entire load of teaching. In 2012, Todaphali had one hundred and thirteen students on its rolls but attendance was less than 50 per cent. A quick survey and audit by Mahendra showed there were a number of 'bogus' enrolments. Cleaning the list, Mahendra pruned the number to eighty which is where the enrolment stands today. The average attendance now is around sixty pupils.

Within days of joining the school, Mahendra realised that the students had absolutely no interest in studies. Disheartened that he would not be able to do anything worthwhile, he began to prepare for the Rajasthan Administrative Services examination. He would bring along his 'GK ki kitab' and prepare for his exam. Quite suddenly, one day, he felt a deep stab of guilt and told himself, '*Yeh galat hai; mujhe inn bacchon ke saath kaam karna hai.*' (This is wrong. I should be teaching these children.) It was almost as though he had sworn himself to an an implacable oath. From that moment, Mahendra was a new man. He put all his energy into planning what he could do for the children; how he could organise them according to their abilities; what kind of activities would interest them; and what exercises would help them. Once he had this worked out, his next aim was to create methods that would enable him to implement this plan. 'My biggest strength in being able to do this was my subject-matter competence. I know how a concept is understood; what needs to be done to make it clear. But what I needed to learn was the patience to transact this in a class of students whose abilities were diverse. I still do not know how I learnt this patience, *shayad maine ek kism ka sankalp liya tha ki main inn sabhi bacchon ko acchhi tarah padaoonga.*' (Maybe, I took an oath that I would teach these children well.)

By nature, Mahendra is reserved, an introvert. He found it difficult to mingle with the parents and community members. He did not have the flair for talking to them about their children's learning, the challenges they and the school face and the kind of support he expects from them. He says this slowed him down. But as he continued to steadfastly work in the school, people came to understand that they had a very special teacher—an earnest and conscientious one from whom their children were learning better. Meanwhile, the members of the Foundation who work closely with teachers recognised his mettle too. They observed his pedagogy, his commitment, his grasp of the subject and lost no time in recommending him as a 'Master Trainer' to the block education authorities.

He knows he is a valuable resource person for the block but is modest, 'Earlier, I would do a lot of "chalk and talk"; a lot of blackboard work, mechanical stuff. But in the last two years, I have been exposed to some really good development programmes. I particularly recall the workshops on fractions and patterns, conducted by Vinod and Dinesh, the maths resource persons of the field institute. I realised how much more I could do in the classroom if I built some good activities. I also learnt to bring out the existing knowledge the children have. It helped me build new concepts on that foundation.'

Mahendra continues to improve his English and attends all workshops on English. 'In a single-teacher school, I have to teach all the subjects. My English is not very good but I must learn if I have to ensure that my children learn.' Mahendra points to a number of English words and phrases that he has got painted on the walls of the school corridor.

It is time to go back to the classroom where, quite uninhibitedly, the children ask us where we have come from; how far Bengaluru is from Abu Road. When, offhand, we draw a map of India on the blackboard and begin marking various places, it becomes a fun-filled exploration for many of them. We ask them to summarise our discussion in a few sentences on the blackboard. Without hesitation, quite a few children volunteer and write some neat short sentences. One of the sentences in Hindi, which we remembered to photograph as a keepsake read, *'Giridhar Bengaluru se aaye hain, aur woh shaher yahan se bahut door hai.'* (Giridhar has come from Bangalore and that city is very far away from here.)

The place value problems—we thought they were intricate—were being solved with aplomb by the children. Mahendra quietly mentioned, 'I try and help a few children develop mental maths abilities. I take them beyond the textbook.'

Mahendra is not over-demonstrative with the children but there is a sense of comfort and equanimity in the relation between the teacher and students. Students from within three kilometres have begun to come to this school and parents from nearby villages also know that GPS, Thodaphali is a good school. Mahendra may be a quiet worker but his work speaks out loud for him.

'Our children go with very good learning levels and the ability to learn independently,' says the taxi driver who became a fine teacher.

SATYANARAYAN BAIRWAL
Government Primary School, Bubariyaphali,
Abu Road Block, Sirohi, Rajasthan

This is the story of a taxi driver who became a teacher, a fine one at that. Mount Abu is one of Rajasthan's most popular resorts, especially for people from the neighbouring state of Gujarat for whom it is a quick weekend getaway. Satyanarayan Bairwal's father drove a tourist taxi for a living, ferrying tourists from Abu Road to the hill station. When Satyanarayan was around eighteen, he began driving the taxi with his father. Father and son would share the drives—if it was a local trip, they would each drive half a day; if it was an overnight journey, they would alternate trips between themselves. Interacting with different types of guests, the young man developed good communication skills and a sense of curiosity about human nature. That is also how Satyanarayan learnt English.

Satyanarayan was keen to study and become a teacher. So, while waiting for his passengers to return to the car, he would study. In time, he acquired his BA degree. He had been a tourist taxi driver for close to seven years before he also obtained his BEd degree. In 1996, when he was twenty-eight-years old, Satyanarayan was selected as a teacher in the Rajasthan education department. His first posting was in the neighbouring block of Reodhar, around forty-two kilometres from his home. For the next ten years, Satyanarayan taught in the government school there, determined to become as good a teacher as possible. He read up, consulted with colleagues and seniors for advice and tried to implement all that in his classroom. What he absorbed early in his career was that all children must receive equal attention and opportunity to develop themselves. He had the sensibility to recognise that children who came from socio-economically disadvantaged backgrounds must see and experience equity and fairness at all times in his school. This was the foundation of his approach to pedagogy.

He completed his MA and got married, interestingly, to a teacher. Immersed in his goal of ensuring that every child was learning, time flew. As results started to show, the department appointed him as the CRP in 2007. Knowing how vulnerable these children were, Satyanarayan was particular in tracking enrolment and retention in his cluster. Three years later, in 2010, Satyanarayan was appointed head teacher at the government primary school in Bubariyaphali, a village in his native Abu Road block. In these eight years, both, the head teacher and the school, have come a long way. For Satyanarayan, these eight years that have seen the turnaround of a dysfunctional school into a vibrant learning centre, have been memorable. He is now fifty-years-old and a couple of years ago, had a serious brush with an illness that he has coped with courageously. Thankfully, he is on the road to recovery and when we met him, no one could discern any decline in his energy or commitment. Despite a jaw surgery, his speech is almost as distinct as it was earlier.

We visited GPS, Bubariyaphali on the day before Holi. At any rural school in North India, on a day before a major festival, one would expect low attendance—never more than 50 per cent. Festivities in the village begin a few days early and families often go to visit relatives. At Bubariyaphali, we were surprised to see (as we quickly counted) fifty-five heads in the milling, happy crowd that quickly surrounded us, greeting us excitedly. Extricating us from his children, Satyanarayan explained, 'You see, I have encouraged my students to also bring their siblings who are below five years to the school. They get used to the school environment and enrol with us as soon as they reach age five. It is a very useful and practical mechanism that has worked well for me.' He then introduced us to his colleague, Aruna Sharma. Aruna, like the head teacher, has also completed her MA and BEd. Between the two of them, they teach all subjects across the five classes. Aruna and Satyanarayan have formed a fine team, the bedrock of their teamwork is mutual respect and a shared commitment towards making Bubariyaphali an exemplary school. Aruna joined the service in 2007 and Bubariyaphali was her first posting. At that time, not only was she the only teacher, but the six-year-old school had also been run with little interest by an earlier teacher who was on deputation there. Enrolment was low and there was a good private school and other government schools not far from the village. Even as she was struggling with these circumstances, Satyanarayan was posted as head teacher. In him, she found a dynamic and zealous leader. Together, they took up the challenge of transforming the school.

The first step was to win back the community's confidence. Satyanarayan decided to go door-to-door, building a relationship and rapport with the parents. He organised monthly PTMs, held vibrant events on Independence Day and Republic Day to build, in his words, 'a shiksha utsav culture' to show the community how serious they are about children's learning. Aruna and Satyanarayan pooled their own money for prizes during these events and invited parents to distribute these to the children. 'I would even meet parents in the evening, after school hours, in the market…' says Satyanarayan recalling from memory those early days of trying to win back the community's trust. The teachers backed their words with their deeds. 'We did this with solid, visible work. *Dekhiye, unn dino mein yeh sab bahut* rocky, *rough ground tha*, (in those days, this was rough and rocky ground)' he points to the fairly large, even playground. Contributing physical labour and money himself; pulling the village Sarpanch into the activities, the head teacher got the ground levelled, cemented the place and had a compound wall erected to make the school secure. He was able to mobilise both SSA funds, as well as funds from the Panchayat for this. They needed some lights and fans for which Aruna and Satyanarayan were happy to contribute Rs 5,000 each.

At the same time, the two teachers also focused on the learning levels of the children. Articulating their approach towards this, Satyanarayan says, 'We were particular about quality. By this, I mean, children developing their understanding, being able to express themselves, and to independently find out things for themselves. We knew that activities to engage and interest children are essential in the early years. Textbooks are only a base; our task is to connect the syllabus and textbooks with the overall objective of why the child must develop an understanding of the topics.' He acknowledges the contribution of nearly fifteen hundred books to the school library by Room to Read. Aruna adds, 'The reading habit is such an important aspect of lifelong learning. Once children begin to enjoy reading, our job becomes one hundred times easier.' She took us to the classroom which also serves as a library and showed a register that has a list of children's names and the books they have borrowed. In the morning assembly and on Saturday afternoons, children also have the opportunity to briefly describe the stories they have read.

This brings us to the morning assembly. The thirty-minute assembly includes oral expression, multiplication tables, general knowledge, mental math, English phrases and stories from books that the children have read. Both teachers invest a lot of attention to the assembly. Interestingly, Satyanarayan adds, '*Subah ki* assembly *se hi mujhe* idea *milta hai ki aaj bacchon ka* mood *kaise hai*. (From the morning assembly, I get an idea about the mood of the children)' And in some subtle manner, he and Aruna use this to pitch the activities, as well as the learning demands of the day. The children look forward to the 'Bal Sabha' on Saturdays when they get a chance to perform and demonstrate their talents—singing, dancing, storytelling and acting. Keeping this on Saturdays, according to Aruna, ensures certain anticipation and excitement throughout the week. Every day, the last period is utilised by the teachers for homework. They are practical and recognise that with little or no learning environment at home, the children are best served by having them do their 'homework' at school.

'I do not try to teach them things like decimals. It is too difficult for them to understand. They will run away,' says Satyanarayan with a laugh and an honesty that can only come from a deep understanding of the cognitive abilities of the children that he has gained over the years. Let me hasten to add that in the block, Satyanarayan has already gained a huge reputation as a fine teacher and his 'place value' classes in maths are recognised as exemplary. In his quest to ensure that every child learns, Satyanarayan is also aware of the special abilities of some children. To them, he poses more challenging problems, especially in mental maths and questions that require higher-order thinking. He wants to prepare at least three to four children for the Navodaya school admission test. He has had some success in this earlier but wants to make this an annual, sustainable goal. With regard to the children of Bubariyaphali, the greatest satisfaction he derives is, in his words, 'When *all* children of Class V—a 100 per cent—every year, continue their education in Class VI at the Upper Primary School.' Satyanarayan adds, 'Some of our children have gone to senior secondary and college. These children go with very good learning levels and the ability to learn independently. That is why they do not face difficulty in higher classes.'

Satyanarayan is a determined man, a fighter both in his chosen profession and in life. His connect with the community is perhaps stronger than ever before; his empathy for them, genuine. '50 per cent of them are really poor labourers as they eke out a livelihood on poorly irrigated land. The other 50 per cent are economically better off; they sell their vegetable produce directly in the Abu Road market without going through middlemen. I belong to each one of them. This school is theirs and we must do our best for their children.' As we leave the school, the children have gathered around both their teachers, happily chattering, completely at ease with them. The teachers seem to not mind and are not unnecessarily quietening them. It is clearly a very happy school.

An aspiring doctor who took to teaching—quirk of fate or destiny?

TILOK CHAND

Government Upper Primary School, Barewada,
Sheoganj Block, Sirohi, Rajasthan

There are six teachers at this school, including the head teacher, Mohanlal Meena. The Upper Primary, Barewada has one hundred and thirty-nine students and has been adjudged an 'Utkrusht Vidyalaya' (school of excellence) by the Rajasthan state education department. Assessed the 'Best School' in the Sheoganj block, the school has also been ranked fourth in Sirohi district. The state department programme for assessing schools is done by a three-member team comprising a Rashtriya Madhyamik Shiksha Abhiyan (RMSA) functionary, and two academic resource persons who spend a day at the school, evaluating not only the infrastructure, cleanliness, hygiene and facilities but also observing the teaching-learning process in classes and interacting with students to get an idea of their reading, comprehension and general awareness levels. While one does take cognisance of these inputs, what convinced me to visit Barewada was that colleagues working with the teachers in Sheoganj strongly recommended that we speak to Tilok Chand, a teacher in that school.

The morning assembly had not yet begun when we entered the school. Students were gathering themselves into class-wise rows, the mike and band set was being set-up and all the six teachers were present. Interestingly, a few boys were sweeping the rooms and corridors. It was, we gathered, a duty that was shared by all students in turns. The assembly too was being managed by a set of students, a responsibility that was rotated among them on a weekly basis. Over the next three hours, we got a sense that not only was the school being run efficiently, but also that the teachers were a cohesive team, deeply involved and very conscious of their responsibility to ensure that Barewada continues to be an excellent school. With the teachers moving to their respective classes, we got the opportunity to be with the head teacher and then meet Tilok Chand.

Head teacher Mohanlal Meena is forty-three and teaches social science to the upper primary classes besides performing administration duties. He came to this school in 2014. Calm and reserved, he is aware that he has an excellent team and wants to ensure that they are content and motivated. One can sense a very light touch, a benign but watchful eye. He has staked out hygiene, maintenance, infrastructure, facilities and relationship with the community as his areas of responsibility. He has done this so that his teachers can concentrate on their teaching responsibilities. The school has eight classrooms, an office, a library, functional toilets and a fairly large playground. Even though the community is not prosperous, it supports the school in every way possible because it has seen that the school is doing its best for their children. 'They are generous people who have made donations voluntarily. They have contributed the green boards in the classrooms and the RO plant for drinking water. They consider this as their school and support us fully,' says Meena making light of his own efforts to mobilise resources from the community.

Tilok Chand came to the school in 2008. He is a native of Jodhpur which is three-hundred-and-twenty kilometres northwest of Sirohi. Born and brought up in the 'blue city', Tilok was a good student throughout his school days. He studied science in school because he wanted to become a doctor but his family circumstances were such that he could not even appear for the pre-medical examination. Reconciled to the fact that he would not become a doctor, he decided to do a BSc in Biology and graduated with first division. As a fresh science graduate, he taught maths and science to Classes V to X at the Sarvodaya Public School, Jodhpur for over four years. Tilok says he will always remain grateful for the experience he gained in those four years. Teaching upper primary and secondary classes enabled him to significantly polish his basics in the subject. He believes this helped his selection in the state education department. After the experience in Sarvodaya, Tilok knew he wanted to be a teacher for life. Taking a bold plunge, he went to the Dogra College of Education in Jammu to do his BEd. 'The BEd programme was in English while I came from a Hindi medium. It was quite difficult initially. But I am hardworking; I come from a hardworking family. My father is sixty-two-years old but still an active and good carpenter. So, I slogged and finished with a fourth rank.' Tilok joined the Rajasthan education service in March 2008. His first (and thus far only) posting has been at Barewada. Married by then, Tilok left his wife and infant son at Jodhpur, took up lodgings in Paldi, three kilometres from Barewada and settled into a job that completely absorbed him. Three years later, he brought his family to Paldi. Of his two sons, the elder in Class VII studies in a government school in Paldi. We asked him, 'Why is your son not in your school?' Tilok replied, 'You see, I come to school riding pillion on my colleague Veeraram's bike. How will I get my son here? The school that he studies in, is within walking distance from our home.'

At Barewada, Tilok began by teaching science and maths to Classes VI, VII and VIII. Later, he asked (almost insisted) for the opportunity to teach maths to the primary classes too. 'The reason is that the early years are crucial for these children who come from disadvantaged backgrounds. I wanted to contribute to developing a strong foundation in maths. Sixty percent of the parents are illiterate. The men are mostly engaged as construction labourers or work under the MNREGA. They migrate for work, many to Gujarat, so only women attend the monthly PTMs, just about 40 per cent of them.' However, irrespective of the family circumstances, all parents are very particular that their children attend school. The day we were at Barewada, the attendance was one hundred and twenty, which Tilok told us is the average attendance throughout the year. After a bit of hesitation, prodded by the head teacher, Tilok adds, 'One of my students scored 100/100 in the Class VIII Board exam.' There was more satisfaction than pride in his voice.

When the A.P.J. Abdul Kalam Avishkar Abhiyan was announced, a hundred schools in the district were selected and given a grant of Rs 15,000 each to pursue a science project. Barewada, under Tilok, designed a project that received the first prize in the district.[10] There is now an active 'Science and Maths Club' in the school and the children participate in model-making, essay-writing, quizzes and debates. Tilok tells us that four students went up to the district finals in each of these categories. With almost paternal pride, he took us to meet his student, Suryaman Singh, who had won the first prize in the science essay-writing competition. In the Bal Mela at Paldi in January 2018, the students of Barewada made models to describe the principles of sound, electricity and magnetism. For Tilok, all these are natural elements of a teaching-learning continuum. 'I want to ensure that every child is engaged, so I want each one of them to join one group or the other so that they are motivated and interested. To help this process,

I try my best to connect the topics with our surroundings. I try and show them some videos and have some PowerPoint presentations too.' Tilok prepares his lesson plans with great care and tries to get children involved by asking them to prepare charts and diagrams too. Tilok explains, 'For topics like the properties of light; or for geometrical concepts, sometimes, I use examples from life.' Then smiling self-consciously, he adds, 'Occasionally, I also use YouTube. My son is smart at these things and helps me download material.' Three students from the school who came in the merit list in the Class VIII Board exam have received laptops under a government scheme to award meritorious students.

Committed to self-development from the beginning, Tilok first attended a training programme for science teachers in 2010, and since then, is a regular resource person and also a 'Master Trainer' for all science and EVS workshops that have been conducted by the DIET of Sirohi district.

As we are about to leave, the head teacher shares another interesting nugget of information about Tilok. 'Do you know that Tilok ji is a trained Scouts teacher? He has been running a Boy Scouts programme at our school for over ten years.' Tilok uses the games/SUPW/arts period on Tuesdays and Fridays to train the thirty-two boys who have enrolled for the Scouts. He personally gets these children khaki uniforms from Sirohi town. We do not even bother to ask him how he manages to fit this in an already packed schedule. We know him well enough to guess that he will shrug his shoulders and say, '*Yeh kuch nahi hai.*' (This is nothing.)

'Decimals, fractions, you name the operation! The children from this school know it all!'

ASHOK SOHAIL

Kailash Chand Jat, Government Primary School, Nadya-ki-Dhani, Uniyara Block, Tonk District, Rajasthan

It took us much longer than we had estimated to reach Nadya-ki-Dhani. Driving from Deoli, bypassing the town of Tonk, all we saw were vast fields of freshly sown mustard for miles. It was almost 3 p.m. and the school would close in an hour. How much could we observe and understand? How would we get the time to interact with children and talk to teachers? Would this visit be an unfortunate miss? We approached the school with such apprehensions through a messy, slushy path in the village with buffaloes on either side up to the school gate. Our eyes and nose warned us of a tabela (cattle shed) right outside the school, which did not seem like a great sign either. But as we entered, we saw a fine, clean premise; a large, well-maintained playground to our left, a number of trees to our right and a perfect avenue of neem trees leading up to the main school building. We heard excited voices from the classrooms as we climbed the steps into the veranda. My colleague Rakesh and I turned right to where Ashok Sohail was teaching maths to the children of Classes III, IV and V. Our other colleague, Deep Chand went left to Kailash Chand Jat's Hindi class for the children of Classes I and II.

There were twenty-three children in Ashok's classroom. Rakesh and I squeezed ourselves into the small space available, careful not to interrupt the class. Usually, in schools when a visitor comes in, the children get up and sing out the rehearsed, 'Good morning/afternoon, sir, how are you?' in a chorus.

Not here, for they were completely immersed in the maths puzzles that their teacher was tossing at them. Ashok grinned a welcome (he was expecting us) and the children too turned around to smile at us but they continued with the lesson. For us, the ensuing thirty-five minutes were a treat. Ashok was challenging the children with questions that required them to mentally do a variety of operations with two-digit numbers. The context Ashok created was that of the market. He 'sent' the children to buy various stationery items. On the board, the price of each item was listed. Like a quizmaster, Ashok would ask a question, 'If you bought three pencils and four erasers, how much would you spend? If you spent Rs 90, what combination of items would you have bought? If you took Rs 100 and bought these three items in these quantities, what is the balance you will receive?' Children from across the room answered; some questions had more than one correct answer; some children made errors but they were doing the calculations in their heads with an agility that could have only come with a complete comprehension of the question, as well as the operation.

Ashok, every now and then, would look at us and grin. I could read the pride and happiness in that grin. He moved to bigger numbers and 'sent' the children to the hardware market to buy articles for construction work at school. There was cement and steel and bricks to be bought. I kept a mental note of the children who were answering; there were four children who were quick as lightning with their answers but seventeen of the twenty-three children answered at least one question. Every child had such an anticipatory smile that Ashok might well have been distributing Deepavali sweets and not asking maths questions. It was past school closure time but no one seemed to care. Ashok was now helping children construct an understanding of decimals. In primary classes, two concepts that both teachers and students struggle with are the concepts of 'fractions' and 'decimals.' But when children have a strong comprehension of numbers, their construction and basic operations, then these concepts can be easily built. Ashok spent a few minutes asking the children to construct a variety of currency denominations to make up Rs 100. The children started in chorus with the simple, 'two Rs 50 notes' and moved on to make combinations of fifty, twenty, ten, five, two- and one-rupee notes. At a particular point in this raucous discussion, Ashok stopped them by saying that the shopkeeper had a problem. He had notes only for Rs 99 and only coins in small denomination for the remaining one rupee. Children now made up the remaining rupee with fifty, twenty-five and ten paisa coins. It was the perfect time for Ashok to introduce the concept of decimal and fraction with the explanation of the fifty paise as half a rupee and as 0.5 rupee. The children constructed the new number as 99 + 0.5 + 0.25 + 0.25. Even as Ashok decided it was enough for the day, the children were racing ahead creating fractions and decimals for two and three rupees.

When we got a few minutes to chat with the children, my colleague Rakesh told them that he came from Jaipur and I, from Bengaluru. We began discussing the distance between these cities from the village of Nadya-ki-Dhani. It quickly led to questions of the relative time it took for us to get there and the children began making accurate estimations of the time it would take by road from Bengaluru to Nadya-ki-Dhani.

We could spend very little time with Kailash Chand but the comfort that the younger children seemed to have in his class was similar to what we saw in Ashok's classroom—free, uninhibited and ready to attempt an answer. They were also easily distracted, as one would expect six- and seven-year-olds to be. Kailash Chand was trying to make the topic of 'vegetables' interesting, making the children of Class I write the word 'tomato' and making the children of Class II construct a couple of simple sentences using the word, 'tomato'. He gave them a little homework to do for that evening and also told them to ask their parents and dada-dadi about all the food preparations that use tomatoes. One of the children immediately said *'juice banatey hain'* (We make juice) to which Kailash laughed and said, *'ghar mein aur bhi poochho.'* (Ask people at home about more.)

In the open courtyard, we thought we would speak to Ashok and Kailash after the children went home but the children refused to leave. Ashok explained this to us saying, *'Jab tak hum nahin jaayenge, bacche nahin jaayenge,* sir (Till we leave, the children won't leave). So, we have to conduct our discussion in their presence.' Since the children were milling around our table, we decided to chat with them. There was water in a metallic jug on the table. What metal is the jug? we asked them. The children did not hesitate to answer; however off-course they were. Steel, said one; brass, said another before Ashok explained that it was copper and that it is good to eat and drink from copper vessels. What would be the volume of the jug? we asked. Pat came the answers, ranging from half-litre to one-litre before they arrived at a consensus that it must be a one-litre jug. Some discussion ensued on milk measuring cans they have in their homes. The estimation of the dimensions of our table was next. Breadth? Two feet, after a few iterations. Length? This was estimated immediately as three feet. The perimeter offered more mental maths practice. Arithmetic, as we know, is not as much about the application of algorithms as about understanding the language. In Hindi, these are called, *'ibarti sawal'* (word problems) in which children can apply the correct arithmetical operation only if they have understood what is being sought. These children were singing out answers.

Ashok had joined the education department in 2001 and moved to Nadya-ki-Dhani in 2010. A graduate with a teaching diploma, he teaches Maths and English. With a deprecatory smile, he mentions that he wishes he could teach English better. Forty-five-year-old Ashok has two children—a daughter, who after her schooling, is preparing to write the NEET medical entrance exam and a son who is in Class XII. Kailash Chand, fifty, has been at Nadya-ki-Dhani since 1999, the year the government established this school under the Rajiv Gandhi Pathshala programme. He joined as a contract teacher (para teacher) and became a *prabodhak* (a full-time employee) in 2008. Both teachers live within a few kilometres of the village.

Kailash, a modest and contented man says, 'The government has given me such a good job, I must do my best every day.' Ashok is the leader and Kailash is happy to fully support him. Ashok, in manner and conversation, is self-confident. His pride in his school and affection for the children is obvious. At times, if one were to take some of his statements in isolation, he would almost come across as boastful. But it may not be so. He values the suggestions and inputs he receives periodically at the maths workshops and the SLDPs that he has attended. He is very keen that his Class V students attempt and clear the entrance examination for the Navodaya school. But he is also candid in expressing what holds him back from doing more than preparing them for the exam, 'The parents are not prepared to take the children to town to write the exam. I am ready to buy the necessary books and stationery but I am afraid to assume the responsibility of taking them to town. What if, god forbid, there is a mishap? I will be held responsible.' The community is an equal mix of Bhils (ST) and the Nath (OBC) community. Most of the parents are illiterate. Only four or five families have enough land of their own to till, the rest have such small holdings that they work as agricultural labourers. 'However, most of them have their own buffaloes and so there is adequate milk for the family,' Kailash Chand informs us. The community is ready to chip in with some small funds, if required. They know their school is good and that Ashok and Kailash Chand are doing a fine job. There is a private school just two kilometres away but Ashok, puffing his chest, just a tad, says, '*Koi nahin jaayega wahan. Kyon jaayega?* (Nobody will go there. Why would they?) Parents can see their children are learning well here.'

The children were still around and it was past 5 p.m. Just outside the gate, we saw three ladies in very bright and colourful clothes, their ghunghat completely covering their faces. One of them had two large steel pots (andas, as they are called in many parts across India) balanced beautifully on her head even as both her hands were free. Kailash and Ashok informed us that the two women are members of the SDMC and one of them is the president. We requested the teachers, the three members of the SDMC and some of the children to pose for a keepsake photograph. We had to take many photos before we could get a good shot because a couple of attention-seeking buffaloes kept ambling into the frame.

4

TEAMWORK: THE PULL OF A SUPERORDINATE GOAL

In the public education system, very often, an entire lifetime of service as a government school teacher can go unnoticed and unrewarded. And yet, it is within this environment that we also have teachers who respond to an inner calling to do their best for children from disadvantaged backgrounds who come to their schools. Often, these teachers are lone rangers in their schools which also means that the fortunes of a school are completely dependent on them. Only when a group of fine teachers come together will a school have a more secure future. Therefore, I had reason to be doubly pleased whenever I observed that there were some schools that were doing well not because of one individual but a cohesive team of teachers.

The remarkable thing that I noticed about this collective ownership of a school among such teams was not merely the fact that they set themselves high goals or that they all worked equally hard but that they seemed comfortable with the knowledge that they had varying abilities. Five teachers across disciplines as varied as English, science, social sciences, maths and first language with different levels of experience, qualifications and pedagogic abilities seemed united by the same level of commitment. This is a valuable lesson for any team in any profession.

Writing about this for the journal of the National Human Resource Development (a pre-eminent body of HR professionals in India), I had called it a version of the much researched and discussed, 'Pygmalion effect'. I argued that something has made these teachers reset the bar for what they expect from themselves and having set it high, they do everything to meet these demanding standards of performance. The Pygmalion effect kicks in from all sides. At some of the Model Schools, the motivation for excellence came from the fact that the teachers have been selected to the position from a large pool of aspirants. For some, it was the realisation that they have been provided an opportunity to teach children from very disadvantaged backgrounds and the children's future depends solely on their efforts. For others, it was a moral compulsion that one of the teachers articulated thus, 'My school is better resourced, both in terms of infrastructure and with teachers, than many other schools. It is my duty, therefore, to provide children with the best possible education.' So, it isn't surprising that what we heard most often from these teams was, *'Kuch karke dikhana hai.'* (I want to achieve something.)

Actions finally decide everything. At some of these schools, within a remarkably short time, at others, after a longer haul, the teachers have implemented a number of simultaneous actions. Unfailingly, these involve extra hours before and after school; coming to school on Sundays and holidays; going door-to-door to meet parents; putting in their personal money to create materials or facilities; and, building their own subject-knowledge. It also means painstakingly prepared child-wise portfolios to track each child's progress. It means identifying children who need extra attention and investing time in supporting them. It means carving out a separate schedule for talented children to train them for admissions to Navodaya schools, the Maths Wizard and various other competitions. The teachers seemed to be filled with purpose and energy, possessed by the ambition to make their school the best in the region. They could not wait to come to school; they did not care if it was well past the time to leave. So, when in the deep interior regions, like Kudalagi or Veerpur Kuraha, we heard teachers say, 'Nothing is a burden for us, we have a shared goal,' it did not sound unreal.

In at least a couple of these schools, the head teacher was, for all practical purposes non-existent, a virtual figurehead; either a person of low energy or poor health. But the rest of the teachers carried the school on their shoulders with no resentment. And invariably, from among this team of teachers with varying abilities, there emerged, a de-facto leader, the one with ideas and conviction who the others willingly followed and supported.

Here, I must also share an interesting observation of teamwork. In many of these schools, when we asked teachers to tell us about themselves, their colleagues jumped in to provide details, taking pride in each other's accomplishments. At one of these schools, the science teacher was preparing her children for the Rashtriya Bal Vigyan Congress. She was good in her subject but new to the job and with little experience in the government school environment. So, helping her was a seasoned colleague, the Hindi teacher who had been at government schools for over twenty years. He shared everything he knew, telling her how in his previous school the science teacher had prepared the children for this competition. The grateful young science teacher, when she spoke to us, remarked that science learning in the school owed much to the Hindi teacher. I stole a quick glance at the Hindi teacher and saw him flush purple in the wintry sunshine of Uttarkashi.

In many ways, this section perhaps pulls together the best attributes described in the other sections and presents stories in which these attributes are present as a collective force. These stories about teamwork among teachers are from schools with varied backgrounds—of well-equipped Model Schools as well as schools that had nearly been ruined by local politics. The teams I feature in this section, do not need supervision or exhortation from outside or above. Indefinably, their expectations have got recalibrated and they are not ready to settle for anything less than the best from themselves. In the process, they re-equip themselves, learn new things, become better professionally and renew their resolve. In normal professional spaces, people rise above themselves only when someone explicitly states such an expectation or for some reward or recognition. Here, in these government schools, as one of the teachers told us, 'Neither are we doing it because we are told, nor with any expectation of a reward in return.' The bugle is from within. No one else can see or hear it. It is for this reason that these teams are remarkable.

'This is not merely a "sarkari naukri". We are here to create the best school in the block.'

SANJAY KUKSAL, MUKESH NAUTIYAL, MEENA BHAT, BINDU GOSAIN, MURARI RAM, SUSHILA RAWAT

Adarsh Primary School, Barethi, Chinyali Block, Uttarkashi District, Uttarakhand

There can be divergent views on the government's policy to create a couple of Model Schools in every block as an exemplar of how high-quality education can be imparted to children at government schools. There can be debates on whether the significantly high resources in terms of teachers, to demonstrate this, in any way, improves systemic excellence or creates sustainable institutional processes. But keeping these broader issues aside, if one were to consider just the implementation of this policy in the Uttarkashi district since the beginning of 2015, it is clear that the government has gone about it in earnest. We saw in the Chinyali, Dunda and Bhatwari blocks of the Ganga valley, and in the Purola and Naugaon blocks of the Yamuna valley that schools designated as Model Schools have indeed been provided with carefully selected teachers in quick time so that they have every chance of success. This is true of the Model Primary School, Badethi, Chinyali block too.

This school, with thirty-eight children in five classes, was like any other village primary school until a few years ago. A number of children from in and around Badethi village attended private schools. In 2015, the department chose to make this a Model School. By 2016, they had invited applications from teachers in the Ganga valley for selection through a test of their subject knowledge. That is how the five new teachers, including the head teacher, Sanjay Kuksal; the maths teacher, Mukesh Nautiyal, the English teacher, Meena Bhat; the science teacher, Bindu Gosain, and the EVS teacher, Murari Ram joined the Adarsh Prathmik Vidyalaya, Badethi in 2016. Sushila Rawat, the Hindi teacher, was the only teacher who had been there earlier.

There is a consistent pattern to how a team of teachers who join a newly designated model school go about their work. To use a cliché, it is a 'mission-mode' approach. This team of six teachers led by the head teacher, Sanjay Kuksal, literally took an oath that they would truly make this an outstanding school. Every model school team in Uttarkashi district has its own story. Here at Badethi, for the past two years, the team has not availed of a single day's casual leave. The six teachers also decided to wear uniforms to show their team spirit and demonstrate to the community that they are proud to belong to the Model School, Badethi. 'This is not a 'sarkari naukri' (government job). We wrote a qualifying exam and came here because we see this as an opportunity to create the best school in the block,' one of the teachers said to us. Within a few months of joining, each teacher had gone door-to-door in the village to communicate how their school was being transformed and how this was the sole purpose of their work at Badethi. It motivated the parents significantly. 'The junoon (passion) that we showed, somehow transmitted itself to the community and they reciprocated with their trust. From thirty-eight children in the academic year 2015-16, the enrolment shot up nearly 300 per cent to one hundred and nine children in 2017. In effect, it meant that around seventy children studying in private schools had been pulled out and enrolled in the Adarsh Vidyalaya, Badethi,' the teacher explained.

This manner of communication and the trust it creates is a virtuous process. Buoyed, the teachers decided to contribute around Rs 7,000 each to add fans in the classrooms and conduct an Annual Day function. On 15 March 2017, the parents and community members of Badethi watched an unforgettably spectacular school Annual Day programme as the children put up skits, music, dance, poetry and speeches to enthral them. Like the teachers of other schools working with a clear vision, the teachers here too realised the importance of the morning assembly. They organised the children into three houses—Alakananda, Mandakini and Bhagirathi—and entrusted them with responsibilities including that of planning and executing the morning assembly. While the head teacher took on the role of front-ending communication with the community; organising and managing parent-teacher and SMC meetings; and, raising calls for financial contributions for the school from the community when needed; the teachers focused all their energies on the children's learning, all-round development, and in ensuring that their team has a shared understanding of the progress of each child, including those who need extra time and attention.

Exemplifying the fine qualities of the teachers at Badethi is the maths teacher, Mukesh Nautiyal. Admittedly, he is not the typical primary school math teacher but in his role as one, there is an excellence that is apparent. We observed his lesson on 'place value', where he introduced the subject, established the concept and ensured that every child had understood it, giving more time to the few who were finding it difficult.

Here is how Nautiyal conducted his lesson on 'place value'. He began by reinforcing the difference between a digit and a number by asking the students to give examples of single, double- and triple-digit numbers, which brought in the concept of units, tens and hundreds. As he did this, he was able to introduce numbers and values in the context of money. From his wallet, he pulled out a couple of notes of different denominations and the discussion veered to the topic of Mahatma Gandhi's picture on our currency notes. A short discussion about Gandhi, India and independence, about India and our society and what Gandhi stood for, followed. He asked the children to connect this to what they had learnt in their weekly general knowledge class and pointed to how two different subjects are related. The class then got into a discussion on the colours of the rupee notes. Steering them back slowly to the subject of constructing numbers, Nautiyal encouraged the children to ask questions, whether for clarification or to satisfy their curiosity. When he felt that the children could construct four-digit numbers, he asked them to announce their roll numbers—single- and double-digit, odd and even—by turns. With this information coming eagerly from them, he proceeded to construct a variety of four-digit combinations using their roll numbers. As he did this, he kept repeating the place value of units, tens, hundreds and thousands. While some of the students were still trying to absorb this, he engaged those who had grasped the concept to start placing the roll numbers in a manner that the highest number could be formed. The energy in the class was sustained, there was also a kind of shared excitement between the teacher and the students about the discovery and understanding of a new concept. Some of the quick-learners started playing a game using different means to construct new numbers. As the class wound down, Mukesh reminded the children of the exercise he had given them the previous week—of jotting down everything in their daily life that is related to mathematics. Obviously, his blackboard did not have space for everything that the children were eager to have included, so with a laugh, he asked them to ease off and explained that he wanted them to appreciate the presence of maths in every aspect, every moment of our lives.

Nautiyal, as we said earlier, is not a run-of-the-mill teacher. Having completed his MSc, BEd and MPhil, he taught at a couple of private engineering colleges for a few years during which time he also acquired his doctoral degree. Married by then, his family pressurised him to take up a government job and that is how Nautiyal applied and got into the Uttarkashi district education department as a primary school teacher. For six months, he served a training period in a school in a remote block of Mori. Later, he was posted to GPS, Kothsankral, Chinyali block where he served for three years, walking four to five kilometres every day from home to school to teach thirty-four children from disadvantaged backgrounds there.

Mukesh Nautiyal is a free and frank conversationalist; candid in admitting that when he began his career, he was not sure he could teach primary school children. His ego and satisfaction seemed to thrive on the fact that he was teaching high-grade maths to engineering students. But slowly, he started finding a strange fulfilment in teaching young children the basics of numeracy and functions of arithmetic. When the SSA made him a Master Trainer for maths in the block, he realised that teaching primary school is far more difficult than teaching older students. One of the turning points in his career, he says, was his meeting with Sanjay Nautiyal of the Foundation and participating in the maths capacity-development workshops. Mukesh also attended the workshop conducted by a faculty of the Azim Premji University and the 'aha' moment for him was when he discovered the power of creating one's own teaching-learning materials. Suddenly, the importance of developing curricular learning material 'ourselves' struck him, he says and now accords great importance to this ability in teachers.

At this school, Nautiyal feels he has all the freedom and resources to do his best. There are enough children to have stimulating and fun interactions with. When one points to the sustained, high-energy in his classroom, Nautiyal says, 'Every child can learn. We have to invest time in them. I love the subject, so even if I have to teach for ten hours after school, I can do it without getting tired. But I just cannot do administrative work and so the head teacher keeps me out of it. My nature is such that when the head teacher asked us to wear uniforms, initially, my ego came in the way. But now I am able to look at this as an experiment. We do not know what will click and how.'

Nautiyal belongs to a large, well-educated, joint family with a number of members employed in various government positions. Anyone who has observed joint families in India will recognise the pulls and pressures of this social system, something that people living independent lives in nuclear families may not experience. Almost every day, in some way, Mukesh Nautiyal is being reminded that his elder brother is an assistant professor in a government college, his younger brother is a PGT teacher of maths in a Kendriya Vidyalaya and his younger sister's husband is also an assistant professor in a government college. So, it will not come as a surprise if he too is tempted to write the qualifying exam for the government's Higher Education Department. It may happen sooner than we think.

'We don't know the answer to this question. But *pata karenge!*'

DHYAN SINGH RAWAT, PRABHA, SURAT LAL, JAGBIR SINGH

Adarsh Upper Primary School, Gangani, Naugaon Block, Uttarkashi District, Uttarakhand

The drive through the pine forests from Uttarkashi to Barkot as one moves from the Ganga to the Yamuna valley is indescribably breathtaking. Travelling northwards from Barkot and crossing the Yamuna, one reaches the village of Gangani. On a clear day, the Bandharpoonch mountain range forms a glorious backdrop, almost like a benediction. In fact, until the late 1970s, the trek to Yamunotri used to start from this village.

In what can be called a luxuriously spacious clearing, is a complex with two schools, a hostel and a large playground.

Established in 1972, there is a primary school for Classes I to V and adjoining it is the Model Upper Primary School for Classes VI to VIII. Across the large field is the Kasturba Gandhi Balika Vidyalaya (KGBV) hostel. There are ninety-seven children enrolled in the Model Upper Primary School, Gangani—twenty-seven boys and seventy girls. The reason for the high proportion of girls is because the fifty girls of the KGBV hostel (started in 2005) are all studying in this school.

Like the other model schools in the state, this too was designated a model school in 2016 and automatically qualified for more resources, including teachers. That is how Dhyan Singh Rawat and Prabha joined the school. Though the appointment to model schools is seen as prestigious and an endorsement of the teachers' abilities, it comes with the responsibility of proving their worth, which makes these teachers work really hard. These two teachers joined Surat Lal, the head teacher of the school since 2001, a veteran who joined the education department in 1976 and Jagbir Singh, the social science teacher who has been with the school since 2006. Jagbir too is an old hand, in his mid-fifties, having joined the department thirty-five years ago.

It is clear that having been given this opportunity to create an 'Adarsh Vidyalaya,' this team of teachers at Gangani is fully committed and charged to do their best. One of the reliable indicators of a well-functioning school is cohesion and teamwork among teachers. At Gangani, the first thing that would strike a visitor is the collegiality among the teachers. As we sit in the sunlit portico, each teacher seems more intent on telling us something about the others, which is, in a way, a clear expression of mutual trust and liking. We also observed how each teacher knows every student, their abilities and difficulties in great detail. That is because the teachers meet at the end of each day for a quick review and identify issues to be addressed. Another sign of a cohesive group is the manner in which the very active Primary School head teacher, Manbir Singh, who has been at Gangani for more than eleven years, is so naturally an integral part of the upper primary team. The teachers of the Upper Primary in turn are eager to contribute to his Primary School. As we sit talking with the teachers, Manbir Singh suddenly gets up, goes into their library and returns with a slim, hardbound book, titled *Ranwalti ki akhaan* (loosely translated, it means proverbs in the Ranwalti dialect), written by Dhyan Singh Rawat.

We tease the story out from Dhyan Singh. When Dhyan Singh saw the rich folklore, proverbs and sayings of Ranwalti slowly disappearing under the dominant Hindi, he decided to undertake a painstaking project to find and document all the proverbs in Ranwalti.* He co-opted his students into this project and together they talked to grandparents and village elders to unearth virtually every proverb. The sweep of the project, the way the children were involved, the fixed pursuit—what Dhyan Singh accomplished, is precious.

In a fascinating footnote to this tale, that afternoon, Dhyan Singh took my colleague Ashish and me to the remote village of Molda and introduced us to ninety-two-year-old Sitaram Bahuguna. Holding him in a respectful embrace, Dhyan Singh said that many of the proverbs in his book were treasures shared by the old man. The village of Molda, only ten miles from Barkot, is a bone-rattling journey up the hill on a narrow muddy path riddled with boulders. For ten years, between 2006 and 2016, Dhyan Singh Rawat and his colleague ran the Upper Primary School, Molda. Both lived in the village,

---

*Ranwalti: A Garhwali dialect spoken in Ranwain, the Yamuna valley of Uttarkashi

leaving their families in town. Dhyan Singh knows everyone in the village and every few metres, someone or the other, from adults to children, stopped to greet him or touch his feet. At Molda, Dhyan Singh had prepared his students to create science projects and compete in the Rashtriya Bal Vigyan Congress. The very first time they participated in 2010, Molda qualified with a second place among twenty other schools from the Naugaon block. When they competed at the district level, Molda emerged as the best among twenty-four teams and qualified to represent the state at the Congress in Jaipur. Dhyan Singh had to plead with the parents to allow their children to travel to Jaipur because the parents could not comprehend the magnitude of their children's achievement. How different is this situation from that in our city schools where parents are so competitive about their children's schoolwork that they don't just help them, they make the projects themselves and even buy readymade ones! Molda's children did everything themselves for their award-winning projects on environmental protection and dwindling water resources. This teacher who put the Molda school on the science map of Uttarakhand is an MA in Hindi and his school had the most rudimentary science materials.

Dhyan Singh is a wiry, fit man in his late forties. He is also an avid trekker. His favourite time of the year is when he goes trekking in the mountains of Uttarkashi with his son who is currently at the National Defence Academy (NDA), Khadakvasla and will be commissioned as an officer in the Indian Army. Dhyan Singh's association with the Foundation goes back to the time of the launch of the LGP in 2006 when he was at the Primary School and then for around ten years at the Upper Primary School. This association has only strengthened over time. He repeatedly asserts that a lot of his understanding of the aims of education, and the ability to translate curricular objectives to lessons and classroom experiences have been gleaned from the numerous capacity-building programmes and the summer and winter workshops. He commands a lot of respect among his peers who listen carefully to his views and suggestions at TLC and VTF.

So, his presence now in the Gangani school is an inspiration for this school to emulate the success of Molda. A wise man, Dhyan Singh has chosen to take a back seat here, allowing the new science teacher, Prabha to take the lead. Prabha, who is a postgraduate in science, teaches maths and science. When colleagues suggested that she prepare students to participate in the Rashtriya Bal Vigyan Congress, Prabha grabbed the idea with alacrity. When we visited the school, two student teams were preparing their projects on 'Medicinal plants in our hills' and 'Local foods and nutrition' for the Congress that was three months away. Browsing through the project reports prepared by the children, one could discern their efforts, as well as, the lightness of the teacher's guiding touch. The material and information gathered were organised and presented in the children's own words. As a result, these children can do an impromptu project presentation before anyone at a short notice. They answer questions confidently but even more importantly, when asked questions to which they do not have answers, they say, '*Pata karenge*' (we will find out). Such is the self-confidence that these children have gained!

All this has come about only in the last one year. Prabha, who is very particular that each of her students gains a sound understanding of maths and science, says that she is beginning to see improvement. There is a visible competence in reading, writing and comprehension. The major challenge before the teachers is to raise the level of learning among the girls from the KGBV. These girls come from extremely difficult backgrounds and the teachers are determined to provide them with extra personal attention. The head teacher, Surat Lal says that earlier, the parents had a poor impression of the school but within a year, they have seen the change. Monthly meetings with parents are held mandatorily and earnestly. Earlier parents would skip these; not anymore. As conversations with teachers go, here too, they talked about the larger aims of education, of creating responsible citizens and lifelong learners; of building self-confidence and an attitude of caring and sharing. Quite appropriately perhaps, the wall in the portico of the Adarsh Upper Primary School, Gangani has the preamble of the Indian constitution prominently painted on it.

'Hamara school, hamare bacche!'

SHANTHIPRASAD, MARKANDEYA PRASAD, CHARAN SINGH ASWAL

Upper Primary School, Derika, Purola Block, Uttarkashi District, Uttarakhand

The Upper Primary School, Derika was established in 1988 and has thirty-four children in Classes VI, VII, VIII. The attendance is uniformly good throughout the year with an average of around thirty to thirty-two students present on most days. Most of the children come from neighbouring villages within three kilometres of the school. It is a neat school though it can do with some refurbishing. What visitors can discern very quickly is a vibrant positive energy, which is largely due to the very natural and amicable interactions between teachers and students. Shanthiprasad, who has been at this school since 2004, has a lot to say about this vibrancy at the Derika Upper Primary.

A native of the same block, Shanthiprasad joined the education service in 2001 when he was in his early thirties. He had passed his Intermediate in science and had the BTC at the time of his first posting to the Mori block. Before this, he had worked as a daily contract clerk in the Public Works Department (PWD) and then for six years as a maths and science teacher in a private school. Mori was a learning experience for Shanthiprasad who realised the tremendous difficulties that children in such remote and disadvantaged places face, which is also why he is able to appreciate the resources, facilities and living comforts of Purola better. Shanthiprasad married early and has four grown-up children. One is an engineer, two of them have completed MA, BEd and the youngest is doing her BEd after her BSc.

Shanthiprasad looks at these fourteen years at Derika as a wonderful journey of personal growth and development. 'When I first came here, we were all old-style and traditional in our thinking. *Pehle ki soch* punishment *ki thi*. (Earlier, our thinking was oriented around punishment.) Now we realise that it only creates resentment and fear. *Ab ki soch* "help and develop" *ki hai*. (Now, we think about "helping and developing").' The change within him, according to Shanthiprasad, is of greater tolerance and patience. And the result is that the children are not intimidated and are free to express themselves and ask questions. The classroom processes and interactions have changed dramatically too. 'People talk of activities in the classroom but we need to have a clear idea of methods and pedagogy. Personally, I use activities only for a concept or theme in which I feel some children may disengage. I also use illustrations from real life, for instance, from their visits to markets.'

Shanthiprasad, who teaches social science and English, is closely associated with the support activities organised for teachers. He is a regular at the various workshops and short-term programmes and says, 'These workshops and discussions at VTF and TLC have helped me in not just clarifying some concepts but also in articulating them better. These are not just a formality of training but are very natural and participative discussions.' Shanthiprasad is among the growing list of teachers in Uttarkashi who write down their reflections and classroom experiences in a diary. But he confesses, 'In a month, *main teen-char baar hi likhta hoon.*' When the Foundation offered Chakmak, the children's monthly magazine on science published by the NGO Eklavya, to schools, Shanthiprasad saw it as a great opportunity to introduce quality reading material to his students. Within the last three years, he has seen a discernible change among children as a result of this exposure. 'Our children at the Upper Primary, Derika, have also started writing their own poems and stories,' he says with visible delight.

Another great source of learning and transformation has been the internet and the WhatsApp revolution. '*Jab se* internet *aaya,* our reading has increased significantly. The mobile phone is the biggest change-maker. I have instant references there. We have also formed a 'Project English' WhatsApp group one year ago with around fifty teachers from Tehri and Uttarkashi. Although our conversations are mostly in Hindi, we discuss a lot about the teaching of English. We do not have any regular occasion to talk in English, so you can imagine how useful such a forum is for us.'

Markandeya Prasad is the head teacher of this school since 2004. He teaches Hindi and Sanskrit. He is a large-hearted man who gives a lot of credit to his colleague, Manbir Singh Rawat, who was at this school for five years before being promoted to an inter-college. If one were to praise the Upper

Primary, Derika in front of Markandeya Prasad, he would, in his modesty, mention that the upper primary schools in Chandeli and Sunali are the best in the block. He would also not fail to add, with great respect that Satyapal Singh ji, who retired a couple of years ago from Sunali, was truly the kind of head teacher everyone should emulate. But cast your eye on the board behind Markandeya Prasad and you will see names of the students who have qualified for the National Means cum Merit Scholarship (NMMS).* Around forty to forty-five children from a district qualify for this scholarship and one can see that every year, at least one to two students from the Upper Primary, Derika are among these, which is an indicator of the quality of learning at this school.

Markandeya is happy that the relationship between the school and the community is good. The SMC monthly meeting is well-attended and its seriousness is well-established. 'We discuss children's progress, seek parents' views and suggestions.' The teachers have discussions among themselves every day; they identify issues and plan steps to address these. Homework is taken seriously and meticulously; each teacher gives feedback to every child. 'Even if there is some backlog, the teachers must complete it latest by Saturday, every week,' the head teacher informs us.

Since this is an SSA school and its expenditure does not fall under the state plan but is a part of non-plan expenditure, there is a recurring problem of delay in salaries. However, the teachers have taken this in their stride. In fact, the teachers are planning to contribute Rs 5,000 each, this year, for refurbishing the school and for

---

*NMMS is sponsored by the central government. The exam seeks to identify meritorious students and fund their education expenses.

procuring the material they need. '*Hamara* school, *hamare bacche*,' Markandeya makes it sound simple. His native village is a hundred miles away but Purola is his home now. His daughter whose dream was to become a doctor, studied at the Navodaya school, Purola and had just qualified for a seat in a medical college. The head teacher says a number of alumni from Derika have done well. He mentions some who have completed nursing, one who has done BIMS, another B. Pharm. and yet another BEd. One of their students has also topped the Class X Board exams.

There is also Charan Singh Aswal, who is new to the school and teaches maths and science in place of Manbir Singh Rawat who moved to the inter-college. It is easy to gauge the positive perception of this school that even new teachers have, from his words, 'I have come here recently and I can clearly see this is a very good school. I have to prepare really well to teach here.'

From dysfunctional to dynamic

YAMUNAPPA, SOMASHEKHAR, SAKHAMBARI, MARIAPPA, GEETHA, YELLAGIRIAPPA

Government Higher Primary School, Maranal, Surpur Block, Yadgir District, Karnataka

There may be a number of reasonably robust frameworks to assess the performance of schools, yet, each school has a unique character that provides an overall, almost intuitive feeling of its quality. As we study and observe schools and teachers, this intuitive feeling plays a key role in corroborating or rejecting what a number of harder metrics might indicate. In rural government schools, with their very specific social contexts and challenges, this becomes crucial. There are sub-texts to this kind of intuitive corroboration. For example, at GHPS, Maranal one observes that at 4 p.m., nearly closing time, teachers are just as involved in discussions among themselves as they were before the morning assembly. The science teacher and the social science teacher are engrossed in their classes, running hands-on work with the learning material, knowing that by the time they finish class and pack up, it will be well past closing time. The old students of the school, along with some youth from the community, are playing cricket in the school playground with the head teacher's permission. And then one also observes the energy, confidence, curiosity and engagement of children in the classrooms. A combination of these indicate a happy environment. If we examine this further, it is a definitive sign that the positive indicators of quality seen through formal frameworks are sustainable and lasting because of the nurturing environment and processes in the school.

Maranal is a village in an interior area with the main road four kilometres away. It is economically secure as its agricultural land is well irrigated. However, over 50 per cent of the children are first-generation learners. At GHPS, Maranal, there are two hundred and five children enrolled in Classes I to VIII and six teachers, including the head teacher, Yamunappa, who is in his mid-fifties and joined the education department in 1984. A man with rich experience, he has been a head teacher for twenty-three years (since 1995) and came to GHPS, Maranal in 2014 after a long stint in a school in neighbouring Narayanpur. Known to be a very supportive leader who actively fosters teamwork, one can see his imprint in Maranal. His colleagues, much younger, are relishing the experience of working with Yamunappa.

Shakhambari, the social science teacher, is the most experienced among the teachers with nearly eighteen years in service. After a troubled period earlier, when she suffered at the hands of a politically well-connected colleague and head teacher, she has, at last, found peace and purpose at Maranal since her posting here in 2015. Somashekar, a livewire science teacher, has been at this school since 2010 and this is his first posting. Mariappa is a recent appointee, who joined in 2016. Geetha teaches Hindi and Yellagiriappa teaches Classes I to III and is adept in using the Nali-Kali pedagogy.

Yamunappa is the backbone. When he came here in 2014, he was faced with a disruptive community and a non-cohesive group of teachers. Around the same time, four teachers from this school were transferred. Rowdy elements were audaciously using the school premises for their drinking sessions in the evenings; there were no functional toilets; and, there was a clear case of spurious enrolment with attendance being less than 30 per cent. Like most head teachers trying to set right a dysfunctional school, Yamunappa began by building a relationship with the community and creating basic facilities. Since there were lady teachers in the school, the first thing he did was to build functional, clean toilets. He then got the SDMC aligned with his immediate priorities. The doors were repaired and the premises renovated and painted. He cleaned up spurious enrolments using Aadhar cards and the enrolment register was pruned down.

His teachers joined Yamunappa and the SDMC members in talking to the community. The manner in which the school was being revived touched a chord with the community and their antagonism reduced considerably. Yamunappa cautioned them not to create noise or nuisance near the school, 'Your children's education will suffer.' He also convinced them to be constructive in their relationship with the school and that his only goal was to provide quality education that would be of lifelong benefit for their children. 'I think this was the most crucial phase of our efforts. We succeeded in establishing a relationship with the community. The community can be strange—from absolute aggression to complete support—it took just a couple of actions on our part for them to completely change their attitude towards the school,' says a calm but visibly amused Yamunappa.

By this time, Yamunappa was also able to get replacements for the transferred teachers. And in this, he was lucky because he got fresh, motivated, almost idealistic young teachers. Each of them could clearly perceive the opportunity that lay before them—to come together in creating a fine school. It unleashed a burst of energy and passion among the teachers. The morning assembly became the starting point of the vibrant school atmosphere. Every teacher and student of the school is punctual and the assembly starts at sharp 9.30 a.m. The midday meal at Maranal is already known in the neighbourhood to be of excellent quality and Yamunappa believes that it is because the cook and helper also share the same passion and know that their contribution is as much appreciated as that of the teachers. The school has instituted the children's cabinet that takes responsibility for organising various activities. The sports teams for kho-kho and kabaddi are being galvanised with the goal of qualifying for district-level competitions. The Annual Day in February is an event where the community gets to see how the school has nurtured and developed the abilities of their children. The joy of seeing 'our children' perform has universal appeal. Every Saturday, the teachers have a review meeting to discuss their classroom experiences, the progress made and difficulties encountered. A neat, up-to-date record of these meetings is maintained in a register. Yamunappa spends time observing the classes and writes a diary with his observations.

The school also organises periodic meetings with parents to update them about the progress of their children.

Yamunappa is one of the head teachers of Surpur who has been associated with various development programmes run by the Foundation. He attended the ten-day programme for head teachers, on school management, in 2004 and subsequent school improvement workshops under the CFSI. By 2011, when other capacity building courses were offered in the district, such as the SLDP, Yamunappa participated actively. Having benefitted from these courses himself, Yamunappa has also encouraged his teachers to participate and teachers Somashekhar, Sakhambari and Mariappa are all regulars at VTF and use the library and resource materials available at TLC.

Individually, each of the teachers has taken ownership of their subjects and classes. Somashekhar, the science teacher is fascinating to watch and makes one want to stick their neck out and predict, 'This teacher will be one of the finest in the district.' Interestingly, he tells us that he scored just 42 per cent in his PUC and it was while he was doing his BSc. that he started developing an interest in science and decided to become a science teacher. Because he has completed MSc and BEd, he is qualified to teach higher classes, which is quite an aspirational position for many qualified teachers like him. However, as a result of his close interactions with members of the Foundation, he says, 'My attitude and approach to teaching has changed and I love teaching lower primary as much as the upper primary. When they sent me for five days to the Centre for Learning in Bengaluru, I saw highly-qualified teachers with PhDs teaching Class IV and V with such passion, it changed me completely and I promised myself that I will teach every class with the same passion.' Somashekhar uses a lot of activities to kindle interest and creates projects and experiments for children to develop an understanding of scientific phenomena. He creates groups that work on understanding smaller units of learning. Somashekar says he has gained much by being a regular at TLC and VTF where he is able to access materials and also bounce ideas off the more experienced teachers and implement these in his classroom. When one observes his classroom, two things become obvious—one, how his children use the various equipment without fear and the manner in which they discuss and help each other; the other is the way Somashekar stimulates their thinking by asking the right questions and allowing them to develop their own arguments and rationale before summarising. 'The purpose is to promote higher-order thinking,' says Somashekar.

When we stepped into Shakhambari's classroom, we saw a stellar example of the teachers' expertise in using teaching aids. She used the globe and maps in a manner that helped the children make clear connections with the topic. Sustaining children's interest is very often a result of the associations they draw from their existing knowledge to assimilate new learning.

A huge advantage at the Maranal school is that barring the head teacher, all other teachers are quite proficient in the use of computers and the internet. As a result of the additional rooms that Yamunappa built, there is a room with five to six computers and children of the upper primary classes have an opportunity to learn and use these. Often, such facilities are poorly used but here at Maranal, because all the teachers are themselves proficient, they have been able to teach basic utilities to the children, who have successfully created PowerPoint Presentations for their projects. In just three years, Maranal has made remarkable progress. From a run-down, dysfunctional school to a vibrant, happy one with a clear vision for continued excellence. Yamunappa is confident that the next KSQAAC assessment will reflect the hard work put in by his colleagues. Assertively, but retaining his poise, he remarks, 'We will do well.'

'The school's alumni have gone on to become engineers, doctors, policemen and accountants.'

SHIVAPPA SAJJAN, SHANKARAGOWDA PATIL, RAJESH MUJAVER, SHIVAKUMAR, KANTHESH, SRIDHAR MALJI, ANNAPPAGOWDER PATIL

Government Higher Primary School,
Maralabhavi, Surpur Block, Yadgir District, Karnataka

Maralabhavi is a village with a population of around one thousand and six hundred people of which 80 per cent belong to the Kuruba community. The rest are STs and there is a sprinkling of Maratha families. This village is in the Hunusigi area of Surpur taluk and not far from the neighbouring district of Vijayapura. Agriculture is the occupation for those who own farms but others earn their livelihood as daily wage labourers and quite a few also migrate in search of seasonal work. Sixty percent of those above thirty-five-years are illiterate and while 70 per cent have toilets constructed in their homes, open defecation continues. A redeeming feature is that child marriage which used to be a sad feature of this village earlier, has now all but disappeared.

In such a scenario, GHPS, Maralabhavi is quite easily the best thing in the area. A physically attractive, neat and clean school that offers everyone a welcome feel; a team of collegial teachers who work cohesively; and evidence of very good learning levels with a track record of children graduating to excellent higher education institutions and livelihoods. The seven teachers and their sustained efforts that have created such a school are fascinating subjects to study.

Shivappa Sajjan joined the education department in 1990 and has been the head teacher here since 2007. Shankaragowda Patil, six years his junior, also joined the school around the same time. Rajesh Mujaver of similar seniority and nearly twenty years of teaching experience joined the school in 2012. The younger teachers include Shivakumar who has been here since 2010; Kanthesh, the science teacher who joined the service in 2007 at this very school; and, Sridhar Malji, the English teacher who has just been posted to Maralabhavi. Interestingly, Annappagowder Patil, trained in the Nali-Kali pedagogy, who taught here for four years till 2003, has, after thirteen years in another school in Surpur, returned to Maralabhavi last year. These teachers live in the neighbouring towns of Hunusigi or Talekote and all of them come to school on their motorbikes.

Head teacher Sajjan and teachers Rajesh and Annappagowder have a long association with the CFSI and have attended various capacity-building courses as a part of this programme. Others have begun their association more recently, after they joined GHPS, Maralabhavi. Sajjan has been trained in Nali-Kali, while the others have attended subject workshops and courses. A couple of years ago, the school also held a mela around the theme of social science to showcase the learning of children to parents and members of the community. The children presented projects on the history of their village and region, that they prepared by talking to elders and seeking out evidence through local explorations to corroborate what they were told.

The school has one hundred and ninety-three children on its rolls and the attendance is always upwards of 80-85 per cent. The attendance was much lower some years ago, but consistent communication with the parents has had its impact. Over time, parents have developed faith in the school and believe that their children are learning well. Now, when the parents migrate for work, they leave their children behind with grandparents so they can continue school. No child from this village goes to private schools; all of them are enrolled at GHPS, Maralabhavi.

If one looks at the school in light of key dimensions, one can easily tick many boxes—appealing environment, clean and functional toilets, separate water for drinking and for cleaning and watering plants, a beautifully-tended garden, and a neat space for assembly and other activities. All teachers arrive punctually by 8.30 a.m., an hour before the start of school because they conduct additional classes for children who require more support. While the RTE (since 2009) makes corporal punishment a punishable offence under the law, Maralabhavi has always had an admirable history of 'no corporal punishment.' Through well-established systems and processes, the teachers have created a culture of independence, responsibility and self-reliance among the children. The school has a children's cabinet that is elected by students of Class III and above. The extremely well-planned morning assembly is executed by the students who take turns to read the news, conduct quizzes, and recite vachanas. A children's bank with passbooks has been created to encourage them to make decisions and procure materials. Active use of the library is encouraged and a register that is maintained shows an interesting range of readers and regular turnover of books. In a simple and effective manner, to motivate more children to borrow books, the students of Class VI and VII introduce a new book, every day, in the morning prayer, with a brief description.

Every Friday, between 3.30 and 4.30 p.m., the children's cabinet conducts a cultural programme that features singing, dancing, theatre, mimicry and the recitation of vachanas. The school's kho-kho and kabaddi teams have qualified up to the block level while the children who have participated in the department's Kalikotsava, have won prizes at the district level in recitation, debates and writing competitions. A good part of the curriculum is transacted with projects that encourage discovery and enquiry. One will find children take up projects ranging from local history to a study of the bio-garden in neighbouring Thinthini; or, a visit to the agricultural college research centre and the village jatra. As a result, children develop an understanding of how things grow, develop and change over time.

Head teacher Sajjan is very particular about early childhood education and personally supervises and teaches children in Classes I to IV. Trained in Nali-Kali, he is acknowledged as one of the best teachers using that pedagogy in the state. He was also named as one of the best teachers on the government's Kannada TV channel, Chandana. The conceptual understanding of children and their ability to engage with subjects beyond textbooks becomes obvious within a few minutes of interacting with them. Sajjan believes, 'this emphasis on developing a sound understanding of basic concepts is why the children go on to do very well in high school.' The latest KSQAAC assessment provides further evidence of Maralabhavi's quality—a top rating on the learning achievements of students. In a very interesting initiative, Kanthesh, runs a science experiment every Wednesday to help create interest in the subject among students and encourage them to develop a spirit of enquiry. He visits TLC regularly and borrows materials from there to conduct his weekly experiments at school.

Most children, after passing out from GHPS, Maralabhavi, go to the Government High School at Salodigi in the neighbouring district of Vijayapura. Sajjan personally takes his students to the high school and helps them complete the admission process. Reports from Salodigi say that these children do extremely well there in their SSLC Board examinations too. The highest score in the taluk in the 2017 SSLC Board exams was secured by a student of Maralabhavi who went on to study at the Government Adarsha High School. The students of the school also do well in PUC exams. 'The topper of the district is our student who then studied at a college in Talikote. Students who have passed out of GHPS, Maralabhavi have become doctors, engineers, policemen and village accountants,' Sajjan tells us. All this adds up to a very strong bond between the school and its alumni. As Kanthesh adds, 'Old students help us during events like Annual Day, Independence Day and the various science or mathematics melas that we organize.' The Annual Day of the school is held every year on the last day of the academic year with the community in full attendance. The relationship with the community is nurtured carefully. 'We are far away from the city and that helps in keeping things simple. No local politics enters the school, the SDMC is duly elected and we nurture the relationship with the community,' says Sajjan.

But there are issues that are a cause of worry for the teachers. The high content of fluoride in the water concerns them greatly and they want to install a water filter at the earliest. With the Panchayat Development Officer being sympathetic to their concern, they are hopeful of getting this done soon. The teachers are also particular that they provide the best possible midday meal with available rations because the children do not have any nutritious food before coming to school. The pressure of administrative paperwork, updating and uploading data is irksome. Kanthesh does a lot of this administrative data updating work for the head teacher using the computer at the TLC. Many of the stories about good schools are about one-man armies or a heroic head teacher but the uplifting aspect of Maralabhavi is that it is a team that is marching forward together.

A wonderful teacher who could have been lost to the powerlooms of Bhiwandi

SHANKAR, KAMLESH
Government Primary School, Kotiyaphali,
Sirohi District, Rajasthan

This is the story of a fine teacher who came into the profession accidentally. It was not some burning desire of his youth. On the contrary, Shankar, was trained to work on power looms as a textile design master. A 'seth' from the Pali district in Rajasthan took the youth to Bhiwandi, a town in the outskirts of Mumbai, that was one of the major hubs for textile production. It was at a powerloom in Bhiwandi that Shankar worked for many years. When he came on a visit to his native village of Deldar, he ran into his childhood friend Omprakash, an employee of the state education department who was the Cluster Resource Coordinator for the area in the Abu Road block. Omprakash who had heard that the government was starting a school in Kotiyaphali village—just two kilometres from Deldar—asked his friend to apply for the post of a para-teacher. 'It was the turning point of my life. I was not a trained teacher. But I always felt that teaching is an excellent profession. *Achanak aisa mauka aaya aur maine* apply *kar diya* (I suddenly got an opportunity and I applied)'. That was in the year 2002. The Government Primary School, Kotiyaphali began with one teacher, Shankar, in one room in the house of Narsabhai, a large-hearted villager. Shankar was already in his mid-thirties when he began his teaching career and realised with a sense of wonder that this was indeed his life's calling. As he threw himself into work, a number of children from the village and nearby surroundings enrolled and Narsabhai's house could not accommodate the growing numbers—nearly sixty children! So, in 2003, the first room of the school was built on land that belonged to the Panchayat. Two years later, the government regularised what till then was a 'makeshift/ alternative' school and sanctioned budgets for the building and some infrastructure. In 2009, another building was constructed. The school now has three classrooms, an open play/ assembly ground and two clean, functional toilets, one each for boys and girls.

During the first five years, Shankar personally planted and nurtured neem, peepal, guava and amla trees. Even during the summer vacations, Shankar would come every alternate day to water the plants so that they do not die in the searing heat. The community observed Shankar's ownership and the children joined in the action. Today, the responsibility of the upkeep of trees and plants rests with the children. Some years ago, in order to provide some kind of secure boundary to the school, Shankar had planted thorny bushes around its periphery. Today, the school has a boundary wall.

GPS Kotiyaphali currently has an enrolment of forty-four children. On an average day, the attendance is around 80 per cent. The children come from very impoverished families. The entire community of Kotiyaphali belongs to the Girasia tribe, who are poor and illiterate farmers with very small holdings and large families with up to six or seven children in each family. These folk cannot even buy basic stationery, even pencils or notebooks for their children. Some large-hearted community members procure stationery in bulk from the town of Palanpur in Gujarat which is just fifty kilometres from Abu Road in Rajasthan. These benefactors or 'bhaamashahs' (as benefactors are called in Rajasthan) have also provided sweaters to these children thrice in the past five years. Shankar does not hesitate to contact them for help and they respond readily. This is because they see the children come happily to school; they notice how well they are learning, interacting and expressing themselves. It is a clear vote of confidence by the community for the school. Shankar, with a touch that is both astute and sincere, ensures that the bhaamashahs distribute the material to the children themselves.

Over the past fifteen years, as a result of the good primary education at this school, a number of young people in the community are educated. Shankar, who has kept a record of the students over the years, tells us that those who passed Class V from his school invariably completed high school. More than 60 per cent of these youngsters are pursuing technical training at the local ITI while some have opted for a BA. Some girls, after their primary education at Kotiyaphali, go to the residential hostel and school for ST children. Among all his tasks, Shankar also has to follow up and persuade the irregular children to come to school. Often, he has to pull them away from sibling-care and goat-rearing duties.

The best thing to have happened, according to Shankar, was that Kamlesh, a young idealistic teacher, joined the school in 2012. Kamlesh comes from a village called Kewarli, which most interestingly, is a village that produces teachers. There are nearly one hundred teachers from this village of five thousand people. For Kamlesh, who is just twenty-seven, Shankar is a father-figure. He admires the simplicity, commitment and passion that Shankar brings to his work. Shankar too developed an instant liking for Kamlesh from the day he arrived at the school. The two of them form an admirable team, planning and executing together, distributing responsibilities and working in perfect harmony. While Kamlesh teaches maths and English, Shankar teaches Hindi and EVS. The assembly at the school bears the stamp of meticulous planning and execution. Speaking almost in unison, both say that the assembly is the best place for children to express themselves, demonstrate and hone their abilities and learn in a harmonious manner. So, when one watches the morning assembly, one notices that the children do a lot of oral exercises such as multiplication tables, counting, rhymes, poetry, and story-telling. There is ample group work and opportunities for all children to participate. Kamlesh points out, 'There is no learning environment at home. Everything has to be done here. So, assembly becomes an important learning space. Hindi is not the language of their homes. They only learn to speak Hindi here. The syllabus is in Hindi, so teaching them to speak and write in Hindi is crucial.' The children of the Kotiyaphali school are also doing well in sports with Class V boys reaching the district finals in wrestling. Shankar also wants us to note that the children are totally honest. 'Even if they find a pencil or a coin, they will come and give it to Kamlesh or me. They seem to be naturally courteous and polite.'

It is again time to take an inconspicuous, quiet seat at the back of the classroom while Shankar takes the children through a topic in EVS. To teach his class about the properties of water, he has a few glass tumblers with water and runs a continuous interactive session. With a spoon of sugar in his hands, he asks children, 'Will this dissolve?' and adds it to the glass of water. He does the same with salt, then with some colours to show how water acquires the character of what is added to it. He talks to them about what floats and what sinks and how oil spreads on water. A child pipes up to exclaim how rainbow colours are seen on oil slicks over puddles on the road. It is a mixed group of children from Classes III, IV and V. All are engaged. When some children discuss among themselves, Shankar allows that and does not consider it disruptive. He lets them finish their argument. As one listens to the children express themselves and write creatively about water on the blackboard, one is able to connect with the teachers' emphasis on children developing the ability to read and write. All too soon, it is time for the midday meal. As the children disperse, I ask Shankar about the deep engagement of children and the manner in which children constructed some excellent sentences. Without a trace of conceit, almost matter-of-fact, he replied, 'Our Class V children's understanding and learning is better than those of the private school.'

Shankar and Kamlesh then show us how they maintain individual child-wise learning portfolios. Kamlesh points out, 'For us, CCE is quite smooth. We are able to maintain up-to-date records without any difficulty. Both of us know every child's learning levels in every subject and where the child is facing difficulty.' As one makes an appreciative comment, Shankar adds that Kamlesh has been instrumental in organising these. 'He is of immense help in administrative work. Being a considerate person by nature, he volunteers help and shares the load.'

The two of them are also committed to their own learning and self-development. Shankar is a regular at VTF and finds the academic discussions in the forum immensely useful. He says,

'*Teen ghante ki charcha hamare beech bahut hi* useful *hoti hai* (Three hours of discussion is very useful for us). For example, in two of the recent meetings, we discussed the teaching of division and methods to describe regional features as a topic in geography. The interactions help us refine our thoughts and explore alternative classroom methods.'

The weaving master who began as a para-teacher in 2002 has come a long way. He became a regular teacher (prabodhak) in 2008 and is now the head teacher. Along the way, he has acquired the STC and the BSTC teacher certifications from DIET, Abu Road. The VTF, being a voluntary initiative, depends a lot on some teachers taking the initiative to keep this going by organising regular meetings and choosing topics that will be relevant and useful to the participants. Here, at the Abu Road block, Shankar is one of the teachers who has assumed the responsibility to lead and organise VTF. Kamlesh is also a regular at the LRC, Kewarli. He looks forward to the maths workshops that are periodically conducted at this centre where teachers who live in the vicinity of Kewarli come together voluntarily. His own children are growing up fast, he says with a smile. The eldest of his three children, a daughter, is doing her MCA. The middle one is doing her Class XII while the youngest, a son, is studying in Class VIII.

There is a certain calmness at Kotiyaphali, an assurance that children are cared for and are learning well. There is an unhurried rhythm that is almost a defining feature of the place. We notice fruit with the midday meal and ask Shankar. Walking to the gate to see us off, he tells us that the children are provided fruit every Thursday by a local social service organisation. He did not have to persuade them to contribute to the school. Such is the groundswell of goodwill for the Government Primary School, Kotiyaphali.

5

HEROES: THEY RECOGNISE NO BARRIERS

All the teachers in this compendium are heroes—as individual performers, as a team or as leaders. So, why am I creating a separate section to feature a few of them? To be honest, as I was organising the stories into sections that in my view best suited them, I realised that with a few teachers and their stories, I just could not do that. Even as I would think that I had found a home for them in one of the sections, there would be aspects that sang out; defied being constrained in any one section. Where could I place the teacher who at great personal risk, converts his classroom into a dormitory at night for the children of migrant parents so that their education does not suffer? What about the head teacher of the girls' school whose students are sent by their parents to the village to look after their brothers but end up as the district's kabaddi champions? In which section could I place the teacher who hauls up a school from zero to a hundred percent attendance and into one of the best schools in the district in an external assessment of the children's learning? Where should I fit the story of the primary school teacher who has ensured that every child in his village, in the past seventeen years, has completed high school?

Many years ago, when the LGP was launched, the idea for it came from what we saw on our numerous visits to rural government schools. We saw some schools and teachers overcome enormous constraints to become exemplary. In identical environments and amidst the same challenges, one school would be remarkable even as another, less than a mile away, would have given up. What mettle were those teachers made of, who completely ignored all constraints, fought and overcame all odds to ensure that every child in the community was enrolled, that every child attended school and was learning? As we unrolled the LGP, we realised that these were not just extraordinary teachers, they were almost eccentric in their zeal. The thought that they could fail, fall foul of authority or make enemies just did not seem to cross their minds. This has remained with me ever since and is perhaps the sub-conscious trigger for this section.

A teacher, whose mother was in the ICU for a month, did not miss school a single day during that period, managing hospital visits before and after work. Another teacher, in another school where not a single child has ever dropped out, knows the name of every child who has been through his school and also what each has gone on to do and become. What kind of people are these teachers? Heroes, mavericks? Or just truly devoted, courageous people? I remember, an elderly villager saying this to me of one of the teachers, '*Yeh duniya ki sabse acchi teacher hain (*She is the best teacher in the world)'. Quizzically, I asked her, '*Duniya ki* (In the world)?' To which she replied, '*Yeh gaon hi toh hamare liye duniya hai* (our village is pretty much the world to us).'

'It is the sports culture in my school that enables equity and mutual respect in the classroom.'

DHARAMVIR SINGH CHAUHAN
Government Upper Primary School, Bijayrampura, Bajpur Block, Udham Singh Nagar District, Uttarakhand

Dharamvir Singh Chauhan was transferred to the Upper Primary School, Bijayrampura in November 2004, within a few months of the school being established. There were just seven children and the head teacher, K.N. Yadav. Within a year, as Yadav and Chauhan mobilised people in the surrounding villages, the enrolment rose to thirty-four. However, the school had no toilets which was an absolute shame as the students included girls in the early adolescent stage. No funds were forthcoming and so, Dharamvir spent Rs 5,500 from his pocket to build temporary toilets for girls. In fact, until 2007, the school had received no funding and Dharamvir was regularly spending his own money for basic upkeep and minimal infrastructure. The economic condition of the village and the surrounding areas is not bad. The villagers work as agricultural labourers and the community comprises of people from the SC/OBC category with around 20 per cent from the Buksa tribe. The Buksa tribe owned land in the past but they have frittered that away according to Dharamvir. Drinking is the menace that has compounded the problems of this community. This was one school where the teachers said the parents have no interest in their children's education. However, over time, Dharamvir and Yadav managed to bypass this obstacle by establishing a strong and direct bond with the students. And this was achieved by Dharamvir's masterstroke of getting the Bijayrampura school to focus on sports. If you now visit the school, you will see how proud the children are of their school and its achievements in sports.

Dharamvir is fifty-two years old and he was twenty-six when he joined the education department. For the first eight years of his teaching career, he worked in a primary school in the Bajpur block before being posted to the Primary School, Khempur in the Gadarpur block in 1999. 'Khempur was the turning point for me,' reminisces Dharamvir. It was there that he had the opportunity of working closely with the head teacher, Ramesh Singh. 'Ramesh Singh had a keen interest in sports and I would accompany him along with the children to various sports events. I got hooked to sports and saw what an important role it plays in children's development. I can never forget my five years with Ramesh Singh.'

So, when he came to Bijayrampura, it was no surprise that Dharamvir began promoting sports. He saw talent bloom among both boys and girls in kabaddi, kho-kho and sprints. 'I realised that the children were so talented that they deserved coaching from an expert. I came to know of a Physical Education expert in the Bajpur Sugar Factory and persuaded him to coach my students. Every day, I would go on my bike to pick him up and bring him to our school so that he could coach our children from 3 p.m. to 7 p.m. I would then drop him back before returning to my own home. Results began to show—our school could win at the cluster and compete at the block level.' Sometime in those early years, Dharamvir also hired a bus with his own money to take twenty-seven children of his school to Kashipur to participate in a sports competition. These children came back to the school with trophies. When the community came to know of it, their amazement and respect for what the school was doing for their children became a defining point in their relationship with the school.

Sports is now institutionalised at the Bijayrampura school with each batch of students seamlessly introducing the joy of sports to successive batches. The school's tradition in sports gets stronger with each passing year. *'Bacche ab khud hi seeti baja lete hain,'* Dharamvir tells us, which is his way of saying that the children know the rules of the games thoroughly. In the past three years, the Bijayrampura school has been the block champion in the two-hundred and four-hundred metre sprints, kabaddi and kho-kho. But Dharamvir knows that he cannot let the pace slacken. So, while he may have stepped back in the actual administration of the sports activities in the school, he has maintained a demanding schedule for children to keep up their practice. Even in winter, the children and Dharamvir stay back in school till 7 p.m.—a work ethic established many years ago that continues. From his own money, he also gets extra milk and provisions for the children participating in the sports competitions. This has inspired his colleagues to contribute too. Some teachers have also begun accompanying the children to competitions. Dharamvir says, *'Mujhe sahyog mil jaaye, mere liye yehi bahut hai* (It's enough if I get co-operation).'

The enrolment at the school has only improved with every year. From thirty-four students in 2005, it rose to fifty-nine in 2008 and gradually reached one hundred and thirty-four in 2016. There is both hard work and some shrewdness behind this. 'I am quite familiar with all these villages that I have roamed around in my initial days. I knew that students from the primary school that is near our school would go to the Shivpuri Junior College (in Uttarakhand upper primary schools are called junior colleges!) which is five kilometres away. I convinced the children and their parents that they should, instead, join our Bijayrampura school after the primary, which I told them is nearer, more convenient and has excellent sports facilities. *Aur hamare* teachers *bhi aa gaye. Mera sochna hai ki bacchon ko jitni ho sakein utni suvidhayein milein.* (Our teachers also came. I believe that we should provide as many facilities as possible to the children.)'

Dharamvir, who has been teaching maths at the school since the beginning, has also started teaching science since 2015. He had completed his Intermediate in science and the BTC before joining the service and has acquired BA and MA (Sociology) degrees while working. A keen learner, when the LGP was launched in 2005-06, Dharamvir quickly got associated with it and understood the benefits of questions that assess conceptual understanding as opposed to rote learning. While that programme introduced him to the benefits of conceptual questions at the primary school level, Dharamvir took the initiative to extend this to the upper primary curriculum, designing such questions for his maths classes. Given his energy and willingness to commit time beyond school hours, it is not surprising that he is also an active participant of the VTF that is held in the block regularly. He has also attended various teacher development workshops organised in the district. He particularly liked the maths workshop held in Dineshpur and remembers, 'The trainers provided many practical inputs for creating teaching-learning material to explain concepts better.' Similarly, he acknowledges the usefulness of the residential winter workshop in science.

'Ashok Kumar of UPS, Patoti is an excellent maths teacher and a very good master trainer who is also now associated with us.' This is a special facet of Dharamvir, this uncanny ability to spot competent people and to co-opt them through informal relationships to contribute to his school. In the classroom, his challenge is to engage every child. He tries to bring each one to the blackboard to practice and prepares his maths kits to consciously include every child. 'Because of the sports culture, the equity and mutual respect in the classroom is much more natural. So even though only ten out of the forty-seven students are good in the subject, the others do not feel left out. After all, many of them are extremely good at sports. So, it is easy for me to use the ten excellent students to teach the others and elevate their levels.' Dharamvir has a keen eye for exceptionally talented students and helps them prepare for the district-level 'Maths Wizard' programme. 'Many years ago, I helped a bright, young child prepare and enter the Navodaya school. Since then, I always try and create space for the exceptional child to compete and excel.'

Sitting in the open ground, in the early winter sun, Dharamvir shares information about his family. His elder son, a B.Tech. in computer science is working in Bengaluru while his younger son, after completing his MSc has interviewed with IIT, Roorkee for their PhD programme. The interesting point to note is that influenced by his mentor, Ramesh Singh, he shifted his two boys from a private school when they were in Class II and enrolled them in his own government school where they studied till Class VIII, after which he sent them to the private Vidya Mandir School in Bajpur.

In 2017, Dharamvir received the block's 'Excellent Teacher Award' in recognition of his school's consistent performance in sports. Even as he shares this information, he does not forget to acknowledge the people who have helped him in this journey. He says that the Deputy BEO of the Bajpur block, Ms Prema Bisht, has been a huge support to him and his school in all their endeavours. He says, 'There is no such thing as extra work. I must do justice to my job and the responsibility given to me. If I have to spend my holidays or late evenings on this, I am not doing anything special.'

'Should we not leave behind something substantial for the school and children that we spend all our working lives?'

AVNISH

Government Model Primary School, Talabpur, Jaspur Block,
Udham Singh Nagar District, Uttarakhand

This is a fact that gets reinforced over and over again—successful institutions are often defined by an individual and not by what is often vaguely referred to as 'the system'. It is also a fact that in many such successful institutions, this individual may not be a formal leader but a driven and dynamic member of the team. Truth be told, in this narrative about the Talabpur School, the head teacher will not get even a passing mention. It is the teacher, Avnish, who has inspired and driven every initiative of the school for the past four years. Much as one's heart soars when one sees an individual create such a transformation, one's mind warns that an institution so dependent on an individual can also be fragile. Let us bear this concern in mind as we look at the work of Avnish at Talabpur.

In April 2013, when Avnish arrived in Talabpur, the school had just seventeen students and three teachers. It was an old school, established in 1949 and like most other schools in the vast plains of this district, had a large space for classrooms and a playground. But everything else was in shambles. Like in many villages in rural India, the sight of rolling green agricultural fields sit without contradiction alongside the difficult living circumstances of the villagers. The Talabpur School caters to children from four villages of which interestingly, three are in Uttar Pradesh as Talabpur is literally on the border of Uttar Pradesh and Uttarakhand. Despite their indigent circumstances, the parents (illiterate, daily wage labourers) have a keen desire that their children receive a good education. Two private schools in the vicinity were believed to be the right choice by parents and it was no surprise that between them, these two schools had three hundred and fifty children on their rolls. Talabpur had seventeen.

Avnish decided that his first task would be to bring children back to this school but he knew that the parents had no confidence in the school and would have little patience. He had to show a few results quickly. He began by teaching the seventeen children through the summer vacation. This stunned the parents; it wasn't something they had seen before. Next, Avnish called for a meeting with the parents and in an open house session, asked them what was the kind of education they desired; what were the things in private schools that they liked. At the end of that meeting, Avnish promised them that they would see changes at the school. The parents seemed sceptical, so Avnish set a deadline, 'Give me three months, *aapko asar dikhega.*'

Avnish and his colleagues began by focusing on just foundational concepts in Classes II and III. They knew this was possible. But they were realistic enough to know that given the poor learning levels, working simultaneously with Classes IV and V and showing an impact there too would be impractical. So, their strategy was to first show that the children in Classes II and III had begun to learn. They insisted that parents meet the teachers every month for a progress review. With hardly any funds available, Avnish spent Rs 10,000 from his pocket and purchased teaching materials. Among these were the ruled handwriting notebooks that he believes are crucial in developing children's handwriting and at the same time giving them a visual pleasure that encourages more practice. Strategically, this was the type of workbook that private schools boasted of and he wanted the community to notice that Talabpur Primary was no less when it came to learning materials.

In the ensuing weeks, as Avnish and his two colleagues began working intensely with the children, parents could see the difference. Soon, they began reciprocating and in a major vote of confidence, sixty-seven children joined the Talabpur Primary School after their parents withdrew them from the two private schools. Avnish had achieved his first significant goal. With the increase in enrolment, Avnish realised how inadequate the school infrastructure was with just two classrooms for eighty-four children across five classes. He began to pressurise the block authorities for funds to build additional rooms. In the meantime, he hired an additional room in the vicinity of the school, paying a rent of Rs 1,500 per month from his own pocket. It is now four years and Avnish still pays the rent for this room.

In 2016, the state government decided that Talabpur would be a Model Primary School. As I have said earlier, at times, the reasons for selecting a school are not clear. Further, not all districts invest the requisite funds on designated model schools. While in our visits to model schools in Uttarkashi, we had seen the district education department commit substantially on infrastructure, here at Talabpur, the department has only tried to ensure a minimum number of teachers to meet the established PTR norm. So, in 2017, Talabpur had five teachers for one hundred and forty-five children. The head teacher is a figure head but mercifully not disruptive. The other teachers cannot match Avnish's 'junoon' but are doing what they can with their own abilities and energy. The village is embroiled in politics which demands cautious handling of relations. But with the school being nominated as a model school, Avnish's next goal has already been thrust upon him—to make it a model school in the true spirit of the concept. This goal, he knows, will challenge him more than the earlier ones he had set for himself. And though he is driven, he is realistic and understands that Talabpur has a long way to go. It also means that he will need to contribute more from his pocket. We were stunned to hear that the money for the painting of the school walls and the compound with relevant learning material that is prescribed in the BALA (Building as Learning Aid) concept of school building has been pumped in by Avnish. He says that when the pending funds from the BEO—which exceed over a lakh—come, he will claim reimbursements. He has also procured twenty-five aluminium-topped folding tables that are used in classrooms as well as for midday meals.

The porch of the school now serves as the fourth classroom. It gets extremely hot in the summer, biting cold in winter and is open to rains in the monsoons. Avnish is soon going to procure thatch blinds to cover the open side and provide some protection. He has also procured an LCD projector and other learning material that is being used meaningfully in the school. For this too, if and when the funds come, he will be able to recover what he has put in from his pocket. His four colleagues have also contributed Rs 10,000 each and these funds will be used to add two tin-roofed rooms (admittedly, temporary structures) so that the school will, at last, have five classrooms. It is a recurring theme in many good schools across rural India how one or two teachers demonstrate heroic ownership, not thinking twice before putting in their money if that means better facilities for the children. The Talabpur community has also begun to chip in and the school has collected nearly one lakh in contribution.

If thus far the story has been about his resourcefulness and passion, it is now time to turn to Avnish, the teacher. To understand the teacher, we have to understand the cardinal principles that Avnish has laid out for himself. These are, '*Har bacche ke saath kaam karenge, woh seekhega,* impact *hoga*; I will not attend any meetings or workshops during school time; during the school hours, I will only be at the school with my children; all the work at school will be academic and all administrative work and reports will be prepared at home before or after school.' Avnish has not availed of a single day's casual leave for years. Not even when his mother was in hospital for twenty-three days and subsequently, another twenty-nine days for a life-saving, gallbladder by-pass surgery. He would visit the hospital early morning or late in the evening. Avnish believes that a significant reason for his effectiveness as a teacher is because of the time he invests at home in planning the lessons for the next day, keeping in mind each child and the examples and exercises that will be best suited, right down to the kind of worksheets that will be used. He is a twenty-hours-on-his-feet person. 'I wake up at five in the morning and go to bed at one, *chaar ghante ki neend mere liye kaafi hai.*'

The morning assembly is a vital part of the academic programme of the school and all children have an equal opportunity to take part in the prayers, stories and creative expression. Spotting talent, special hobbies and interests of the children and providing space for these in the assembly, according to Avnish, enable a smooth and organic absorption of values—'accha-bura' (good and bad), 'mil ke kaam karna' (teamwork)—in his words. The school library is the other crucial component of learning. Room to Read has helped set it up and Avnish and his colleagues encourage the children to borrow books and read. Children, through these processes, are independent and engaged. A look at some of their compositions and answers to questions reflects this. To a question in Hindi,

'What is the word for a person who sings songs, the expected answer would be 'gaayak' but a child had written 'singer' (in Hindi) which had been accepted as a correct response by the teachers of the school.

Avnish personally teaches and takes care of Classes I and II as he believes this is the most important stage in a child's education. The children of the two classes sit separately so that Avnish can give them better attention. Classes IV and V are usually combined while Class III is flexible, either separate or combined with the higher two depending on the topic or subject being taught. Avnish also teaches maths in Classes IV and V. Saturday at the Talabpur Primary is a 'no-academics day' devoted to cleaning, maintenance, games, a musical bal-sabha and such all-round development activities. Attendance at the school is over 90 per cent on most days. Children are usually absent only when their parents take them on long vacations to attend weddings in the family. Avnish has the phone number of every parent and has established the rule that no child can be absent without the parents first informing him.

Many years ago, when Avnish was at the Primary School, Teerath III, the school participated in the LGP and he got an opportunity to learn and adopt improved assessment methods in his pedagogy. He also became the Resource Person for the programme at the Jaspur block. A few years later, as a progression to the programme, when the district administration formed a thirty-member Academic Resource Group, Avnish was nominated to it and attended a ten-day programme conducted by the Vidya Bhawan Society, Udaipur. Ten years later, he can still accurately recall every session of that programme, identifying what he liked best and also what he did not. Avnish now regularly attends the meetings of the VTF as well as the summer and winter workshops conducted by the

Foundation's field institute at Dineshpur. He is straightforward in his opinion, 'I get turned off by artificial and intellectually hypocritical discussions at the training programmes and workshops. So, my suggestion to the organisers would be to always conduct workshops that provide teachers clear ideas that they can try out in their classrooms.'

He is also clear and direct in explaining everything that he has done at Talabpur and for those who fail to consider the wonderful and transformative impact that his work is yielding, it may even come across as a bit of chest-thumping. Another reason to take his words seriously is that the man is unsparing even in self-assessment. I asked him where he thinks Talabpur is on the quality scale when it comes to learning and education. His response with a vehement shake of the head was, 'The learning levels at Talabpur are still lower than what we had achieved at the Teerath III School. There, more than 70 per cent of the children were able to do well in the learning assessment. Here, the percentage is much lower. Of the four years here, we have spent two in just establishing ourselves and creating some basic facilities.'

Avnish was an excellent student in school, did well in Intermediate and then graduated with a BSc in industrial chemistry scoring high marks. He was about to prepare for the UPSC exam when his father, a science teacher and the sole breadwinner of the family, passed away, suddenly. As his dependent, Avnish was offered a teaching position. This was in 2001; Avnish was just twenty years old. He embraced this turn of events with a positive outlook and the memory of his father as a fine teacher became his inspiration. He has, since, completed his MA through correspondence and with sixteen years of teaching behind him, Avnish believes that becoming a teacher was the best thing to have happened to him. His wife is a teacher too in a school just across the border, in Uttar Pradesh. Avnish drops her to school in the morning before coming to Talabpur. Perhaps, Avnish's devotion to the school is also motivated by his family. His mother and sister always join him in the celebrations of Independence Day and Republic Day at the school and insist on buying and distributing sweets to the children.

It will only be befitting to end this essay in Avnish's own words, 'We strive all our lives to leave much for our own families when we pass away, so, when we work as teachers with our school and our children for forty years, should we not leave behind something substantial and solid for them?'

Scraped knees, buoyant spirits and remarkable confidence—how a girl's school in Uttarakhand produces kabaddi champions

DURGESH NANDINI YADAV
Kanya Upper Primary School, Damta, Naugaon Block, Uttarkashi District, Uttarakhand

The Girls' Upper Primary School, Damta is a short but steep descent off the road. One hundred and five girls are enrolled in Classes VI to VIII and of these, sixty-four belong to the SC and ST and thirty-eight to the OBC categories. It was with a mixed feeling of despair and hope that we learnt from Durgesh Nandini Yadav, the head teacher, how these girls come to study at Damta. 'There are seventeen villages around Damta and these villages send their boys to study in private schools here. The boys have to take up rooms in Damta and so the parents send their sisters to cook and look after them. It is these girls who join our school. So, for my colleagues and me, our mission is to make school a life-changing experience for these girls.' With this background, it is easy to understand why the dynamic head teacher has a mission statement prominently displayed in her school 'All round development through a balance of scholastics, sports, arts and culture.'

Durgesh's life revolves around the lives of the girls who study in her school. Damta Kanya was established fairly recently, in 2011, and Durgesh has been here since the beginning as the head teacher. It is, in her words, a second lease of life with a fresh new mission and purpose for her. In her mid-forties, Durgesh has seen her share of challenges. She speaks little about those but one can sense that her stout-hearted character has helped her overcome some difficult times. Durgesh joined the education department twenty years ago after completing her MSc and BEd and was for many years a teacher at the Primary School, Rikhaura in the same block of Naugaon. She is not a native of the hills but is from Dehradun or thereabouts. For years, she has seethed at the attitude of a patriarchal society towards girls and their education, which is why she sees this school as an opportunity of a lifetime to convert her angst into constructive energy for the progress and development of girls. Ever-smiling, confident and full of ideas and plans for her school, her positivity is contagious.

Talking to the articulate and confident twelve- to fourteen-year-old girls at the Damta School, it is obvious that Durgesh is translating her vision into action. Supported superbly by her two colleagues, Savita Chamoli and Ushakiran Rawat, she is trying to ensure that there is an ideal balance between classroom, scholastic and other activities that will develop all-round capabilities in her children. She sees this manifest itself in her students as self-confidence, poise and the ability to face and solve problems in their lives.

Durgesh is conscious of the fact that she comes from a family of educated people and had an environment at home that helped her learning, an advantage her students are deprived of. Which is why all the hundred and five girls receive her personal attention. It translates into extra hours every evening after school when the three teachers work with identified children to help them with their studies. Among the remarkable teaching practices in this school is how language learning is encouraged through the writing of original compositions, poems, and how the use of maps in geography classes encourages children to develop visual learning and spatial thinking in a manner not often see in many classrooms.

Even as the three teachers pay full attention to academics, they are also pulling together various initiatives to enable the children to fulfil their potential and interests in sports, literature and fine arts. 'Mind and body' is a conjugation that Durgesh uses frequently. She has declared Saturdays as 'no-studies day,' a day exclusively for games, singing, art and painting. When she came to know of a good trainer for judo and karate, she persuaded him to come and teach these martial arts to her students. She also focused on building a team for kabaddi. Durgesh recognises that not only does every child have some talent but a different one at that. Therefore, cultural activities in the school go hand-in-hand with judo, karate and kabaddi. With their own money, Durgesh and her colleagues have purchased lezim sets, dumb-bells and judo uniforms. In fact, Durgesh and her colleagues also contribute around Rs 1,500 every month for various things such as fans in the classroom, teaching-learning materials and to meet some incidental expenses. Damta Kanya is an SSA school and quite often, the salaries of the teachers are delayed by a few months. But Durgesh, Savita and Ushakiran have learnt to take this in their stride. It does not dampen their commitment in any way.

In all that Durgesh is spearheading, her colleague, Savita Chamoli is a loyal lieutenant. Savita too has been with the school since the beginning and is also a veteran, having joined the education department in 1995. Her energy is unflagging. Ask her about it and she replies with a smile, 'We should not be idle for a minute, the mind should always be focused on things to do, new things to learn and apply. I want these girls to develop a questioning mind and ask me things that I do not know; things that I have to study to tell them about. The one thing I love here as compared to my earlier schools is the mutual trust and friendship among us teachers. It creates immense energy and therefore, I never feel overworked or bored.'

At Damta, the 'Bhojan-mata'—the lady who prepares and serves the midday meal at the school—is an integral member of Durgesh's team and this is obvious from the way she too, during a chat, was able to clearly explain the vision of the school and its various activities. It is extremely rare to come across a person who prepares and serves the midday meal to not only be aware of the school's day-to-day activities but also its larger intent and purpose.

Since these children, who are at a pre/early adolescent stage, are encouraged by Durgesh to ask questions about anything that they are curious or concerned about, she says, they ask questions that they would otherwise not have the courage to ask even their mothers, 'As a result, these girls are able to consult the doctor at the Community Health Centre without any hesitation.'

Leadership among students has evolved organically. A student with an interest in health and medicine takes the responsibility of maintaining the health register, while the girls who are outstanding at kabaddi, coach the school team. Damta School's kabaddi team has progressed through the block- and district-levels to win awards at the state level and the students have represented Uttarakhand in national tournaments. When we called out to students who have represented the block, district or state, a dozen girls stepped out. These champions play and practice in the school courtyard that is uneven and has granite rocks jutting out. We asked the girls, 'How many scraped knees?' Amid laughter, all hands went up.

This lone teacher manages a school of 105 for the past several years now!

ASHOK

Lower Primary School, Hemmadagi, Rukmapur Cluster, Surpur Block, Yadgir District, Karnataka

---

Ashok is truly who one would call an unsung hero. If you happen to spend a day in his school, you cannot but be deeply moved by what this gentleman is achieving single-handedly in a remote hamlet in Karnataka. He was just twenty when he joined the Karnataka education service in the year 2000. The Lower Primary School, Hemmadagi was his first posting and Ashok has been at this school for seventeen years now. Hemmadagi village has a population of less than a thousand. A mix of Kuruba, SC, ST and the Lingayat communities, most of them are hard put, managing at a bare sustenance level. Open defecation is still the norm and you will hardly find a house with a toilet. But over the past seventeen years, since Ashok has been at the school, this community has recognised the value of education and all children go to school.

Ashok's journey as a teacher is a story of self-discovery, self-learning and continuous improvement. He describes his initial years as a teacher at this outpost as a lonely period; also, one of trial and error. Although he was equipped with a TCH, after his PUC, he had no practical experience. He would employ traditional processes and struggle with pedagogy, unable to understand how children learn. It was at the CFSI in 2004 that he received his first valuable training. As part of this programme, teachers were trained on the Nali-Kali pedagogy and Ashok embraced it, mastering and internalising it in content and spirit. A burning desire came from within because Ashok wanted to be as good a teacher as he could be and he saw in the pedagogy the opportunity to teach his students well. 'Earlier, with my traditional methods, ten out of twenty children would learn. With Nali-Kali, it takes more time and effort but every child learns.' Because of his excellent command over Nali-Kali, he is also a district resource person for training teachers in this pedagogy.

Ashok's commitment to every child is evident from the fact that since he came to LPS, Hemmadagi, not one child has dropped out of school. After the children pass out of his school, he also makes sure that each one of them is admitted to the higher primary school. Issues of sibling care, domestic work and the absence of an Anganwadi in the village are roadblocks that he has managed to navigate around in order to ensure that at least in this small hamlet, the core objectives of Universal Elementary Education are achieved.

There are a hundred and five children in this school which has two rooms on either side of a road and to manage the five classes, Ashok must cross this road several times a day. When he arrived here seventeen years ago, the small and remote village of Hemmadagi had no bus service and so Ashok took up lodgings in the nearby village of Sugur. Staying at Sugur made it possible for him to reach the school every day by 8 a.m. and leave as late as he wanted to. This facilitated the bond he wanted to build with the children. With a disarming smile, he says, 'I also saved money as the cost of living in the village was less than what I would have spent living in a town. I continued to stay in Sugur village after my marriage and my son too studies in my school.'

If you visit this school and can ignore its rather unsightly and battered building and the lack of basic facilities, you will see energetic, enthusiastic children, fearless and inquisitive. While Ashok is busy teaching Classes I to III (taught collectively), if you stop by at the Classes IV and V across the road, you will be surprised to see the children working independently and building upon the concepts that Ashok has taught them. Four to five children take charge and help the others. They create their own problems in maths and solve these involving all their classmates, taking care to include even the odd child who has trouble grasping it. Their quickness and sharpness are distinctively different from those in many other schools. 'Fifty percent of my work is done by these children. After all, there are hundred and five students and unless I co-opt the children, it will be humanly impossible for me to teach them all. I have helped the children form a cabinet that is responsible for opening the school every morning, cleaning it and closing it in the evening. It has been running smoothly for eight years now; even if I am delayed by a few minutes, children ensure that the school starts on time; they organise the morning assembly and prayer by themselves.' In the KSQAAC assessment in 2016, LPS, Hemmadagi was among the best schools in both mathematics and EVS. Ashok's focus is already on bettering this, 'The school must improve in the language assessment next time.'

The mutual attachment between the children and Ashok is obvious. Since a learning environment is missing in their homes, Ashok insists on giving them some work every day to do at home. He makes it a point to check and comment on every child's homework. Before leaving for the day, he completes all his administrative paperwork. Over the years, grateful students have formed an Old Students Association and are deeply invested in the school, be it in the setting up of a library or to stand-in for Ashok if he has to go out. Ashok explains his wonderful relationship with the community simply, 'It is nothing special. I do my work and they respect it. I do not interfere in the village community affairs except when it comes to SDMC elections. Those, I ensure are conducted fairly.'

The sad part of this remarkable story is that Ashok has been the sole teacher in the school for many years. A second teacher who was posted here used political influence to get deputed to a more convenient location. An irate community, in a show of solidarity, protested by locking up the school and calling in the attention of local media, including TV channels. The protest was successful and the second teacher has recently been posted back to the school. Ashok, meanwhile, continues with the same zeal, seeking every avenue for his own learning and development. Although the TLC is almost eighteen kilometres from his home, Ashok is a regular visitor, keenly discussing aspects of material development and pedagogy with his fellow teachers. Much respected for his expertise in Nali-Kali, Ashok's contribution to these forums is appreciated by everyone. Some people leave you with a lasting impression of their goodness. Ashok has that intangible charisma.

'Two classrooms in this school double up as a night hostel for students whose parents migrate seasonally, so that they do not miss school!'

ACHAPPA GOWDER

Government Higher Primary School, Jumalpur Dodda Thanda, Surpur Block, Yadgir District, Karnataka

Achappa Gowder is an institution in the village of Jumalpur Dodda Thanda. And with good reason. He joined the education department in 1999 and his first and only posting has been at this school, which means he has been here for over eighteen years and the fortunes of the village, the school and his own life are interwoven in a story-like manner. His native village is just twelve kilometres away, where he has a twelve-acre farm. The farm is looked after by his nephew; Achappa's time and attention are only for his school. The enrolment numbers in this school have been stable for many years. It was three hundred children and five teachers when he joined the school and it is three hundred and fifty children and five teachers now, eighteen years later. In all the years that Achappa has been at the school, three head teachers have come and gone; Achappa made many suggestions to them but none of the head teachers paid heed to his advice. Now, since October 2015, Achappa is the acting head teacher, after the previous one was transferred.

What Achappa inherited was an old building—four rooms in a row of which only two were usable (the other two were too badly run-down); no functional toilets because of disuse; and no provision for drinking water.

Jumalpur Thanda is a hamlet in the southern part of Surpur block. The nearest town is an hour's drive while the district headquarters of Yadgir is 120 kilometres away. Over 75 per cent of the community belongs to SC and ST. Apart from a few people with small landholdings, the rest depend on work as agricultural labourers. Invariably, for many months in the year, such work is not available and the people of Jumalpur Dodda Thanda have no choice but to migrate seasonally in search of livelihood. They are gone for months, every year, to places like Belagavi, Jamakhandi and Bengaluru. In the past, from October to April, only one hundred and fifty students of the three hundred and fifty would attend school. The rest would move with their parents, returning months later. It was such a confounding problem that Achappa could think of nothing less radical—perhaps foolhardy too—than converting the school into a residential hostel and convincing the parents to leave their children behind during the six months of their absence from the village. For this, he first needed to repair and refurbish the school infrastructure. Achappa and his four colleagues moved as a team on mission-mode for he had already won them over by telling them that they were all at par, 'I am not the head teacher, only in-charge head teacher.'

His first target was to build attractive new rooms in place of the dilapidated structure. Two years prior to this, the budget had been sanctioned but the previous head teacher had neither acted on it nor informed anyone and the money had lapsed. It had led to a showdown between him and Achappa, who had sworn, 'I will get it done.' Later, as acting head teacher, Achappa went to the Deputy Programme Coordinator's office and obtained approval for three buildings and got the budget re-allocated. These funds were deposited into the school account and the construction began. Achappa was determined to make the school building look attractive and he personally supervised it at every stage. From the time the land was levelled, to when the construction began and as it progressed, Achappa was present—from 8 a.m. to 8 p.m., every day. And because of his hawk-eyed supervision, the school saved money. What would have normally cost Rs 40,000 was accomplished with Rs 25,000! Achappa used the money thus saved to repair and make the toilets functional. This remarkable person had also saved enough money to install a water storage (Sintex) tank.

Achappa then turned his attention to organising an eyecatching inaugural event for the opening day of the academic year, 2016. He knew that the new building, the freshwater tank and functioning toilets would bring great cheer to the community, the children and the teachers. He knew this kick-off event could be crucial to gain their confidence in the school and he was right. Such was the confidence and trust, that Achappa could now talk to the parents about leaving their children behind when they migrated seasonally for work. And sensing a positive mood, Achappa seized the moment to announce his daring new plan—he was going to use two classrooms as residential dormitories for the children whose parents would migrate. Recalling this momentous decision, Achappa says, 'This was possible only because the parents felt assured of their children's safety and wellbeing.' Achappa could only accommodate up to thirty children in the school at night and for the remaining, he convinced the parents to leave them with their elderly relatives and grandparents. He exhorted the other members of the community to take responsibility of the children whose parents were away. Incredible as it sounds, this is how eight girls and twenty-two boys now live in GHPS, Jumalpur Dodda Thanda under this audacious 'hostel' initiative. The school manages to provide dinner and breakfast for these thirty children out of the midday meal budget itself. Three teachers take turns to stay overnight in the 'hostel' and provide supervision and care. Moved by these efforts, grateful parents and some members of the community are also contributing money to support this initiative.

Achappa did not stop here. When you visit Jumalpur Thanda School, you will notice that the students wear strikingly good-quality uniforms. The story behind this is that Achappa refused to accept the standard uniforms that the BEO's office organised through established suppliers. Instead, he got the funds of Rs 54,000 transferred to the school account, went personally to buy superior quality cloth, sought out a good tailor and got the uniforms stitched. And he did all this at a lower cost. The well-entrenched 'commission' system was derailed by this man's boldness and he does not worry that he might be creating enemies in the process.

Attendance at the school is back to decent levels and Achappa's next mission is to improve the learning levels of the children. For this, he has organised extra teaching and coaching—'parihara bodhane' (remedial teaching), as he calls it—after school by the three teachers. He has installed speakers in every class and the state education department's Keli-Kali radio programme is implemented exactly the way it was intended to be. Achappa's reason for implementing the radio programme with all the sincerity is because he had seen it implemented in a school in the Kushtagi taluk and had also observed the positive response from the children there. That he learns from others and is keen to adopt good practices and processes from them is evident when he says, 'I have been greatly influenced by my visit to the school in Kushtagi. I am also deeply influenced by Head Master Sangaiah of GHPS, Gedhalamari. I want to do similar things here at Jumalpur Dodda Thanda.'

Achappa knows that some of the steps that he has taken may not be permanent and may fizzle away when he leaves the school but he looks at this current assignment as an opportunity of a lifetime. He could never get things done earlier when his pleas and suggestions were ignored by previous head teachers. Now that he can, twenty-four hours in a day seem less. Achappa's association with the Foundation is just five years old but during this association, one of the programmes that has had a profound impact on him was the exposure visit to exemplary schools. 'I have only done twenty-five percent of what the school in Kushtagi has done. Give me two more years, Jumalpur Thanda will become a Model School. I have to motivate the village sahukar (money-lender) to donate more money for the school facilities. What we have managed is no magic, just hard work and cooperation of my colleagues. My children do not leave school even after the evening bell. They sit here, play here, do their homework here and water the plants.' When Hulagappa, the Foundation's local representative, mooted the idea of a school mela, Achappa brought the same energy to this enterprise. Last year, he held this fair, calling it a 'Kalika Mela' (a learning fair) and showcased to the community the learning of the children around themes in geography, history and general science.

Every year, five to six children out of the twenty-five applicants from GHPS, Jumalpur Dodda Thanda qualify for admission to the Morarji schools. Achappa wants this to increase. 'Give me two more years…' he repeats this throughout our conversation like a fervent mantra. The children of Jumalpur Dodda Thanda will perhaps realise only after some years what a great difference Achappa has made to their lives. And even after they grow up, they will always remember this fearless and eccentric man.

'There is nothing better or more important than being a primary school teacher.'

BASAVARAJ DALAVAI
Government Lower Primary School, Peeranayaka Thanda,
Surpur Block, Yadgir District, Karnataka

PN Thanda (it is generally referred to by its initials) is a hamlet in Kakkera area of the Surpur taluk. Surpur is one of the most disadvantaged taluks in Karnataka, ranking 201 among its 202 blocks on the Human Development Index. Within this taluk, Kakkera is the most deprived. Economically, the condition is not very sorry because of the remunerative paddy cultivation but in terms of the quality of life, Kakkera is pitiful. With the one hundred and eight hamlets spread across it in dire need of electricity, roads, sanitation and literacy, it symbolises years of political neglect. Drinking and gambling are a norm.

So how remarkable is it that in such a region, the Government Lower Primary School is easily one of the most outstanding schools in the entire block. But this was not always so. The school, established in 1992, languished in apathy for many years. Even in those initial years, it had an enrolment of a hundred children but only on paper—just two children attended school. Soon, the three teachers posted there were also moved out.

All this changed in 2007 when a one-man army, in the form of a short, twenty-four-year-old Basavaraj Dalavai, arrived at PN Thanda. If ever there is a justification for giving the entire credit of a school's outstanding performance to one man, it is here at PN Thanda. This was Basavaraj's first posting after joining the education department and he has been in this school since then. Basavaraj had got this job with much difficulty after completing his PUC and TCH, and so he took on the challenge before him as an opportunity to bring about a significant change. PN Thanda had one hundred and forty homes spread across five habitations mainly comprising the SC, ST and Kuruba communities. Basavaraj went to each of the one hundred and forty homes, introduced himself and talked to the parents. Every morning, including Sundays, he would visit people's homes as early as 8.30 a. and was so persistent that parents were compelled to listen to him and children started trickling back to school, slowly.

Basavaraj began the next phase of his work inside the school. He spent every minute of the day with the children, providing individual attention, organising them into groups for tasks, reviewing their learning and insisting that when they went back home, they tell their parents about their day at the school. Parents soon saw that their children were learning and within a year, by 2008, fifty children were coming to the school regularly. Basavaraj kept up the tempo by teaching during summer holidays and in order to execute this effectively, he also arranged midday meals for the children during holidays when the service is otherwise not available. He knew that there was no reading material or learning environment in their homes and that on Sundays, the children helped their parents by taking the cattle to graze in the fields. Basavaraj began to teach on Sundays too. With each day, they made some progress. The children were bright and eager and they loved Basavaraj for the way he helped and challenged them. They looked forward to school and by 2010, Basavaraj had managed to attract every child back to the school. A 100 per cent attendance became a norm at PN Thanda by 2011.

The change that Basavaraj has been able to create in this single-teacher school is evident from a few simple indicators.

Every year, on an average, eight to nine girls who finish Class V from this school get admission into Kasturba Gandhi Balika Vidyalaya (KGBV) residential schools. Basavaraj personally takes them there and settles them in KGBV hostels in Bengaluru, Bagalakote and Kalaburgi. Interestingly, he does not take them to KGBV, Yadgir where they did not get a good response when they first went there. Many children have also joined the Morarji school in the Shahpur block after successfully clearing the entrance test. In the state conducted KSQAAC assessment of 2016, PN Thanda ranked fourth among the schools in the taluk. Another sign of progress is how from 2007 when almost all parents were illiterate, now ten years on, as many as 70 per cent of them sign their children's progress cards, having been taught basic literacy by their own children.

Basavaraj is an avid learner himself. During the last seven years, he has acquired BA and BEd degrees through correspondence; and has become computer literate too. He has a computer at home on which he browses the internet and also compiles data that the block and district authorities ask him for. He is up-to-date with all information as a result of this data collation and processing ability. Basavaraj was a keen learner when the CFSI was being implemented in Surpur and learnt to use the Nali-Kali pedagogy very capably. When the TLC was established at Kakkera, Basavaraj became an active participant in its various voluntary seminars and activities. He acknowledges that the TLC at Kakkera and the workshops conducted by the Foundation have helped him develop relevant material for his classroom and has also helped him in the manner in which he transacts certain themes. Over the years, Basavaraj has unfailingly attended workshops and courses offered in the district. Whether it was a head teachers workshop by Sunny Tharappan or the summer workshop on the pedagogy of social science, he was there, absorbing every interaction.

Every Sunday, Basavaraj assumes charge as the resource person for maths in the free coaching programme that is organised in Kakkera for children to prepare for the Navodaya and Morarji schools. He relates the interesting background of his ability to teach maths, 'I was very poor in maths till PUC, but after becoming a teacher, I learnt maths by myself because I wanted to teach my children well enough to do well in the Navodaya entrance exams. My maths is now so good that I can teach high-school students.'

In the past four years, Basavaraj has organised three school melas—two on social sciences and one on language. In fact, those who have watched PN Thanda closely over the years, believe that the first mela conducted in 2010 was a turning point in demonstrating the learning of the children to the community, especially the parents. In 2011, PN Thanda was recognised as the best among the Surpur schools in CFSI.

Though a native of Belagavi, Surpur is now Basavaraj's home. His father is still an active agriculturist and tends to his farm with support from one of Basavaraj's brothers who is a village accountant. Another brother is a havaldar in the Army while his third brother is a police constable. Basavaraj who came to PN Thanda as a bachelor is now married and has two children, a boy aged seven and a girl of four. His son studies at the PN Thanda School in Class II. Basavaraj has established a record of sorts that will be tough to beat—he has been present in his school every day since he joined it in 2007 and has not availed a single day's casual leave in the past four years. He practices yoga every day; wakes up at 5 a.m.; is at the school at sharp 9 a.m. and leaves only by 5.30 p.m. He reads at home for two hours every day and turns in by 10.30 p.m.

Over the years, his students have developed an enduring bond with him. Every day, at least seven to eight alumni drop by at the school on some pretext or the other, but the main reason is that their day is not complete without seeing Basavaraj. When Basavaraj has to leave school to attend meetings, an alumnus from the 'Old Student Sangha' steps in to hold the fort. Sadly, hardly any government functionary visits the school. Kakkera, as we said, is one of the most disadvantaged regions and Basavaraj is trying to ensure that the children of PN Thanda acquire a good education and go on to do well in life and become socially responsible citizens. There is a complete conviction in his voice as he says, 'There is nothing better or more important than being a primary school teacher. Nothing can ever equal the respect that I get here.'

THE LAST WORD: WHY THESE STORIES MUST BE TOLD

Is the work ethic of the government school teachers worse than that of business (private) sector employees? That question may sound silly in an age where the government school teacher has been effectively made the 'folk-devil'—the creature responsible for all failings of our education—while the private sector is feted as the paragon of industriousness. But we have learnt the hard way that silly questions are worth asking and answering. Do the stars and the sun really revolve around the earth? Was the 'witch' really responsible for the outbreak of cholera?

From 2002 to 2016 we have worked (and continue to do so) with lakhs of government school teachers. These were not brief, but sustained interactions. We did not encounter the folk-devil—across the jungles, the mountains, and the deserts of the country. Villages and small-towns where these teachers live or commute to, and my colleagues live there as well, are places that are hardly visited by anyone from the outside, including the self-assured critics of the teacher.

One of the starkest contradictions between the folk-devil narrative of the teacher and the reality that we observed in these years was about 'teacher absenteeism'. Popular discourse—including in parts of the higher echelons of government—backed by some 'scholarly' research talked of absenteeism of

30 to 50 per cent. We had never seen absenteeism rates, even remotely of this order. 'Absenteeism' refers to teachers playing hooky, that is, not showing up at work, without taking leave or without some other reasonable cause.

All our experience of fifteen years with lakhs of teachers was discounted by the self-assured critics as 'anecdotal', though they may have been speaking from hearsay or a sample size of fifty. So, we decided to conduct a research study on teacher absenteeism. The study was published in 2017, as a part of the Field Studies in Education series of the Azim Premji University. It discovered the teacher absenteeism number to be 2.5 per cent. Teachers felt vindicated by the study. Unconcerned about the facts, some people said that we were trying to 'protect' the teachers.

The week that the study was published I was travelling in Uttarkashi district. A widely circulated local Hindi newspaper published a sensational headline 'Inspections across the district discover 26 teachers missing!'. The word used for 'missing' in Hindi was 'nadaarad', which is as negative as can be. The next day the newspaper was forced to issue a clarification. Only one teacher was missing, five were on sanctioned leave and the other twenty had been sent by the Department of Education for training. In this little incident lies the tale of how misleading interpretations are consistently used to feed the folk-devil narrative.

Our research study found that about 18 per cent teachers were not in their school. 2.5 per cent were absent without any cause (playing hooky), 6 per cent were on leave, and about 11 per cent were out for some other bona-fide work (e.g. sent on training). While writing our report and its headlines—we pointedly talked about this break up, leaving no room for the 18 per cent number to be brandished as the 'absenteeism' number. This exactly was the secret of the sensational tale of the newspaper story.

In today's age of many low-quality media outlets, this behaviour is unsurprising. I won't use the same brush for the researchers whose papers have fed this false narrative, but these papers have indeed fuelled the scapegoating of teachers. Buried in the footnotes or in a table in the latter pages of these papers is the same tale, that their headline number of 25-30 per cent is not absenteeism but absence including with good cause, and that absenteeism is around 3-4.5 per cent. The authors of some of these papers have usually not tried to clarify matters, as their paper have been merrily used to propel a blatant falsehood.

And when teachers have protested this patently false narrative, it has been taken as the whining of the guilty.

Clearly, if so many teachers are not in school, education suffers. But the point is that for most of this problem the teachers cannot be blamed in any way—it is the system that has to solve the issues of how to resource adequately, for example, factoring for leave, anticipating other work and training that teachers may have to be involved with, etc.

1-2 per cent absenteeism even in a factory or a bank is unsurprising. And this is even though the capacity to catch absence without good cause is near perfect in such business organisations and its consequences (docking of pay, disciplinary action etc) are clear and severe. So, it should be a wonder that the teacher absenteeism is quite comparable to this number—even though the capacity of the system to catch such truancy and then punish is very limited, given the remoteness of most schools.

But at the end of this book which is all about public-school teachers, the truth about the myth of absenteeism, won't surprise you, even if you did not know it before. You have got to know such teachers better. Page after page you have encountered teachers who go beyond their commonly understood job description, while facing tough conditions, and with very limited resources.

And this is not the story of a few teachers here and there. The numbers are so large that it is hard to keep track. We have over 200 Teacher Learning Centres (TLCs) across small towns in fifty districts across five states. These TLCs have a library, a couple of computers, a few sports kits, experimental kits and resources, and other such things of interest to teachers and children. Thousands of teachers come regularly to these TLCs, to participate in learning sessions or workshops that we conduct, or just to read and borrow books, or to chat with their fellow teachers.

Much of this activity happens after school hours or on holidays and the participation is voluntary, i.e. no one is 'ordering' the teachers to participate. So, the teachers invest their personal time to do all this, and their own money on the commute, which for some is quite a bit, all of their own volition.

Though I know the answer by now, I keep asking such teachers 'why do you come here?'. Some are more articulate than others, but the gist of all answers is the same 'we want to learn to teach better'. And when probed further with 'why do you want to teach better?', the answers range from 'we must do our jobs as best as possible' to 'the future of these children is in our hands' to 'our work shapes society, so this is our duty', and more.

None of this would happen in business organisations. Employees of business organisations are not going to invest their own time (say a Sunday) to learn to do their jobs better and spend their own money to access this learning.

THE LAST WORD

I have spent about a couple of decades in business before moving full time to the Foundation. Many of you may have similar experience. We know that even imagining that our business colleagues (the average employee) would spend their Sundays learning to do their jobs better without any external incentive, and that too regularly, is ludicrous.

Why do teachers do things like this? Let's dig deeper, underneath the answers that they give.

It is not as though a large number of teachers have become teachers because they saw it as their life's calling. There are a few, but most of them have certainly not set out to change the world. The vast majority of them take up the profession as a secure job with decent salary. These are much the same kind of motivations that drive people to take up jobs in stable, 'good' business organisations. So, the average teacher is very much the average person of this country—no more or less fired up by any noble intentions when taking up the profession.

So, what is going on? It's not hard to understand.

Teachers are surrounded by children, unsurprisingly so. This is every day of their working life. The average humans' response to children may vary for many reasons, but at the core is deeply determined by the evolutionary disposition to take care of the young of the species. Put simply, adults naturally feel for children; if they see them day after day, they develop bonds, and they start caring for them. Except for the very few teachers at the extremities of personality disposition distribution, teachers care for their students, because that is just natural. Even the gruff teachers, or (most of) even those who regularly mete out corporal punishment, have an underlying relationship of care with their students. This doesn't excuse the gruff or punitive behaviour—but it does tell of the complex human dynamic that underlies the teacher-student relationship.

Teachers are also acutely aware that good education can transform the life of children. And for the students that government school teachers teach—most of whom are from disadvantaged backgrounds—this is even more true. For most such students, education is the only path—not only out of poverty, but also out of the shackles of social hierarchies.

Now let's put these two things together. Teachers care for their students and they know that their work is one of the few things that can really help improve the lives of these kids. Isn't it just natural that most teachers would feel the urge to do as much as they can? Not all teachers may do it all the time or even most of the time—but this potent force is in there and animating all teachers—leaving aside very few.

However, there is another thing at play. Whether or not anyone else can make out—a teacher knows how successful s/he is as a teacher. They can assess how much are the children actually learning, i.e., how effective are they themselves in playing their roles. This knowledge gives direction to the force animating the teacher—to try to teach better.

The social, psychological, and moral landscape of the teacher's role really has no equivalent in the world of 'jobs.' It is quite unique. The closest analogy—and one can arrive at this through just common sense—is that of a parent. The teacher is a 'quasi-parent', even if s/he doesn't know or want to be. So, teachers will do things for the good of their students, which cannot be explained or understood, unless seen in the context of the unique nature of the teachers' role.

The irony of our education system is that instead of harnessing this potentially powerful positive human dynamic, it often dilutes and deflates it. It does so by diminishing the role of a teacher, by treating them as the lowest rung of the vast government hierarchy, by disempowering them, by not providing them even the basic resources and conditions for their work, by fostering an inspectorial culture, and by too often just plainly disrespecting them.

It is the inherent power of this positive human dynamic, combined with the sheer spirit of teachers, and sometimes the support of good officers or the community that we see the kind of stories that you have read of in this book.

Let me end with some things that we, this country, needs to do—from policy to real action on the ground, for teachers, such that our education becomes equitable and high quality.

First, how can we expect teachers to remain engaged and motivated if the most basic physical working conditions are inadequate to appalling? If they don't have access to functioning toilets and running water, electricity supply is disrupted, and not even a small working space to themselves? If we respect the profession of teaching, then it will first reflect in the education system providing them these basic things.

Second, their struggle to get even the most rudimentary of learning resources and material must be put to a stop. All teachers will have adequate learning material to transact the curriculum. This ranges from books and experimental kits to pencils and paper.

Third, teachers must not be given other tasks. They must be allowed to focus on their teaching and on their students. Teachers must not be pulled out for other kinds of work such as surveys, distribution of public services, local elections, etc. Repetitious data demands on the teacher from the system must also be eliminated by intelligent use of information technology.

Fourth, an adequate number of teachers must be appointed. Today, an estimated 2 million teaching jobs are vacant across the country, while we altogether have 9 million teachers. That's a large deficit. Teachers are handling more students than they can, across multiple grades, and often teaching subjects that they have themselves not studied.

Fifth, teachers must not face discriminatory service conditions. Lakhs of 'para-teachers' across the country perform the same role as other teachers in their schools, but get paid half to one-fourth. All such cadres of teachers must be given service conditions and compensation equivalent to other teachers, after going through the relevant qualifications where required. Also, compensation and service conditions must be equalized across primary to high school.

Sixth, teachers must be provided support for professional development and growth. This must be based on their own needs and not driven by some centralised, impersonal system. This will entail providing sustained high-quality education and opportunities for peer learning. It will also mean objective assessment of their work and recognition for good work, enabled by development-oriented supervision. This in turn must be enabled by appropriate capacity development of school leaders and other leaders of the education system.

Seventh, the teacher preparation system (BEd), which has about 18,000 teacher education institutions (TEI), must be overhauled to eliminate rampant corruption and dysfunction; TEIs that are nothing more than 'degree-selling-shops' must be shut down. The curricula must be reimagined—appropriate to the complex and critical role that teachers play, and all TEIs must have high-quality teaching-learning.

Eighth, most importantly, the culture of the education system—including in schools— must be based on trust and must empower and enable teachers. It must foster creativity and initiative, and curricular innovation. Teachers must be treated as valued professionals, not as the bottom-most rung in the vast government hierarchy. This must reflect in the daily behaviour of the education system's leaders.

This is not a full or comprehensive list of matters, but it does cover some of the more important ones.

If we want to truly transform our education, we need to fire up the human positivism of teachers to its maximum. And we will be a different country. This book is a great preview of what that would be like.

ANURAG BEHAR
CEO, Azim Premji Foundation

ABBREVIATIONS

BEO	:	Block Education Officer
BRC	:	Block Resource Centre/Block Resource Coordinator
BRCF	:	Block Resource Centre Facilitator
BRP	:	Block Resource Person
BSTC	:	Basic School Training Certificate
BTC	:	Basic Teaching Certificate
CBSE	:	Central Board for Secondary Education
CCE	:	Continuous and Comprehensive Evaluation
CRC	:	Cluster Resource Centre
CRP	:	Cluster Resource Person
CRCF	:	Cluster Resource Centre Facilitator
DDPI	:	Deputy Director of Public Instruction
DEO	:	District Education Officer
DIET	:	District Institute of Education and Training
DPEP	:	District Primary Education Programme
DSERT	:	Department of State Educational Research and Training
ECCE	:	Early Childhood Care and Education
KSQAAC	:	Karnataka School Quality Assessment and Accreditation Council
LGP	:	Learning Guarantee Programme
LRC	:	Learning Resource Centre
LPS	:	Lower Primary School
MEO	:	Mandal Education Officer
MHRD	:	Ministry of Human Resource Development
MLA	:	Member of Legislative assembly
MP	:	Mandal Panchayat
MRP	:	Mandal Resource Person

NCERT	:	National Council for Educational Research and Training
NCF	:	National Curriculum Framework
OBC	:	Other Backward Classes
PRI	:	Panchayati Raj Institution
PS	:	Primary School
PTA	:	Parent Teacher Association
PTR	:	Pupil-Teacher Ratio
PUC	:	Pre-University Course
REET	:	Rajasthan Eligibility Examination for Teachers (Formerly known as RTET)
RTE	:	Right to Education
SC	:	Scheduled Caste
SCERT	:	State Council for Educational Research and Training
SDC	:	School Development Committee
SDMC	:	School Development and Monitoring Committee
SDP	:	State Domestic Product
SEC	:	School Education Committee
SGT	:	Secondary Grade Teacher
SIDA	:	Swedish International Development Authority
SIERT	:	State Institute of Educational Research and Training
SIIDCUL	:	State Infrastructure and Industrial Development Corporation of Uttarakhand Ltd, a government of Uttarakhand Enterprise.
SLDP	:	School Leadership Development Programme
SMC	:	School Management Committee
SSA	:	Sarva Shiksha Abhiyan
SSLC	:	Secondary School Leaving Certificate
ST	:	Scheduled Tribe
TCH	:	Teacher Certificate Higher
TET	:	Teacher Eligibility Test
TLC	:	Teacher Learning Centre
TLM	:	Teaching-Learning Material
TPR	:	Teacher-Pupil Ratio
UPS	:	Upper Primary School
VTF	:	Voluntary Teacher Forum

GLOSSARY

A

Adarsha Vidyalaya (also known as 'Model School' or 'Utkrusht Vidyalaya' in some states): A government scheme that has been implemented in some states with the objective of providing access to high-quality school education through exemplar or model schools.

Anganwadis: Meaning the 'courtyard shelter,' these are rural childcare centres started in 1975 as part of the Integrated Child Development Scheme of the Ministry of Women and Child Development of the Government of India to combat child hunger and malnutrition by providing supplementary nutrition to children in the age group of three to six years. Pre-school activities and non-formal pre-school education are also provided.

B

Bhil: Primarily an ethnic group of people in West India who speak the Bhil languages, a subgroup of the Western Zone of the Indo-Aryan languages. As of 2013, Bhils were the largest tribal group in India.

Block Resource Centre (BRC): Established in each block of every district in the country under the Sarva Shiksha Abhiyan to conduct in-service teacher training; provide academic support to teachers and schools on a regular basis, and; to help in community mobilisation activities.

Buksa: Indigenous people living mainly in the Indian states of Uttarakhand and Uttar Pradesh. They have been granted the Scheduled Tribe status.

C

Child-Friendly School Initiative (CFSI): A joint programme of the government of Karnataka and the Azim Premji Foundation in the Surpur block of Yadgir district to promote comprehensive school improvement covering teacher capabilities, school environment, children's learning, well-being and all-round development.

Cluster Resource Centre (CRC): There are several in each block covering a small number of schools within easy reach. Each CRC has a Cluster Resource Person/Cluster Resource Coordinator whose role is to provide academic support to teachers and schools on a regular basis and help in community mobilisation activities.

Continuous and Comprehensive Evaluation (CCE): A process of assessment, mandated by the Right to Education Act, 2009. The main aim is to evaluate every aspect of each child in school with the aim to decrease the workload on the student by means of continuous evaluation through a number of small tests throughout the year in place of a single test at the end of an academic programme. As part of this system, students' marks are replaced by grades which are evaluated through a series of curricular and extra-curricular evaluations along with academics.

D

District Institute for Education and Training (DIET): Established in each district of the country by the Indian government as a centre of guidance for educational institutes and schools of a district. As part of their mandate, these institutes offer a pre-service teacher education diploma and provide academic and resource support at the grassroot level for in-service training of teachers.

Department of State Educational Research and Training (DSERT, also known as SCERT or SIERT in some states): Established at the state level to provide overall academic leadership in school education and for improving the quality of education provided in primary and secondary schools in the states.

G

Garasia: A general or open category ruling tribe inhabiting the Indian states of Rajasthan and Gujarat. Garasia settlements are found in the Rajasthan districts of Pali, Sirohi, Udaipur and Dungarpur, and the Gujarat districts of Sabarkantha and Banaskantha.

J

Jawahar Navodaya Vidyalaya (JNV): Conceived as part of the National Policy for Education 1986 (NPE 1986), this is an alternate residential school system for gifted children, predominantly from rural India. They are fully residential and co-educational schools affiliated to Central Board of Secondary Education (CBSE), New Delhi, with Classes from grades VI to XII. The scheme provides for opening of one JNV in each district of the country. Admission to Class VI of the JNVs requires qualification in the entrance exam designed, developed and conducted by the CBSE and is conducted annually throughout the country.

K

Karnataka School Quality Assessment and Accreditation Council (KSQACC): Constituted as an organisation in the department of school education, Government of Karnataka, the council is tasked with assessing quality of education and acting as an accreditation body. It had earlier been constituted in 2006 as the Karnataka Schools Quality Assessment Organisation (KSQAO) and performed a similar role.

Kasturba Gandhi Balika Vidyalaya (KGBV): Residential girls' secondary school run by the government for the weaker sections of India. The scheme, introduced by the Government of India in August 2004, then integrated with the Sarva Shiksha Abhiyan, provides educational facilities to girls belonging to Scheduled Castes, Scheduled Tribes, Other Backward Classes, minority communities and families below the poverty line in educationally backward blocks.

Kalikotsava: Meaning, the festival of learning, it is an initiative of the Government of Karnataka to identify special learning outcomes in language, maths, science in primary school children and presenting these before the community, so as to create a positive response from the community. Successful students at the block level receive a citation and certificate. Participation certificates are also given to all participants at all levels.

Keli-Kali: A radio programme designed and implemented by the DSERT, the academic wing of the Department of Public Instruction, Government of Karnataka. It is broadcast for the students of Classes I to VIII, Monday to Friday on 13 stations of All India Radio. The schedule and topics of the broadcast are prepared and supplied to all schools and teachers/ subject teachers at the beginning of a new academic year.

L

Learning Guarantee Programme (LGP): A joint initiative of the respective state governments of Karnataka, Madhya Pradesh, Gujarat, Uttarakhand and Rajasthan and the Azim Premji Foundation that was implemented in these states between 2003 and 2008. This was a voluntary programme for schools to participate in an independent assessment of their quality based on the three parameters of Universal Elementary Education (UEE), namely, enrolment, attendance and learning. The main purpose of the programme was to bring about a change in the assessment of student learning—from testing rote learning to testing conceptual understanding while also recognising the schools that fulfilled these criteria.

Learning Resource Centre (LRC): An Azim Premji Foundation initiated centre in the districts where its field institutes are established. These are located in towns where a larger number of teachers have their residences and serve as venues for teachers to gather, discuss academic issues and access necessary teaching material. Launched with the intent to improve the quality in educational development at all stages of education, this centre is called the LRC in Rajasthan and the Teacher Learning Centre (TLC) in other states.

M

Model School. Please see Adarsha Vidyalaya.

Morarji Desai Residential Schools: Established by the Government of Karnataka to provide free residential education to students of Classes VI to X. Under the Minorities department, these schools have 50 per cent reservation for minorities while the schools under Zila Panchayats are reserved for SC & ST. Students who have passed Class V are eligible to write the entrance exam for admission to Class VI. Family income is also a criterion for admission.

Maths Wizard: Conducted for the children of Class V by the education department of the Government of Uttarakhand to encourage those who have a flair in maths. Children progress from cluster to block and then district level competitions. The department conducts a similar programme for students of Class V in English called 'Spelling Genius.'

N

National Children's Science Congress (also, Rashtriya Bal Vigyan Congress): A nationwide science communication programme started in the year 1993 under the Department of Science and Technology, Government of India. The primary objective is to provide a forum to children in the age group of 10-17 years to exhibit their creativity and ability in solving a societal problem experienced locally using the methods of science.

Navodaya Vidyalaya: see Jawahar Navodaya Vidyalaya

Nali-Kali: An initiative of the Government of Karnataka, launched in 2001, it was first piloted as a small UNICEF-assisted pilot project in HD Kote, Mysore district. Meaning joyful learning, it is a multi-grade, multi-level (MGML) activity-based learning programme for primary classes based on the methodology developed by the Rishi Valley Institute for Educational Resources (RIVER). It was expanded to cover nearly fourteen thousand schools by 2009 and the state education department is considering significant modifications to the programme.

P

Pratibha Karanji: An education department of Karnataka programme for primary and secondary schools where cultural and literary competitions are held at cluster, block, district and state levels. It provides children a common platform to participate and be recognised.

R

Rajiv Gandhi Swarna Jayanti Pathshala: Initiated to bring schools to areas/habitations where there were still no primary schools, by August 1999, twelve thousand schools had been started under this scheme which is an adaptation of the Shiksha Karmi scheme and draws from the Education Guarantee Scheme of Madhya Pradesh.

Rashtriya Bal Vigyan Congress: See National Children's Science Congress.

Remedial Teaching Programme: Called 'Parihara Bodhane' in Karnataka, this is a programme that aims to provide additional academic support and accelerated learning to children who have never been enrolled, have dropped out or who require additional support. It was renamed Accelerated Learning Programme since educationists pointed out the undesirable labelling of children if the programme is referred to as 'remedial' teaching.

Rishi Valley Institute for Educational Resources (RIVER): The teacher training and resource development wing of the Rishi Valley Rural Education Centre that designed the Multi-Grade, Multi-Level (MGML) methodology, the essence of which is activity and task-oriented pedagogy and that children will learn at their own pace and manage their learning themselves if the teaching-learning process is joyful. Nali-Kali in Karnataka and Activity-based Learning programme in Tamil Nadu and a few other states are based on these principles.

Room to Read: A non-profit organisation which seeks to transform the lives of millions of children in low-income communities by focusing on literacy and gender equality in education. Working in collaboration with local communities, partner organisations and governments, it seeks to develop literacy skills and a habit of reading among primary school children, and support girls to complete secondary school with life skills to succeed in school and beyond.

S

Sarva Shiksha Abhiyan (SSA): A programme aimed at universalisation of elementary education as mandated by the 86th Amendment to the Constitution of India making free and compulsory education for all children between the ages of 6 to 14 years a fundamental right. It is implemented by the central government in partnership with state governments through a district-level decentralised management framework involving local bodies.

School Development and Monitoring Committee (SDMC) or School Management Committee (SMC): Committee consisting of parents and teachers to encourage community participation and ownership for the effective management of government schools. The head teacher is the secretary and one parent, the president of the committee. The members and president are elected by the parents of students of the school.

School Leadership Development Programme (SLDP): Government of Karnataka and the Azim Premji Foundation conceptualised and implemented this programme to build and enhance the capacity of school heads on a long-term and continuous basis. The same was also implemented with necessary modifications for head teachers of Primary and Upper Primary Schools in Uttarakhand.

School Head Teachers Programme: The ten-day training programme for head teachers of Surpur Block was conducted in 2004 jointly by the education department and the Azim Premji Foundation as a part of the Child-Friendly School Initiative.

T

Teaching Learning Centres (TLC): See Learning Resource Centres (LRC).

Teacher Certificate Higher (TCH): Two-year teacher diploma course after PUC/Class XII in Karnataka till 2002; subsequently replaced by the equivalent two-year DEd (Diploma in Education).

U

Utkrusht Vidyalaya: See Adarsha Vidyalaya.

V

Voluntary Teacher Forums (VTF): A self- and peer-learning platform for continued professional development of teachers from government schools organised and run by the Azim Premji Foundation. It is a network of teachers that has been formed through voluntary participation. The informal group meets periodically on its own initiative and not as a part of any department directive.

ACKNOWLEDGEMENTS

I thank my colleagues in the field who, because of their deep and sustained engagement on ground, were able to suggest a pool of good teachers for this study. Many of them, despite their pressing work schedules, accompanied me to schools. Their insights and timely interjections during the school visits were invaluable. And of course, they also knew the best roadside eateries where we could either start or end a long day.

Udham Singh Nagar District: Rajiv Sharma, Azhar Zubair, Jaishankar Chaubey, Sanjay Yadav, Amit Chandra, Kulwant Singh Kanta, Ashwini, Rajkumar, Vijay Kumar Pandey, Arun Kumar Nautiyal, Deepa Rani

Yadgir District: Rudresh S., Gururajrao Kulkarni, Adiveppa Kuri, Ramesh S. Patil, Anwar M., Hulagappa S. Goundi, Gururaj Kulkarni, Shivanand Hadapada, Vinod Kumar, Ramesh M. Kulkarni, Khaja Azeemuddin Fareedi, Mallappa Hadapada

Uttarkashi District: Ashish Tripathi, Pramod Penyuli, Sanjay Rawat, Sanjay Semwal, Sanjeev Bijliyan, Saurabh Thakur

Tonk District: Vikas Chandra Roy, Rakesh Tewary, Devendra Joshi, Narendra Jat, Dilip Chugh, Kailash Baroda, Mahesh Sharma, Rajendra, Anil Gupta, Umakant Sharma, Rajender Singh

Sirohi District: Rakesh Tewary, Vinod, Vikram Sharma, Tirang Rangsanamei, Ali Mohammad Khan, Amol Kate, Jyoti Srivastava

At the University: Umashanker Periodi, Enakshi Bhar, Harini Nagendra, Syed Shamshad Hussain, Rishikesh B.S., Sujatha Puranik, Subrat Kumar Mishra

*

I thank every teacher I met during my visit to their schools. For allowing me into their schools and classrooms to observe and take notes; for the freedom to interact with the children. I will always remain grateful to them for spending time, sometimes well beyond school hours, talking to me. They spoke to me most cordially and openly, giving me glimpses of their lives as teachers, their hopes and aspirations, their difficulties and frustrations. It was an honour to be with them. I hope I have done justice in presenting what these teachers so graciously shared with me.

Udham Singh Nagar District

Jaspur Block: Dharmender Kumar, Avnish Kumar Chauhan, Alok Kumar, Jitendra Singh

Khatima Block: Tapanshil, Ishwar Chand Maurya, Kamala Bhandary, Dharampal Gangwar, Anita Rawat, Gobilal, Siya Nand, Suman

Rudrapur Block: Shikha Gangwar, Krishna Kumar Sharma, Keerti Nidhi Sharma, Pankaj Pandey, Ravi Mohan, Manju Bisht, Vinay Prabha Pathak, Pradeep Pandey

Kashipur Block: Harish Chandrasingh Rawat, Kiran Sharma, Anil Kumar Sharma, Zahiruddin, Sohail Khan, Usha Sharma

Gadarpur Block: Raghuvendra Singh, Ankur Arora, Amandeep Kaur

Sitargunj Block: Meena Rana, Ramjanam Chouhan, Sangeeta Gupta, Ramkishore, Dayashankar Sharma, Jagjit Kaur, Mobina Malik, Ompal, Ravikumar, Daler Singh

Bajpur Block: Dharamveer Singh Chouhan, Vidya Lohari, Shivani Agarwal, Rajender Saxena, Sabeena Khatum, Bharat Rawal, Rachna Varma

Yadgir District

Surpur Block: Sharanabasaiah Hiremath, Babu Lamani, G.N. Biradhar, Kashilingaiah Ganachari, Channabasaiah B. Navani, Ramesh Vanakihaal, Shreeshaila M.G., Basappa Abyal, Giriappa Asangi, Manjunatha Kattimani, Veeresh Hiremath, Prabhudeva Yadav, Rajugowda Mudigoudar, Achappa Gowdar, Sangaiah Bachal, Renuka Pujari, Manjunatha Siddanna, Mallappa Guli, Sharanagagouda Patil, Basavaraj Dalwai, Basavagouda Choudri, Ayub Jamadar, Mallikarjun Nandelli, Siddaram Birajdar, Parameshwariah Hiremath, Mallanna Sajjan, Sushma G., Ashoka K., Rajanna Gotur, Shivananda Biradar, Sharanagowda Patil, Dundappa Kolkar, Basavaraj Neelgar, Shivappa Sajjan, Shankargowda Patil, Rajesh Mujawar, Annappagowda Patil, Shivakumar Bandoli, Kanthesh Halagimani, Shridhar Malji, Yamunappa Kuri, Somashekar Bakli, Shakambari Hiremath, Mariappa Hosamani, Yalagudappa Tippanna, Geetha Hatrikihal, Rajashekhar Chillal, Kashiba Basarakod, Jayashree Hiremath, Kausar Banu, Shobha Bhandari, Fareeda Begum, Lingaiah Kallurmatha

Uttarkashi District

Bhatwari Block: Rekha Chamoli, Manju Rana, Rameshwari Lingwal, Darbeshwari Bahuguna, Shoorveer Singh Kharola,

Chandramohan Singh, Narendra Singh Chauhan, Kushla Prasad Bhat, Balwant Singh Bisht, Saira Bano, Madhulika Thapliyal, Pavitra Rawat

Dunda Block: Ajay Nautiyal, Sunita Rana, Chandan Singh, Jaiveer Agarwal, Rekha Aswal, Urmila Nautiyal

Chinyali Block: Rajni Negi, Mukesh Nautiyal, Murari Rana, Susheela Rawat, Meena Bhatt, Bindu Gusain Padiyar, Sanjay Kuksal

Purola Block: Chandrabhushan Bijlawan, Suresh Shah, Shanti Prasad, Charan Singh Aswal, Markandey Prasad Semwal, Jagat Mishrawan, Kulwanti Rawat

Naugaon Block: Sarita, Vinod Maithani, Yashpal Singh, Puneeta Rana, Praveena Puri, Surat Lal (Retired in March 2018), Dhyansingh Rawat, Manbir Singh Chouhan, Jagbir Singh Jayada, Prabha Bhatt, Vijaya Rawat, Durgesh Nandini Yadav, Savita Chamoli, Ushakiran Bisht, Sangeeta Bahuguna

Tonk District

Unniyara Block: Ashok Soyal, Kailash Chand Jat

Malpura Block: Kamalchand Mali, Radheshyam Choudhary, Mahaveer Swami, Abdul Hameed, Kishanlal Gujjar, Vishnukanta Parashar

Nevai Block: Ladulal Bairwa, Rajesh Gurjar, Niranjan Sawariya, Jainarayan Meena, Ramprasad Koli, Dhannalal Varma, Shankarlal Meena, Bhagwati Ramanwal, Subhash Kumavat, Devendra Sharma

Peeplu Block: Mukesh Kumar Sharma, Abdul Wajid

Tonk Block: Prakashchandra Regar, Narendra Kumar Gautam, Surajban Choudhary, Mohanlal Harrawat, Kaluram Yadav

Todarai Singh Block: Satyanarayan Mali, Maya Jat, Ompal Prajapat, Mathuralal Raigar, Ramesh Chandra Meena, Rajaram Meena, Pankaj Kumar Verma, Pradhan Kumar Bairwa, Yogesh Prasad Mahavar

Deoli Block: Vijay Bisht, Kailashchandra Pancholi, Kaluram Yadav, Mansaur Bai Choudhary, Govind Prajapat

<u>Sirohi District</u>

Reodhar Block: Ramesh Chandra Pal, Ramraj Gujjar, Yunus Gouri, Geeta Singh

Abu Road Block: Mahendra Kumar Dabi, Shankar Lal Barot, Kamlesh Rajpurohit, Satyanarayan Bairwa, Chetana Vishwa, Shweta, Jagdish Kumar Barot, Pankaj Mathur, Pakaram Meena

Sheoganj Block: Tilok Chand, Veerendra Ratoi, Veera Ram, Nahar Singh, Veena Rathore, Shaitan Singh, Mahinder Kumar, Bhupender Kumar Detha

Sirohi Block: Mewaram Chaudhary, Dinesh Prajapat, Pankaj Kumar Sharma, Ghani Khan, Bhanwarlal Choudhary, Durjandan Charan

Pindwara Block: Sumit Panjabi, Gopal Raval, Dewaram

*

A special note of thanks to my colleague, Shefali Tripathi Mehta.

I needed enormous editorial help to bring this book to its final shape. Shefali helped me from the very early stages of its draft, taking proprietorial responsibility in re-organising and rearranging the sections and chapters and selecting the stories that feature here. She was uncompromisingly tough on me to ensure consistency in style and most painstaking in copy-editing.

Shefali is a writer and author. She writes on social issues, travel, parenting and disability awareness. Her most recent book, *Stuck like Lint*, a collection of stories was published in 2017. She volunteers with the charity Arushi and curates Gond art to support tribal artists.

I have been most fortunate that Shefali helped edit this book.

*

I must thank my friend and colleague, Anurag Behar, the CEO of Azim Premji Foundation for the concluding essay. Not only was he most encouraging at every stage of the book but in a signal of how much he valued this effort, offered to write this essay. I could not have had a better conclusion that ties up the essence of what I wanted to convey through the stories of the extraordinary teachers.

I thank Adwait Pawar for the five lovely sketches that set the tone for each of the five chapters. I am deeply touched by how enthusiastically Sachin Mulay, Radhika Motani and Manjusha Muthiah helped with the design and worked closely with the illustrator.

I thank Karthik Venkatesh, my commissioning editor, for believing in the larger purpose of this book—to convey to readers that there are many unsung heroic teachers in rural India who go way beyond their call of duty to provide every child the best possible education. To convey that in many government schools, equity and quality have reclaimed their place. Karthik is himself an educator, having run a school for years. There could not be a more empathetic editor. It becomes so much more fun, when both author and editor share the passion.

REFERENCES

While this book is a compilation of a more comprehensive study, the author has periodically written articles on various aspects and attributes of excellent schools and teachers. Some parts of the stories featured here have previously been published as short articles.

Unshackling the vice-like grip of hierarchy in our country. *Times of India.* September 1, 2018.

https://timesofindia.indiatimes.com/city/bengaluru/unshackling-the-vice-like-grip-of-hierarchy-in-our-country/articleshow/65638094.cms

Consolidating small schools without compromising access. *Deccan Herald.* August 26, 2018.

https://www.deccanherald.com/consolidating-small-schools-689375.html

One teacher at a time. *Deccan Herald.* July 7, 2018.

https://www.deccanherald.com/opinion/main-article/one-teacher-time-679549.html

The principal practices that make govt schools good. *Times of India.* April 21, 2018.

https://timesofindia.indiatimes.com/city/bengaluru/the-principal-practices-that-make-govt-schools-good/articleshow/63862702.cms

The good work by government schools gets ignored. *Times of India.* April 14, 2018. https://timesofindia.indiatimes.com/city/bengaluru/the-good-work-by-government-schools-gets-ignored/articleshow/63764801.cms

Teacher's zeal is key. *Deccan Herald.* February 16, 2018. https://www.deccanherald.com/content/659922/teachers-zeal-key.html

Teachers at Uttarakhand model schools go the extra mile to bring quality education to children from poor families. *Firstpost.* Feb 9, 2018.

https://www.firstpost.com/india/teachers-at-uttarakhand-model-schools-go-the-extra-mile-to-bring-quality-education-to-children-from-poor-families-4343599.html

Ordinary women, extraordinary stories: These teachers in rural India's schools are real-life heroes. *Firstpost.* January 11, 2018.

https://www.firstpost.com/living/ordinary-women-extraordinary-stories-these-teachers-in-rural-indias-schools-are-real-life-heroes-4290209.html

Internet and WhatsApp are revolutionising Uttarakhand's schools, giving teachers a forum for self-development. *Firstpost.* November 26, 2017.

https://www.firstpost.com/india/internet-and-whatsapp-are-revolutionising-uttarakhands-schools-giving-teachers-a-forum-for-self-development-4228733.html

Scraped knees and spirited minds: How an Uttarakhand girls' school defied odds to become kabaddi champion. *Firstpost.* November 17, 2017.

https://www.firstpost.com/india/scraped-knees-and-spirited-minds-how-an-uttarakhand-girls-school-defied-odds-to-become-kabaddi-champion-4212803.html

Teacher education critical missing piece. *Deccan Herald.* November 4, 2017.

https://www.deccanherald.com/content/641124/teacher-education-critical-missing-piece.html

In Uttarkashi schools, a poem inspires teachers to reflect on classroom interactions, make learning fun for students. *Firstpost.* October 25, 2017.

https://www.firstpost.com/india/in-uttarkashi-schools-a-poem-inspires-teachers-to-reflect-on-classroom-interactions-make-learning-fun-for-students-4173415.html

Support the village teacher. *Deccan Herald.* September 5, 2017.

https://www.deccanherald.com/content/631622/support-village-teacher.html

In Karnataka's Surpur, Government School Teachers Inspire Hope. *The Wire.* May 18, 2017.

https://thewire.in/education/karnataka-surpur-government-schools

NOTES

1. For a recent study, refer to Azim Premji University, 2019, *Educational Expectations, Aspirations and Structural Constraints.* https://azimpremjiuniversity.edu.in/SitePages/pdf/Educational-Expectations-Aspiratons-and-Structural-Constraints-Field-Studies-in-Education-Jan-2019.pdf
2. ASER (2018), *Annual Status of Education Report*, ASER Centre, Pratham, New Delhi. http://img.asercentre.org/docs/ASER%20 2018/Release%20Material/aserreport2018.pdf
3. B.S. Rishikesh, *Observations of school practices: Learning Guarantee Programme*, Azim Premji Foundation's *Learning Curve*, Issue V, March 2005
4. Azim Premji University, 2017, *Teacher Absenteeism Study*, https://azimpremjiuniversity.edu.in/SitePages/pdf/Field-Studies-in-Education-Teacher-Absenteeism-Study.pdf
5. World Bank, *World Development Report 2018: Learning to Realize Education's Promise*, Washington, DC: World Bank. doi:10.1596/978-1-4648-1096-1. http://www.worldbank.org/en/publication/wdr2018
6. J.P. Naik, *Equality, Quality and Quantity: The elusive triangle in Indian education*, Allied Publishers. 1975.
7. National Council of Educational Research and Training (NCERT), 1971, *Education and national development (Report of Education Commission [1964—66] Vol. 3)*, New Delhi: Higher Education http://archive.org/details/ReportOfTheEducationCo mmission1964-66D.S.KothariReport

8. Government of India, 1986, National Policy for Education; Ministry of Human Resource Development, New Delhi. http://mhrd.gov.in/sites/upload_files/mhrd/files/upload_document/npe.pdf
9. Ministry of Human Resource Development Annual Report, 2005, http://mhrd.gov.in/sites/upload_files/mhrd/files document-reports/AR2005-06.pdf
10. Earlier, Rashtriya Avishkar Abhiyan—a national award instituted by the Ministry of Human Resource Development to nurture the spirit of inquiry and creativity, love for science and mathematics and effective use of technology amongst children.

www.ingramcontent.com/pod-product-compliance
Lightning Source LLC
LaVergne TN
LVHW010311070526
838199LV00065B/5526